ISBN: 978129027791

Published by:
HardPress Publishing
8345 NW 66TH ST #2561
MIAMI FL 33166-2626

Email: info@hardpress.net
Web: http://www.hardpress.net

SIGILLVM · VNIVERSITATIS · CALIFORNIENSIS

FIAT LVX

MDCCCLXVIII

EX LIBRIS

WOMAN TRIUMPHANT
(*LA MAJA DESNUDA*)

BY
VICENTE BLASCO IBAÑEZ

TRANSLATED FROM THE SPANISH
BY
HAYWARD KENISTON

WITH A SPECIAL INTRODUCTORY NOTE BY THE AUTHOR

NEW YORK
E. P. DUTTON & COMPANY
681 FIFTH AVENUE

INTRODUCTORY NOTE TO THE ENGLISH TRANSLATION

THE title of this novel in the original, *La maja desnuda,* "The Nude Maja," is also the name of one of the most famous pictures of the great Spanish painter Francisco Goya.

The word *maja* has no exact equivalent in English or in any of the modern languages. Literally, it means "bedecked," "showy," "gaudily attired," "flashy," "dazzling," etc., and it was applied at the end of the eighteenth century and at the beginning of the nineteenth to a certain class of gay women of the lower strata of Madrid society notorious for their love of dancing and their fondness for exhibiting themselves conspicuously at bull-fights and all popular celebrations. The great ladies of the aristocracy affected the free ways and imitated the picturesque dress of the *maja;* Goya made this type the central figure of many of his genre paintings, and the dramatist Ramón de la Cruz based most of his *sainetes*—farcical pieces in one act—upon the customs and rivalries of these women. The dress invented by the *maja,* consisting of a short skirt partly covered by a net with berry-shaped tassels, white *mantilla* and high shell-comb, is considered all over the world as the national costume of Spanish women.

When the novel first appeared in Spain some years ago, a certain part of the Madrid public, unduly evil-minded, thought that it had discovered the identity of the real persons whom I had taken as models to draw my characters. This claim provoked a scandalous sensation and gave my book an unwholesome notoriety. It was thought that the protagonists of *La maja desnuda* were an illustrious Spanish painter of world-wide fame, who is my friend, and an aristocratic lady very celebrated at the time but now forgotten. I protested against this unwarranted and fantastic interpretation. Although I draw my characters from life, I do so only in a very fragmentary way (like all the great creative novelists whom I admire as masters in the field of fiction), using the materials gathered in my observations to form completely new types which are the direct and legitimate offspring of my own imagination. To use a figure: as a novelist I am a painter, not a photographer. Although I seek my inspiration in reality, I copy it in accordance with my own way of seeing it; I do not reproduce it with the mechanical servility of the photographic camera.

It is possible that my imaginary heroes are vaguely reminiscent of beings who actually exist. Subconsciousness is the novelist's principal instrument, and this subconsciousness frequently mocks us, leading us to mistake for our own creation the things which we have unwittingly observed in Nature. But despite this, it is unfair, as well as risky, for the reader to assign the names of real persons to the characters of fiction, saying, "This is So-and-so."

It would be equally unfair to consider this novel as audacious or of doubtful morality. The artistic world which I describe in *La maja desnuda* cannot be expected to have the same conception of life as the conventional world. Far from believing it immoral, I consider this one of the most moral novels I have ever written. And it is for this reason that, with a full realization of the standards demanded by the English-reading public, I have not hesitated to authorize the present translation without palliation or amputation, fully convinced that the reader will not find anything in this novel objectionable or offensive to his moral sense. Morality is not to be found in words but in deeds and in the lessons which these deeds teach.

The difficulty of adequately translating the word *maja* into English led to the adoption of "Woman Triumphant" as the title of the present version. I believe it is a happy selection; it interprets the spirit of the novel. But it must be borne in mind that the woman here is the wife of the protagonist. It is the wife who triumphs, resurrecting in spirit to exert an overwhelming influence over the life of a man who had wished to live without her.

Renovales, the hero, is simply the personification of human desire, this poor desire which, in reality, does not know what it wants, eternally fickle and unsatisfied. When we finally obtain what we desire, it does not seem enough. "More: I want more," we say. If we lose something that made life unbearable, we immediately wish it back as indispensable to our happiness. Such are we: poor deluded children who cried yesterday for what we scorn to-day and shall want again to-morrow; poor deluded beings plunging across the span of life on the Icarian wings of caprice.

VICENTE BLASCO IBAÑEZ.

New York, January, 1920.

WOMAN TRIUMPHANT

WOMAN TRIUMPHANT

PART I

I

It was eleven o'clock in the morning when Mariano Renovales reached the Museo del Prado. Several years had passed since the famous painter had entered it. The dead did not attract him; very interesting they were, very worthy of respect, under the glorious shroud of the centuries, but art was moving along new paths and he could not study there under the false glare of the skylights, where he saw reality only through the temperaments of other men. A bit of sea, a mountainside, a group of ragged people, an expressive head attracted him more than that palace, with its broad staircases, its white columns and its statues of bronze and alabaster—a solemn pantheon of art, where the neophytes vacillated in fruitless confusion, without knowing what course to follow.

The master Renovales stopped for a few moments at the foot of the stairway. He contemplated the valley through which you·approach the palace—with its slopes of fresh turf, dotted at intervals with the sickly little trees—with a certain emotion, as men are wont to contemplate, after a long absence, the places familiar to their youth. Above the scattered growth the ancient church of Los Jerónimos, with its gothic masonry, outlined against the blue sky its twin towers and ruined arcades.

The wintry foliage of the Retiro served as a background
for the white mass of the Casón. Renovales thought of
the frescos of Giordano that decorated its ceilings. Afterwards, he fixed his attention on a building with red walls
and a stone portal, which pretentiously obstructed the
space in the foreground, at the edge of the green slope.
Bah! The Academy! And the artist's sneer included in
the same loathing the Academy of Language and the
other Academies—painting, literature, every manifesta-
tion of human thought, dried, smoked, and swathed, with
the immortality of a mummy, in the bandages of tradi-
tion, rules, and respect for precedent.

A gust of icy wind shook the skirts of his overcoat, his
long beard tinged with gray and his wide felt hat, beneath the brim of which protruded the heavy locks of
his hair, that had excited so much comment in his youth,
but which had gradually grown shorter with prudent
trimming, as the master rose in the world, winning fame
and money.

Renovales felt cold in the damp valley. It was one of
those bright, freezing days that are so frequent in the
winter in Madrid. The sun was shining; the sky was
blue; but from the mountains, covered with snow, came
an icy wind, that hardened the ground, making it as
brittle as glass. In the corners, where the warmth of the
sun did not reach, the morning frost still glistened like
a coating of sugar. On the mossy carpet, the sparrows,
thin with the privations of winter, trotted back and forth
like children, shaking their bedraggled feathers.

The stairway of the Museo recalled to the master his
early youth, when at sixteen he had climbed those steps
many a time with his stomach faint from the wretched
meal at the boarding-house. How many mornings he had
spent in that old building copying Velásquez! The place
brought to his memory his dead hopes, a host of illusions

that now made his smile; recollections of hunger and humiliating bargaining to make his first money by the sale of copies. His large, stern face, his brow that filled his pupils and admirers with terror lighted up with a merry smile. He recalled how he used to go into the Museo with halting steps, how he feared to leave the easel, lest people might notice the gaping soles of his boots that left his feet uncovered.

He passed through the vestibule and opened the first glass door. Instantly the noises of the world outside ceased; the rattling of the carriages in the Prado; the bells of the street-cars, the dull rumble of the carts, the shrill cries of the children who were running about on the slopes. He opened the second door, and his face, swollen by the cold, felt the caress of warm air, buzzing with the vague hum of silence. The footfalls of the visitors reverberated in the manner peculiar to large, unoccupied buildings. The slam of the door, as it closed, resounded like a cannon shot, passing from hall to hall through the heavy curtains. From the gratings of the registers poured the invisible breath of the furnaces. The people, on entering, spoke in a low tone, as if they were in a cathedral; their faces assumed an expression of unnatural seriousness, as though they were intimidated by the thousands of canvases that lined the walls, by the enormous busts that decorated the circle of the rotunda and the middle of the central salon.

On seeing Renovales, the two door-keepers, in their long frock-coats, started to their feet. They did not know who he was, but he certainly was *somebody*. They had often seen that face, perhaps in the newspapers, perhaps on match-boxes. It was associated in their minds with the glory of popularity, with the|high honors reserved for people of distinction. Presently they recognized him. It was so many years since they had seen him there! And the two attendants, with their caps covered with gold-braid in their hands and with an obsequious smile, came forward towards the great artist.

"Good morning, Don Mariano. Did Señor de Renovales wish something? Did he want them to call the curator?" They spoke with oily obsequiousness, with the confusion of courtiers who see a foreign sovereign suddenly enter their palace, recognizing him through his disguise.

Renovales rid himself of them with a brusque gesture and cast a glance over the large decorative canvases of the rotunda, that recalled the wars of the 17th century; generals with bristling mustaches and plumed slouch-hat, directing the battle with a short baton, as though they were directing an orchestra, troops of arquebusiers disappearing downhill with banners of red and blue crosses at their front, forests of pikes rising from the smoke, green meadows of Flanders in the backgrounds—thundering, fruitless combats that were almost the last gasps of a Spain of European influence. He lifted a heavy curtain and entered the spacious salon, where the people at the other end looked like little wax figures under the dull illumination of the skylights.

The artist continued straight ahead, scarcely noticing the pictures, old acquaintances that could tell him nothing new. His eyes sought the people without, however, finding in them any greater novelty. It seemed as though they formed a part of the building and had not moved from it in many years; good-natured fathers with a group of children before their knees, explaining the meaning of the pictures; a school teacher, with her well-behaved and silent pupils who, in obedience to the command of their superior, passed without stopping before the lightly clad saints; a gentleman with two priests, talking loudly, to show that he was intelligent and almost at home there; several foreign ladies with their veils caught up over their straw hats and their coats on their arms, consulting the catalogue, all with a sort of family air, with identical expressions of admiration and curiosity, until Renovales wondered if they were the same ones he had seen there years before, the last time he was there.

As he passed, he greeted the great masters mentally; on one side the holy figures of El Greco, with their greenish or bluish spirituality, slender and undulating; beyond, the wrinkled, black heads of Ribera, with ferocious expressions of torture and pain—marvelous artists, whom Renovales admired, while determined not to imitate them. Afterwards, between the railing that protects the pictures and the line of busts, show-cases and marble tables supported by gilded lions, he came upon the easels of several copyists. They were boys from the School of Fine Arts, or poverty-stricken young ladies with run-down heels and dilapidated hats, who were copying Murillos. They were tracing on the canvas the blue of the Virgin's robe or the plump flesh of the curly-haired boys that played with the Divine Lamb. Their copies were commissions from pious people; a *genre* that found an easy sale among the benefactors of convents and oratories. The smoke of the candles, the wear of years, the blindness of devotion would dim the colors, and some day the eyes of the worshipers, weeping in supplication, would see the celestial figures move with mysterious life on their blackened background, as they implored from them wondrous miracles.

The master made his way toward the Hall of Velásquez. It was there that his friend Tekli was working. His visit to the Museo had no other object than to see the copy that the Hungarian painter was making of the picture of *Las Meninas*.

The day before, when the foreigner was announced in

his studio, he had remained perplexed for a long while,
looking at the name on the card. Tekli! And then all
at once he remembered a friend of twenty years before,
when he lived in Rome; a good-natured Hungarian, who
admired him sincerely and who made up for his lack of
genius with a silent persistency in his work, like a beast
of burden.

Renovales was glad to see his little blue eyes, hidden
under his thin, silky eyebrows, his jaw, protruding like
a shovel, a feature that made him look very much like the
Austrian monarchs—his tall frame that bent forward
under the impulse of excitement, while he stretched out
his bony arms, long as tentacles, and greeted him in
Italian:

"Oh, *maestro, oaro maestro!*"

He had taken refuge in a professorship, like all artists
who lack the power to continue the upward climb, who
fall in the rut. Renovales recognized the artist-official
in his spotless suit, dark and proper, in his dignified
glance that rested from time to time on his shining boots
that seemed to reflect the whole studio. He even wore
on one lapel of his coat the variegated button of some
mysterious decoration. The felt hat, white as meringue,
which he held in his hand, was the only discordant feature
in this general effect of a public functionary. Renovales
caught his hands with sincere enthusiasm. The famous
Tekli! How glad he was to see him! What times they
used to have in Rome! And with a smile of kindly superiority he listened to the story of his success. He
was a professor in Budapest; every year he saved money
in order to go and study in some celebrated European
museum. At last he had succeeded in coming to Spain,
fulfilling the desire he had cherished for many years.

"Oh, *Velásquez! uel maestro, caro Mariano!*"

And throwing back his head, with a dreamy expression

in his eyes, he moved his protruding jaw covered with reddish hair, with a voluptuous look, as though he were sipping a glass of his sweet native Tokay.

He had been in Madrid for a month, working every morning in the Museo. His copy of *Las Meninas* was almost finished. He had not been to see his "Dear Mariano" sooner because he wanted to show him this work. Would he come and see him some morning in the Museo? Would he give him this proof of his friendship? Renovales tried to decline. What did he care for a copy? But there was an expression of such humble supplication in the Hungarian's little eyes, he showered him with so many praises of his great triumphs, expatiating on the success that his picture *Man Overboard!* had won at the last Budapest Exhibition, that the master promised to go to the Museo.

And a few days later, one morning when a gentleman whose portrait he was painting canceled his appointment, Renovales remembered his promise and went to the Museo del Prado, feeling, as he entered, the same sensation of insignificance and homesickness that a man suffers on returning to the university where he has passed his youth.

When he found himself in the Hall of Velásquez, he suddenly felt seized with religious respect. There was a painter! *The* painter! All his irreverent theories of hatred for the dead were left outside the door. The charm of those canvases that he had not seen for many years rose again—fresh, powerful, irresistible; it overwhelmed him, awakening his remorse. For a long time he remained motionless, turning his eyes from one picture to another, eager to comprise in one glance the whole work of the immortal, while around him the hum of curiosity began again.

"Renovales! That's Renovales!"

The news had started from the door, spreading through the whole Museo, reaching the Hall of Velásquez behind his steps. The groups of curious people stopped gazing at the pictures to look at that huge, self-possessed man who did not seem to realize the curiosity that surrounded him. The ladies, as they went from canvas to canvas, looked out of the corner of their eyes at the celebrated artist whose portrait they had seen so often. They found him more ugly, more commonplace than he appeared in the engravings in the papers. It did not seem possible that that "porter" had talent and painted women so well. Some young fellows approached to look at him more closely, pretending to gaze at the same pictures as the master. They scrutinized him, noting his external peculiarities with that desire for enthusiastic imitation which marks the novice. Some determined to copy his soft bow-tie and his tangled hair, with the fantastic hope that this would give them a new spirit for painting. Others complained to themselves that they were beardless and could not display the curly gray whiskers of the famous master.

He, with his keen sensitiveness to praise, was not long in observing the atmosphere of curiosity that surrounded him. The young copyists seemed to stick closer to their easels, knitted their brows, dilated their nostrils, and moved their brushes slowly, with hesitation, knowing that he was behind them, trembling at every step that sounded on the inlaid floor, full of fear and desire that he might deign to cast a glance over their shoulders. He divined with a sort of pride what all the mouths were whispering, what all the eyes were saying, fixed absent-mindedly on the canvases only to turn toward him.

"It's Renovales—the painter Renovales."

The master looked for a long while at one of the copyists—an old man, decrepit and almost blind, with heavy convex spectacles that gave him the appearance of a sea-monster, whose hands trembled with senile unsteadiness. Renovales recognized him. Twenty years before, when he used to study in the Museo, he had seen him in the same spot, always copying *Los Borrachos.* Even if he should become completely blind, if the picture should be lost, he could reproduce it by feeling. In those days they had often talked together, but the poor man could not have the remotest suspicion that the Renovales whom people talked so much about was the same lad who on more than one occasion had borrowed a brush from him, but whose memory was scarcely preserved in his mind, mummified by eternal imitation.

Renovales thought of the kindness of the chummy Bacchus and the gang of ruffians of his court, who for half a century had been supporting the household of the copyist, and he fancied he could see the old wife, the married children, the grandchildren—a whole family supported by the old man's trembling hand.

Some one whispered to him the news that was filling the Museo with excitement and the copyist, shrugging his shoulders disdainfully, raised his moribund glance from his work.

And so Renovales was there, the famous Renovales! At last he was going to see the prodigy!

The master saw those grotesque eyes like those of a sea-monster, fixed on him, with an ironical gleam behind the heavy lenses. The grafter! He had already heard of that studio, as splendid as a palace, behind the Retiro. What Renovales had in such plenty had been taken from men like him who, for want of influence, had been left behind. He charged thousands of dollars for a canvas, when Velásquez worked for three *pesetas* a day and Goya painted his portraits for a couple of doubloons. Deceit, modernism, the audacity of the younger generation that lacked scruples, the ignorance of the simpletons that believe the newspapers! The only good thing was right there before him. And once more shrugging his shoulders scornfully, he lost his expression of ironical protest and returned to his thousandth copy of *Los Borrachos*.

Renovales, seeing that the curiosity about him was diminishing, entered the little hall that contained the picture of *Las Meninas*. There was Tekli in front of the famous canvas that occupies the whole back of the room, seated before his easel, with his white hat pushed back to leave free his throbbing brow that was contracted with a tenacious insistence on accuracy.

Seeing Renovales, he rose hastily, leaving his palette on the piece of oil-cloth that protected the floor from spots of paint. Dear master! How thankful he was to him for this visit! And he showed him the copy, minutely accurate but without the wonderful atmosphere, without the miraculous realism of the original. Renovales approved with a nod; he admired the patient toil of that gentle ox of art, whose furrows were always alike, of geometric precision, without the slightest negligence or the least attempt at originality.

"Ti piace?" he asked anxiously, looking into his eyes to divine his thoughts. *"È vero? È vero?"* he repeated with the uncertainty of a child who fears that he is being deceived.

And suddenly calmed by the evidences of Renovales' approval, that kept growing more extravagant to conceal his indifference, the Hungarian grasped both of his hands and lifted them to his breast.

"Sono contento, maestro, sono contento."

He did not want to let Renovales go. Since he had had the generosity to come and see his work, he could not let him go away, they would lunch together at the hotel where he lived. They would open a bottle of Chianti to recall their life in Rome; they would talk of the merry Bohemian days of their youth, of those comrades of various nationalities that used to gather in the Café del Greco,—some already dead, the rest scattered through Europe and America, a few celebrated, the majority vegetating in the schools of their native land, dreaming of a final masterpiece before which death would probably overtake them.

Renovales felt overcome by the insistence of the Hungarian, who seized his hands with a dramatic expression, as though he would die at a refusal. Good for the Chianti! They would lunch together, and while Tekli was giving a few touches to his work, he would wait for him, wandering through the Museo, renewing old memories.

When he returned to the Hall of Velásquez, the assemblage had diminished; only the copyists remained bending over their canvases. The painter felt anew the influence of the great master. He admired his wonderful art, feeling at the same time the intense, historical sadness that seemed to emanate from all of his work. Poor Don Diego! He was born in the most melancholy period of Spanish history. His sane realism was fitted to immortalize the human form in all its naked beauty and fate had provided him a period when women looked like turtles, with their heads and shoulders peeping out between the double shell of their inflated gowns, and when men had a sacerdotal stiffness, raising their dark, ill-washed heads above their gloomy garb. He had painted what he saw; fear and hypocrisy were reflected in the eyes of that world. In the jesters, fools and humpbacks immortalized by Don Diego was revealed the forced merriment of a dying nation that must needs find distraction in the monstrous and absurd. The hypochondriac temper of a monarchy weak in body and fettered in spirit by the terrors of hell, lived in all those masterpieces, that inspired at once admiration and sadness. Alas for the artistic treasures wasted in immortalizing a period which without Velásquez would have fallen into utter oblivion!

Renovales thought, too, of the man, comparing with a feeling of remorse the great painter's life with the princely existence of the modern masters. Ah, the munificence of kings, their protection of artists, that people talked about in their enthusiasm for the past! He thought of the peaceful Don Diego and his salary of three *pesetas* as court painter, which he received only at rare intervals; of his glorious name figuring among those of jesters and barbers in the list of members of the king's household, forced to accept the office of appraiser of masonry to improve his situation, of the shame and humiliation of his last years in order to gain the Cross of Santiago, denying as a crime before the tribunal of the Orders that he had received money for his pictures, declaring with servile pride his position as servant of the king, as though this title were superior to the glory of an artist. Happy days of the present, blessed revolution of modern life, that dignifies the artist, and places him under the protection of the public, an impersonal sovereign that leaves the creator of beauty free and ends by even following him in new-created paths!

Renovales went up to the central gallery in search of another of his favorites. The works of Goya filled a large space on both walls. On one side the portraits of the kings and queens of the Bourbon decadence; heads of monarchs, or princes, crushed under their white wigs; sharp feminine eyes, bloodless faces, with their hair combed in the form of a tower. The two great painters had coincided in their lives with the moral downfall of two dynasties. In the Hall of Velásquez the thin, bony,

fair-haired kings, of monastic grace and anæmic pallor,
with their protruding under-jaws, and in their eyes an
expression of doubt and fear for the salvation of their
souls. Here, the corpulent, clumsy monarchs, with their
huge, heavy noses, fatefully pendulous, as though by
some mysterious relation they were dragging on the
brain, paralyzing its functions; their thick underlips,
hanging in sensual inertia; their eyes, calm as those of
cattle, reflecting in their tranquil light indifference for
everything that did not directly concern their own well-
being. The Austrians, nervous, restless, vacillating with
the fever of insanity, riding on theatrical chargers, in
dark landscapes, bounded by the snowy crests of the
Guadarrama, as sad, cold and crystallized as the soul of
the nation; the Bourbons, peaceful, adipose, resting—surfeited—on their huge calves, without any other thought
than the hunt of the following day or the domestic in-
trigue that would set the family in dissension, deaf to
the storms that thundered beyond the Pyrenees. The
one, surrounded by brutal-faced imbeciles, by gloomy pet-
tifoggers, by Infantas with childish faces and the hollow
skirts of a Virgin's image on an altar; the others bringing
as a merry, unconcerned retinue, a rabble clad in bright
colors, wrapped in scarlet capes or lace mantillas,
crowned with ornamental combs or masculine hats—a
race that, without knowing it, was sapping its heroism in
picnics at the Canal or in grotesque amusements. The
lash of invasion aroused them from their century-long
infancy. The same great artist that for many years had
portrayed the simple thoughtlessness of this gay people,
showy and light-hearted as a comic-opera chorus, afterwards painted them, knife in hand, attacking the Mame-
lukes with the agility of monkeys, felling those Egyptian
centaurs under their slashes, blackened with the smoke
of a hundred battles, or dying with theatrical pride by

the light of a lantern in the gloomy solitude of Moncloa, shot by the invaders.

Renovales admired the tragic atmosphere of the canvas before him. The executioners hid their faces, leaning on their guns; they were the blind executors of fate, a nameless force, and before them rose the pile of palpitating, bloody flesh; the dead with strips of flesh torn off by the bullets, showing reddish holes, the living with folded arms, defying the murderers in a tongue they could not understand, or covering their faces with their hands, as though this instinctive movement could save them from the lead. A whole people died, to be born again. And beside this picture of horror and heroism, in another close to it, he saw Palafox, the Leonidas of Saragossa, mounted on horseback, with his stylish whiskers and the arrogance of a blacksmith in a captain-general's uniform, having in his bearing something of the appearance of a popular chieftain, holding in one hand, gloved in buckskin, the curved saber, and in the other the reins of his stocky, big-bellied steed.

Renovales thought that art is like light, which acquires color and brightness from the objects it touches. Goya had passed through a stormy period; he had been a spectator of the resurrection of the soul of the people and his painting contained the tumultuous life, the heroic fury that you look for in vain in the canvases of that other genius, tied as he was to the monotonous existence of the palace, unbroken except by the news of distant wars in which they had little interest and whose victories, too late to be useful, had the coldness of doubt.

The painter turned away from the dames of Goya, clad in white cambric, with their rosebud mouths and with their hair done up like a turban, to concentrate his attention on a nude figure, the luminous gleam of whose flesh seemed to throw the adjacent canvases in a shadow.

He contemplated it closely for a long time, bending over the railing till the brim of his hat almost touched the canvas. Then he gradually moved away, without ceasing to look at it, until, at last, he sat down on a bench, still facing the picture with his eyes fixed upon it.

"Goya's *Maja*. The *Maja Desnuda!*"

He spoke aloud, without realizing it, as if his words were the inevitable outburst of the thoughts that rushed into his mind and seemed to pass back and forth behind the lenses of his eyes. His expressions of admiration were in different tones, marking a descending scale of memories.

The painter looked with delight at the gracefully delicate form, luminous, as though within it burned the flame of life, showing through the pearl-pale flesh. A shadow, scarcely perceptible, veiled in mystery of her femininity; the light traced a bright spot on her smoothly rounded knees and once more the shadow reached down to her tiny feet with their delicate toes, rosy and babyish.

The woman was small, graceful, and dainty; the Spanish Venus with no more flesh than was necessary to cover her supple, shapely frame with softly curving outlines. Her amber eyes that flashed slyly, were disconcerting with their gaze; her mouth had in its graceful corners the fleeting touch of an eternal smile; on her cheeks, elbows and feet the pink tone showed the transparency and the moist brilliancy of those shells that open their mysterious colors in the secret depths of the sea.

"Goya's *Maja*. The *Maja Desnuda!*"

He no longer said these words aloud, but his thought and his expression repeated them, his smile was their echo.

Renovales was not alone. From time to time groups of visitors passed back and forth between his eyes and the picture, talking loudly. The tread of heavy feet

shook the wooden floor. It was noon and the bricklayers
from nearby buildings were taking advantage of the
noon hour to explore those salons as if it were a new
world, delighting in the warm air of the furnaces. As
they went, they left footprints of plaster on the floor;
they called out to each other to share their admiration
before a picture; they were impatient to take it all in at
a single glance; they waxed enthusiastic over the war-
riors in their shining armor or the elaborate uniforms of
olden times. The cleverest among them served as guides
to their companions, driving them impatiently. They
had been there the day before. Go ahead! There was
still a lot to see! And they ran toward the inner halls
with the breathless curiosity of men who tread on new
ground and expect something marvelous to rise before
their steps.

Amid this rush of simple admirers there passed, too,
some groups of Spanish ladies. All did the same thing
before Goya's work, as if they had been previously
coached. They went from picture to picture, commenting on the fashions of the past, feeling a sort of longing
for the curious old crinolines and the broad mantillas
with the high combs. Suddenly they became serious,
drew their lips together and started at a quick pace for
the end of the gallery. Instinct warned them. Their
restless eyes felt hurt by the nude in the distance; they
seemed to scent the famous *Maja* before they saw her
and they kept on—erect, with severe countenances, just
as if they were annoyed by some rude fellow's advances
in the street—passing in front of the picture without
turning their faces, without seeing even the adjacent
pictures nor stopping till they reached the Hall of
Murillo.

It was the hatred for the nude, the Christian, century-
old abomination of Nature and truth, that rose instinc-

tively to protest against the toleration of such horrors in a public building which was peopled with saints, kings and ascetics.

Renovales worshiped the canvas with ardent devotion, and placed it in a class by itself. It was the first mani-. festation in Spanish history of art that was free from scruples, unhampered by prejudice. Three centuries of painting, several generations of glorious names, suc-ceeded one another with wonderful fertility; but not until Goya had the Spanish brush dared to trace the form of a woman's body, the divine nakedness that among all peoples has been the first inspiration of nascent art. Renovales remembered another nude, the Venus of Velásquez, preserved abroad. But that work had not been spontaneous; it was a commission of the monarch who, at the same time that he was paying foreigners lavishly for their studies in the nude, wished to have a similar canvas by his court-painter.

Religious oppression had obscured art for centuries. Human beauty terrified the great artists, who painted with a cross on their breasts and a rosary on their sword-hilts. Bodies were hidden under the stiff, heavy folds of sackcloth or the grotesque, courtly crinoline, and the painter never ventured to guess what was beneath them, looking at the model, as the devout worshiper contem-plates the hollow mantle of the Virgin, not knowing whether it contains a body or three sticks to hold up the head. The joy of life was a sin. In vain a sun fairer than that of Venice shone on Spanish soil, futile was the light that burned upon the land with a brighter glow than that of Flanders: Spanish art was dark, lifeless, sober, even after it knew the works of Titian. The Renais-sance, that in the rest of the world worshiped the nude as the supreme work of Nature, was covered here with the monk's cowl or the beggar's rags. The shining landscapes were dark and gloomy when they reached the canvas; under the brush the land of the sun appeared with a gray sky and grass that was a mournful green; the heads had a monkish gravity. The artist placed in his pictures not what surrounded him, but what he had within him, a piece of his soul—and his soul was fettered by the fear of dangers in the present life and torments in the life to come; it was black—black with sadness, as if it were dyed in the soot of the fires of the autos-de-fé.

That naked woman with her curly head resting on her folded arms was the awakening of an art that had lived in isolation. The slight frame, that scarcely rested on the green divan and the fine lace cushions, seemed on the point of rising in the air with the mighty impulse of resurrection.

Renovales thought of the two masters, equally great, and still so different. One had the imposing majesty of famous monuments—serene, correct, cold, filling the horizon of history with their colossal mass, growing old in glory without the centuries opening the least crack in their marble walls. On all sides the same façade—noble, symmetrical, calm, without the vagaries of caprice. It was reason—solid, well-balanced, alien to enthusiasm and weakness, without feverish haste. The other was as great as a mountain, with the fantastic disorder of Nature, covered with tortuous inequalities. On one side the wild, barren cliff; beyond, the glen, covered with blossoming heath; below, the garden with its perfumes and birds; on the heights, the crown of dark clouds, heavy with thunder and lightning. It was imagination in unbridled career, with breathless halts and new flights —its brow in the infinite and its feet implanted on earth.

The life of Don Diego was summed up in these words: "He had painted." That was his whole biography. Never in his travels in Spain and Italy did he feel curious to see anything but pictures. In the court of the Poet-king, he had vegetated amid gallantries and masquerades, calm as a monk of painting, always standing before his canvas and model—to-day a jester, to-morrow a little Infanta—without any other desire than to rise in rank among the members of the royal household, to see a cross of red cloth sewed on his black jerkin. He was a lofty soul, enclosed in a phlegmatic body that never tormented him with nervous desires nor disturbed the calm of his work with violent passions. When he died the good Dona Juana, his wife, died too, as though they sought each other, unable to remain apart after their long, uneventful pilgrimage through the world.

Goya "had lived." His life was that of the nobleman-artist—a stormy novel, full of mysterious amours. His pupils, on parting the curtains of his studio, saw the silk of royal skirts on their master's knees. The dainty duchesses of the period resorted to that robust Aragonese of rough, manly gallantry to have him paint their cheeks, laughing like mad at these intimate touches. When he contemplated some divine beauty on the tumbled bed, he transferred her form to the canvas by an irresistible impulse, an imperious necessity of reproducing beauty; and the legend that floated about the Spanish artist connected an illustrious name with all the beauties whom his brush immortalized.

To paint without fear or prejudice, to take delight in reproducing on canvas the glory of the nude, the lustrous amber of woman's flesh with its pale roses like a sea-shell, was Renovales' desire and envy; to live like the famous Don Francisco—a free bird with restless, shining plumage in the midst of the monotony of the human barn-yard; in his passions, in his diversions, in his tastes, to be different from the majority of men, since he was already different from them in his way of appreciating life.

But, ah! his existence was like that of Don Diego—unbroken, monotonous, laid out by level in a straight line. He painted, but he did not live. People praised his work for the accuracy with which he reproduced Nature, for the gleam of light, for the indefinable color of the atmosphere, and the exterior of things; but something was lacking, something that stirred within him and fought in vain to leap the vulgar barriers of daily existence.

The memory of the romantic life of Goya made him think of his own life. People called him a master; they bought everything he painted at good prices, especially if it was in accordance with some one else's tastes and contrary to his artistic desire; he enjoyed a calm existence, full of comforts; in his studio, almost as splendid as a palace, the façade of which was reproduced in the illustrated magazines, he had a wife who was convinced of his genius and a daughter who was almost a woman and who made the troop of his intimate pupils stammer with embarrassment. The only evidences of his Bohemian past that remained were his soft felt hats, his long beard, his tangled hair and a certain carelessness in his dress; but when his position as a "national celebrity" demanded it, he took out of his wardrobe a dress suit with the lapel covered with the insignia of honorary orders and played his part in official receptions. He had thousands of dollars in the bank. In his studio, palette in hand, he conferred with his broker, discussing what sort of investments he ought to make with the year's profits. His name awakened no surprise or aversion in high society, where it was fashionable for ladies to have their portraits painted by him.

In the early days he had provoked scandal and protests by his boldness in color and his revolutionary way of seeing Nature, but there was not connected with his name the least offence against the conventions of society. His women were women of the people, picturesque and repugnant; the only flesh that he had shown on his canvases was that of a sweaty laborer or the chubby child. He was an honored master, who cultivated his stupendous ability with the same calm that he showed in his business affairs.

What was lacking in his life? Ah! Renovales smiled ironically. His whole life suddenly came to mind in a tumultuous rush of memories. Once more he fixed his glance on that woman, shining white like a pearl amphora, with her arms above her head, her breasts erect and triumphant, her eyes resting on him, as if she had known him for many years, and he repeated mentally with an expression of bitterness and dejection:

"Goya's *Maja,* the *Maja Desnuda!*"

II

As Mariano Renovales recalled the first years of his life, his memory, always sensitive to exterior impressions, called up the ceaseless clang of hammers. From the rising of the sun till the earth began to darken with the shadows of twilight the iron sang or groaned on the anvil, jarring the walls of the house and the floor of the garret, where Mariano used to play, lying on the floor at the feet of a pale, sickly woman with serious, deep-set eyes, who frequently dropped her sewing to kiss the little one with sudden violence, as though she feared she would not see him again.

Those tireless hammers that had accompanied Mariano's birth, made him jump out of bed as soon as day broke and go down to the shop to warm himself beside the glowing forge. His father, a good-natured Cyclops —hairy and blackened—walked back and forth, turning over the irons, picking up files, giving orders to his assistants with loud shouts, in order to be heard in the din of the hammering. Two sturdy fellows, stripped to the waist, swung their arms, panting over the anvil, and the iron—now red, now golden—leaped in bright showers, scattered in crackling sprays, peopling the black atmosphere of the shop with a swarm of fiery flies that died away in the soot of the corners.

"Take care, little one!" said the father, protecting his delicate curly-haired head with one of his great hands.

The little fellow felt attracted by the colors of the glowing iron, till with the thoughtlessness of childhood he sometimes tried to pick up the fragments that glowed on the ground like fallen stars.

His father would push him out of the shop, and outside the door—black with soot—Mariano could see stretching out below him in the flood of sunlight the fields with their red soil cut into geometric figures by stone walls; at the bottom the valley with groups of poplars bordering the winding, crystal stream, and before him the mountains, covered to the very tops with dark pine woods. The shop was in the suburbs of a town and from it and the villages of the valley came the jobs that supported the blacksmith—new axles for carts, plowshares, scythes, shovels, and pitchforks in need of repair.

The incessant pounding of the hammers seemed to stir up the little fellow, inspiring him with a fever of activity, tearing him from his childish amusements. When he was eight years old, he used to seize the rope of the bellows and pull it, delighting in the shower of sparks that the current of air drove out of the lighted coals. The Cyclops was gratified at the strength of his son, robust and vigorous like all the men of his family, with a pair of fists that inspired a wholesome respect in all the village lads. He was one of his own blood. From his poor mother, weak and sickly, he inherited only his propensity toward silence and isolation that sometimes, when the fever of activity died out in him, kept him for hours at a time watching the fields, the sky or the brooks that came tumbling down over the pebbles to join the stream at the bottom of the valley.

The boy hated school, showing a holy horror of letters. His strong hands shook with uncertainty when he tried to write a word. On the other hand, his father and the other people in the shop admired the ease with which he could reproduce objects in a simple, ingenuous drawing, in which no detail of naturalness was lacking.

His pockets were always full of bits of charcoal and he never saw a wall or stone that had a suggestion of whiteness, without at once tracing on it a copy of the objects that struck his eyes because of some marked peculiarity. The outside walls of the shop were black with little Mariano's drawings. Along the walls ran the pigs of Saint Anthony, with their puckered snouts and twisted tails, that wandered through the village and were supported by public charity, to be raffled on the festival of the saint. And in the midst of this stout procession stood out the profiles of the blacksmith and all the workmen of the shop, with an inscription beneath, that no doubt might arise as to their identity.

"Come here, woman," the blacksmith would shout to his sick wife when he discovered a new sketch. "Come and see what our son has done. A devil of a boy!"

And influenced by this enthusiasm, he no longer complained when Mariano ran away from school and the bellows rope to spend the whole day running through the valley or the village, a piece of charcoal in his hand, covering the rocks of the mountain and the house walls with black lines, to the despair of the neighbors. In the tavern in the Plaza Mayor he had traced the heads of the most constant customers, and the innkeeper pointed them out proudly, forbidding anyone to touch the wall for fear the sketches would disappear. This work was a source of vanity to the blacksmith when Sundays, after mass, he went in to drink a glass with his friends. On the wall of the rectory he had traced a Virgin, before which the most pious old women in the village stopped with deep sighs.

The blacksmith with a flush of satisfaction accepted all the praises that were showered on the little fellow as if they belonged in large part to himself. Where had that prodigy come from, when all the rest of his family were such brutes? And he nodded affirmatively when the village notables spoke of doing something for the boy. To be sure, he did not know what to do, but they were right; his Mariano was not destined to hammer iron like his father. He might become as great a personage as Don Rafael, a gentleman who painted saints in the capital of the province and was a teacher of painting in a big house, full of pictures, in the city. During the summer he came with his family to live in an estate in the valley.

This Don Rafael was a man of imposing gravity; a saint with a large family of children, who wore a frock-coat as if it were a cassock and spoke with the suavity of a friar through his white beard that covered his thin,' pink cheeks. In the village church they had a wonderful picture painted by him, a *Purísima,* whose soft glowing colors made the legs of the pious tremble. Besides, the eyes of the image had the marvelous peculiarity of looking straight at those who contemplated it, following them even though they changed position. A veritable miracle. It seemed impossible that that good gentleman who came up every morning in the summer to hear mass in the village, had painted that supernatural work. An Englishman had tried to buy it for its weight in gold. No one had seen the Englishman, but every one smiled sarcastically when they commented on the offer. Yes, indeed, they were likely to let the picture go! Let the heretics rage with all their millions. The *Purísima* would stay in her chapel to the envy of the whole world—and especially of the neighboring villages.

When the parish priest went to visit Don Rafael to speak to him about the blacksmith's son, the great man already knew about his ability. He had seen his drawings in the village; the boy had some talent and it was a pity not to guide him in the right path. After this came the visits of the blacksmith and his son, both trembling when they found themselves in the attic of the country house that the great painter had converted into a studio, seeing close at hand the pots of color, the oily palette, the brushes and those pale blue canvases on which the rosy, chubby cheeks of the cherubim or the ecstatic face of the Mother of God were beginning to assume form.

At the end of the summer the good blacksmith decided to follow Don Rafael's advice. As long as he was so good as to consent to helping the boy, he was not going to be the one to interfere with his good fortune. The shop gave him enough to live on. All it meant was to work a few years longer, to support himself till the end of his life beside the anvil, without an assistant or a successor. His son was born to be somebody, and it was a serious sin to stop his progress by scorning the help of his good protector.

His mother, who constantly grew weaker and more sickly, cried as if the journey to the capital of the province were to the end of the world.

"Good-by, my boy. I shall never see you again."

And in truth it was the last time that Mariano saw that pale face with its great expressionless eyes, now almost wiped out of his memory like a whitish spot in which, in spite of all his efforts, he could not succeed in restoring the outline of the features.

In the city his life was radically different. Then for the first time he understood what it was his hands were striving for as they moved the charcoal over the white-washed walls. Art was revealed to his eyes in those silent afternoons, passed in the convent where the provincial museum was situated, while his master, Don Rafael, argued with other gentlemen in the professor's hall, or signed papers in the secretary's office.

Mariano lived at his protector's house, at once his servant and his pupil. He carried letters to the dean and the other canons, who were friends of his master and who accompanied him on his walks or spent social evenings in his studio. More than once he visited the locutories of nunneries, to deliver through the heavy gratings presents from Don Rafael to certain black and white shadows, which attracted by this sturdy young country boy, and aware that he meant to be a painter, overwhelmed him with the eager questions born of their seclusion. Before he went away they would hand him, through the revolving window, cakes and candied lemons or some other goody, and then, with a word of advice, would say good-by in their thin, soft voices, which sifted through the iron of the gratings.

"Be a good boy, little Mariano. Study, pray. Be a good Christian, the Lord will protect you and perhaps you will get to be as great a painter as Don Rafael, who is one of the first in the world."

How the master laughed at the memory of the childish simplicity that made him see in his master the most marvelous painter on earth! . . . Mornings, when he attended the classes in the School of Fine Arts, he grew angry at his comrades, a disrespectful rabble, brought up in the streets, sons of mechanics, who, as soon as the professor turned his back, pelted each other with the crumbs of bread meant to wipe out their drawings, and cursed Don Rafael, calling him a "Christer" and a "Jesuit."

The afternoon Mariano passed in the studio, at his master's side. How excited he was the first time he placed a palette in his hand and allowed him to copy on an old canvas a child St. John which he had finished for a society! . . . While the boy with his forehead wrinkled in his eagerness, tried to imitate his master's work, he

listened to the good advice that the master gave him,
without looking up from the canvas over which his an-
gelic brush was running.

Painting must be religious; the first pictures in the
world had been inspired by religion; outside of it, life
offered nothing but base materialism, loathsome sins.
Painting must be ideal, beautiful. It must always represent pretty subjects, reproduce things as they ought to
be, not as they really are, and above all, look up to
heaven, since there is true life, not on this earth, a valley
of tears. Mariano must modify his instincts—that was
his master's advice—must lose his fondness for drawing coarse subjects—people as he saw them, animals in
all their material brutality, landscapes in the same form
as his eyes gazed upon.

He must have idealism. Many painters were almost
saints; only thus could they reflect celestial beauty in the
faces of their madonnas. And poor Mariano strove to
be ideal, to catch a little of that beatific serenity which
surrounded his master.

Little by little he came to understand the methods
which Don Rafael employed to create these masterpieces
which called forth cries of admiration from his circle of
canons and the rich ladies that gave him commissions
for pictures. When he intended to begin one of his
Purísimas, which were slowly invading the churches and
convents of the province, he arose early and returned to
his studio after mass and communion. In this way he
felt an inner strength, a calm enthusiasm, and, if he felt
depressed in the midst of the work, he once more had
recourse to this inspiring medicine.

The artist, besides, must be pure. He had taken a vow
of chastity after he had reached the age of fifty, somewhat late to be sure, but it was not because he had not
known before this certain means of reaching the per-

fect idealism of a celestial painter. His wife, who had grown old in her countless confinements, exhausted by the tiresome fidelity and virtue of the master, was no longer anything but the companion who gave the responses when he prayed his rosaries and Trisagia at night. He had several daughters, who weighed on his conscience like the reproachful memory of a disgraceful materialism, but some were already nuns and the others were on the way, while the idealism of the artist increased as these evidences of his impurity disappeared from the house and went to hide away in a convent where they upheld the artistic prestige of their father.

Sometimes the great painter hesitated before a *Purísima,* which was always the same, as if he painted it with a stencil. Then he spoke mysteriously to his disciple:

"Mariano, tell the gentlemen not to come to-morrow. We have a model."

And when the studio was closed to the priests and the other respectable friends, with heavy step in came Rodríguez, a policeman, with a cigarette stub under his heavy bristling mustache and one hand on the handle of his sword. Dismissed from the gendarmerie for intoxication and cruelty, and finding himself without employment, by some strange chance he began to devote himself to serving as a painter's model. The pious artist, who held him in a sort of terror, nagged by his constant petitions, had secured for him this position as policeman, and Rodríguez took advantage of every opportunity to show his rough appreciation, slapping the master's shoulders with his great hands and blowing in his face, his breath redolent with nicotine and alcohol.

"Don Rafael, you are my father. If anybody touches you, I'll fix him, whoever he is."

And the ascetic artist, with a feeling of satisfaction at

this protection, blushed and waved his hands in protest against the frankness of the rude fellow with his threats for the men he would "fix."

He threw his helmet on the ground, handed his heavy sword to Mariano, and like a man that knows his duty, took out of the bottom of a chest a white woolen tunic and a piece of blue cloth like a cloak, placing both garments on his body with the skill of practice.

Mariano looked at him with astonished eyes but without any temptation to laugh. They were mysteries of art, surprises that were reserved only for those who, like him, had the good fortune to live on terms of intimacy with the great master.

"Ready, Rodriguez?" Don Rafael asked impatiently.

And Rodríguez, erect in his bath robe with the blue rag hanging from his shoulders, clasped his hands and lifted his fierce gaze to the ceiling, without ceasing to suck the stub that singed his mustache. The master did not need the model except for the robes of the figure, to study the folds of the celestial garment, which must not reveal the slightest evidence of human contour. The possibility of copying a woman had never passed through his imagination. That was falling into materialism, glorifying the flesh, inviting temptation; Rodríguez was all he needed; one must be an idealist.

The model continued in his mystic attitude with his body lost in the innumerable folds of his blue and white raiment, while under it the square toes of his army boots stuck out, and he held up his grotesque, flat head, crowned with bristling hair, coughing and choking from the smoke of the cigar, without ceasing to look up and without separating his hands clasped in an attitude of worship.

Sometimes, tired out by the industrious silence of the master and the pupil, Rodríguez uttered a few grumbles that little by little took the form of words and finally developed into the story of the deeds of his heroic period, when he was a rural policeman and "could take a shot at anyone and pay for it afterward with a report." The *Purisima* grew excited at these memories. His hands separated with a tremble of murderous joy, the carefully arranged folds were disturbed, his bloodshot eyes no longer looked heavenward, and with a hoarse voice he told of tremendous beatings he administered, of men who fell to the ground writhing with pain, the shooting of prisoners which afterwards were reported as attempts to escape; and to give greater relief to this autobiography which he declaimed with bestial pride, he sprinkled his words with interjections as vulgar as they were lacking in respect for the first personages of the heavenly court.

"Rodríguez, Rodríguez!" exclaimed the master, horror-stricken.

"At your command, Don Rafael."

And the *Purisima,* after passing the stub from one side of his mouth to the other, once more folded his hands, straightened up, showing his red-striped trousers under the tunic, and lost his gaze on high, smiling with ecstasy, as if he contemplated on the ceiling all his heroic deeds of which he felt so proud.

Mariano was in despair before his canvas. He could never imitate his illustrious master. He was incapable of painting anything but what he saw, and his brush, after reproducing the blue and white raiment, stopped, hesitating at the face, calling in vain on imagination. After futile efforts it was the grotesque mask of Rodríguez that appeared on the canvas.

And the pupil had a sincere admiration for the ability of Don Rafael, for that pale head veiled in the light of its halo, a pretty, expressionless face of childish beauty, which took the place of the policeman's fierce head in the picture.

This sleight-of-hand seemed to the boy the most astounding evidence of art. When would he reach the easy prestidigitation of his master!

With time the difference between Don Rafael and his pupil became more marked. At school his comrades gathered around him, recognizing his superiority and praising his drawings. Some professors, enemies of his master, lamented that such talent should be lost beside that "saint-painter." Don Rafael was surprised at what Mariano did outside of his studio—figures and landscapes, directly observed which, according to him, breathed the brutality of life.

His circle of serious gentlemen began to discover some merit in the pupil.

"He will never reach your height, Don Rafael," they said. "He lacks unction, he has no idealism, he will never paint a good Virgin—but as a worldly painter he has a future."

The master, who loved the boy for his submissive nature and the purity of his habits, tried in vain to make him follow the right way. If he would only imitate him, his fortune was made. He would die without a successor and his studio and his fame would be his. The boy only had to see how, little by little, like a good ant of the Lord, the master had gathered together a fair sized future with his brush. By virtue of his idealism, he had his country house there in the village, and no end of estates, the tenants of which came and visited him in his studio, carrying on endless discussions over the payment and amount of the rents in front of the poetic Virgins. The Church was poor because of the impiety of the times, it could not pay as generously as in other centuries, but commissions were numerous, and a Virgin in all her purity was a matter of only three days—but young Renovales made a troubled, wry face, as if a painful sacrifice were demanded of him.

"I can't, Master. I'm an idiot. I don't know how to invent things. I paint only what I see."

And when he began to see naked bodies in the so-called "life" class he devoted himself zealously to this study, as if the flesh caused in him the most violent intoxication. Don Rafael was appalled by finding in the corners of his house sketches that portrayed shameful nudes in all their reality. Besides, the progress of his pupil caused him some uneasiness; he saw in his painting a vigor that he himself had never had. He even noted some falling-off in his circle of admirers. The good canons, as always, admired his Virgins, but some of them had their portraits painted by Mariano, praising the skill of his brush.

One day he said to his pupil, firmly:

"You know that I love you as I would a son, Mariano, but you are wasting your time with me. I cannot teach you anything. Your place is somewhere else. I thought you might go to Madrid. There you will find men of your stamp."

His mother was dead; his father was still in the blacksmith shop, and when he saw him come home with several duros, the pay for portraits he had made, he looked on this sum as a fortune. It did not seem possible that anyone would give money in exchange for colors. A letter from Don Rafael convinced him. Since that wise gentleman advised that his son should go to Madrid, he must agree.

"Go to Madrid, my boy, and try to make money soon, for your father is old and will not always be able to help you."

At the age of sixteen, Renovales landed in Madrid

and finding himself alone, with only his wishes for his guide, devoted himself zealously to his work. He spent the morning in the Museo del Prado, copying all the heads in Velásquez's pictures. He felt that till then he had been blind. Besides, he worked in an attic studio with some other companions and evenings painted water-colors. By selling these and some copies, he managed to eke out the small allowance his father sent him.

He recalled with a sort of homesickness those years of poverty, of real misery, the cold nights in his wretched bed, the irritating meals—Heaven knows what was in them—eaten in a bar-room near the Teatro Real; the discussions in the corner of a café, under the hostile glances of the waiters who were provoked that a dozen long-haired youths should occupy several tables and order all together only three coffees and many bottles of water.

The light-hearted young fellows stood their misery without difficulty and, to make up for it, what a fill of fancies they had, what a glorious feast of hopes! A new discovery every day. Renovales ran through the realm of art like a wild colt, seeing new horizons spreading out before him, and his career caused an outburst of scandal that amounted to premature celebrity. The old men said that he was the only boy who "had the stuff in him"; his comrades declared that he was a "real painter," and in their iconoclastic enthusiasm compared his inexperienced works with those of the recognized old masters—"poor humdrum artists" on whose bald pates they felt obliged to vent their spleen in order to show the superiority of the younger generation.

Renovales' candidacy for the fellowship at Rome caused a veritable revolution. The younger set, who swore by him and considered him their illustrious captain, broke out in threats, fearful lest the "old boys" should sacrifice their idol.

When at last his manifest superiority won him the fellowship, there were banquets in his honor, articles in the papers, his picture was published in the illustrated magazines, and even the old blacksmith made a trip to Madrid, to breathe with tearful emotion part of the incense that was burned for his son.

In Rome a cruel disappointment awaited Renovales. His countrymen received him rather coldly. The younger men looked on him as a rival and waited for his next works with the hope of a failure; the old men who lived far from their fatherland examined him with malignant curiosity. "And so that big chap was the blacksmith's son, who caused so much disturbance among the ignorant people at home! . . . Madrid was not Rome. They would soon see what that *genius* could do!"

Renovales did nothing in the first months of his stay in Rome. He answered with a shrug of his shoulders those who asked for his pictures with evident innuendo. He had come there not to paint but to study; that was what the State was paying him for. And he spent more than half a year drawing, always drawing in the famous art galleries, where, pencil in hand, he studied the famous works. The paint boxes remained unopened in one corner of the studio.

Before long he came to detest the great city, because of the life the artists led in it. What was the use of fellowships? People studied less there than in other places. Rome was not a school, it was a market. The painting merchants set up their business there, attracted by the gathering of artists. All—old and beginners, famous and unknown—felt the temptation of money; all were seduced by the easy comforts of life, producing works for sale, painting pictures in accordance with the suggestions of some German Jews who frequented the studios, designating the sizes and the types that were in style in order to spread them over Europe and America.

When Renovales visited the studios, he saw nothing but *genre* pictures, sometimes gentlemen in long dress coats, others tattered Moors or Calabrian peasants. They were pretty, faultless paintings, for which they used as models a manikin, or the families of *ciociari* whom they hired every morning in the Piazza di Espagna beside the Sealinata of the Trinity; the everlasting country-woman, swarthy and black-eyed, with great hoops in her ears and wearing a green skirt, a black waist and a white head-dress caught up on her hair with large pins; the usual old man with sandals, a woolen cloak and a pointed hat with spiral bands on his snowy head that was a fitting model for the Eternal Father. The artists judged each other's ability by the number of thousand lire they took in during a year; they spoke with respect of the famous masters who made a fortune out of the millionaires of Paris and Chicago for easel-pictures that nobody saw. Renovales was indignant. This sort of art was almost like that of his first master, even if it was "worldly" as Don Rafael had said. And that was what they sent him to Rome for!

Unpopular with his countrymen because of his brusque ways, his rude tongue and his honesty, which made him refuse all commissions from the art merchants, he sought the society of artists from other countries. Among the cosmopolitan group of young painters who were quartered in Rome, Renovales soon became popular.

His energy, his exuberant spirits, made him a congenial, merry comrade, when he appeared in the studios of the Via di Babuino or in the cholocate rooms and cafés of the Corso, where the artists of different nationalities gathered in friendly company.

Mariano, at the age of twenty, was an athletic fellow,

a worthy scion of the man who was pounding iron from morning till night in a far away corner of Spain. One day an English youth, a friend of his, read him a page of Ruskin in his honor. "The plastic arts are essentially athletic." An invalid, a half paralyzed man, might be a great poet, a celebrated musician, but to be a Michael Angelo or a Titian a man must have not merely a privileged soul, but a vigorous body. Leonardo da Vinci broke a horseshoe in his hands; the sculptors of the Renaissance worked huge blocks of marble with their titanic arms or chipped off the bronze with their gravers; the great painters were often architects and, covered with dust, moved huge masses. Renovales listened thoughtfully to the words of the great English æstheticist. He, too, was a strong soul in an athlete's body.

The appetites of his youth never went beyond the manly intoxications of strength and movement. Attracted by the abundance of models which Rome offered, he often undressed a *ciociara* in his studio, delighting in drawing the forms of her body. He laughed, like the big giant that he was, he spoke to her with the same freedom as if she were one of the poor women that came out to stop him at night as he returned alone to the Academy of Spain, but when the work was over and she was dressed—out with her! He had the chastity of strong men. He worshiped the flesh, but only to copy its lines. The animal contact, the chance meeting, without love, without attraction, with the inner reserve of two people who do not know each other and who look on each other with suspicion, filled him with shame. What he wanted to do was to study, and women only served as a hindrance in great undertakings. He consumed the surplus of his energy in athletic exercise. After one of his feats of strength, which filled his comrades with enthusiasm, he would come in fresh, serene, indifferent, as

though he were coming out of a bath. He fenced with
the French painters of the Villa Medici; learned to box
with Englishmen and Americans; organized, with some
German artists, excursions to a grove near Rome, which
were talked about for days in the cafés of the Corso.
He drank countless healths with his companions to the
Kaiser whom he did not know and for whom he did not
care a rap. He would thunder in his noisy voice the
traditional *Gaudeamus Igitur* and finally would catch two
models of the party around the waist and with his arms
stretched out like a cross carry them through the woods
till he dropped them on the grass as if they were feathers.
Afterwards he would smile with satisfaction at the admiration of those good Germans, many of them sickly
and near-sighted, who compared him with Siegfried and
the other muscular heroes of their warlike mythology.

In the Carnival season, when the Spaniards organized
a cavalcade of the Quixote, he undertook to represent the
knight Pentapolin—"him of the rolled-up sleeves,"—and
in the Corso there were applause and cries of admiration
for the huge biceps that the knight-errant, erect on his
horse, revealed. When the spring nights came, the
artists marched in a procession across the city to the
Jewish quarter to buy the first artichokes—the popular
dish in Rome, in the preparation of which an old Hebrew
woman was famous. Renovales went at the head of the
carciofalatta, bearing the banner, starting the songs
which were alternated with the cries of all sorts of animals; and his comrades marched behind him, reckless
and insolent under the protection of such a chieftain. As
long as Mariano was with them there was no danger.
They told the story that in the alleys of the Trastevere
he had given a deadly beating to two bullies of the dis-
trict, after taking away their stilettos.

Suddenly the athlete shut himself up in the Academy

and did not come down to the city. For several days
they talked about him at the gatherings of artists. He
was painting; an exhibition that was going to take place
in Madrid was close at hand and he wanted to take to it
a picture to justify his fellowship. He kept the door of
his studio closed to everyone, he did not permit comment nor advice, the canvas would appear just as he
conceived it. His comrades soon forgot him and Renovales ended his work in seclusion, and left for his
country with it.

It was a complete success, the first important step on
the road that was to lead him to fame. Now he remembered with shame, with remorse, the glorious uproar his
picture "The Victory of Pavia" stirred up. People
crowded in front of the huge canvas, forgetting the rest
of the Exhibition. And as, at that time, the Government
was strong, the Cortes was closed and there was no
serious accident in any of the bull-rings, the newspapers,
for lack of any more lively event, hastened in cheap
rivalry to reproduce the picture, to talk about it, publishing portraits of the author, profiles, as well as front
views, large and small, expatiating on his life in Rome
and his eccentricities, and recalled with tears of emotion
the poor old man who far away in his village was pounding iron, hardly knowing of his son's glory.

With one bound Renovales passed from obscurity to
the light of apotheosis. The older men whose duty it
was to judge his work became benevolent and extended
kindly sympathy. The little tiger was getting tame.
Renovales had seen the world and now he was coming
back to the good traditions; he was going to be a painter
like the rest. His picture had portions that were like
Velásquez, fragments worthy of Goya, corners that recalled El Greco; there was everything in it, except Renovales, and this amalgam of reminiscences was its chief

merit, what attracted general applause and won it the first medal.

A magnificent début it was. A dowager duchess, a great protectress of the arts, who never bought a picture or a statue but who entertained at her table painters and sculptors of renown, finding in this an inexpensive pleasure and a certain distinction as an illustrious lady, wished to make Renovales' acquaintance. He overcame the stand-offishness of his nature that kept him away from all social relations. Why should he not know high society? He could go wherever other men could. And he put on his first dress-coat, and after the banquets of the duchess, where his way of arguing with members of the Academy provoked peals of merry laughter, he visited other salons and for several weeks was the idol of society which, to be sure, was somewhat scandalized by his *faux pas,* but still pleased with the timidity that overcame him after his daring sallies. The younger set liked him because he handled a sword like a Saint George. Although a painter and son of a blacksmith, he was in every way a respectable person. The ladies flattered him with their most amiable smiles, hoping that the fashionable artist would honor them with a portrait gratis, as he had done with the duchess.

In this period of high-life, always in dress clothes from seven in the evening, without painting anything but women who wanted to appear pretty and discussed gravely with the artist which gown they should put on to serve as a model, Renovales met his wife Josephina.

The first time that he saw her among so many ladies of arrogant bearing and striking presence, he felt attracted towards her by force of contrast. The bashfulness, the modesty, the insignificance of the girl impressed him. She was small, her face offered no other beauty than that of youth, her body had the charm of delicacy.

Like himself, the poor girl was there out of a sort of condescendence on the part of the others; she seemed to be there by sufferance and she shrank in it, as if afraid of attracting attention. Renovales always saw her in the same evening gown somewhat old, with that appearance of weariness which a garment constantly made over to follow the course of the fashions is wont to acquire. The gloves, the flowers, the ribbons had a sort of sadness in their freshness, as if they betrayed the sacrifices, the domestic exertions it had taken to procure them. She was on intimate terms with all the girls who made a triumphal entrance into the drawing-rooms, inspiring praise and envy with their new toilettes; her mother, a majestic lady, with a big nose and gold glasses, treated the ladies of the noblest families with familiarity; but in spite of this intimacy there was apparent around the mother and daughter the gap of somewhat disdainful affection, in which commiseration bore no small part. They were poor. The father had been a diplomat of some distinction who, at his death, left his wife no other source of income than the widow's pension. Two sons were abroad as attachés of an embassy, struggling with the scantiness of their salary and the demands of their position. The mother and daughter lived in Madrid, chained to the society in which they were born, fearing to abandon it, as if that would be equivalent to a degradation, remaining during the day in a fourth-floor apartment, furnished with the remnants of their past opulence, making unheard-of sacrifices in order to be able in the evening to rub elbows worthily with those who had been their equals.

Some relative of Doña Emilia, the mother, contributed to her support, not with money (never that!) but by loaning her the surplus of their luxury, that she and her daughter might maintain a pale appearance of comfort.

Some of them loaned them their carriage on certain

days, so that they might drive through the Castellana and
the Retiro, bowing to their friends as the carriages
passed; others sent them their box at the Opera on evenings when the bill was not a brilliant one. Their pity
made them remember them, too, when they sent out invitations to birthday dinners, afternoon teas, and the like.
"We mustn't forget the Torrealtas, poor things." And
the next day, the society reporters included in the list
of those present at the function "the charming Señorita
de Torrealta and her distinguished mother, the widow of
the famous diplomat of imperishable memory," and Doña
Emilia, forgetting her situation, fancying she was in the
good old times, went to everything, in the same black
gown, annoying with her "my dears" and her gossip the
great ladies whose maids were richer and ate better than
she and her daughter. If some old gentleman took refuge
beside her, the diplomat's wife tried to overwhelm him
with the majesty of her recollections. "When we were
ambassadors in Stockholm." "When my friend Eugénie
was empress. . . ."

The daughter, endowed with her instinctive girlish
timidity, seemed better to realize her position. She would
remain seated among the older ladies, only rarely ven-
turing to join the other girls who had been her boarding-
school companions and who now treated her condescendingly, looking on her as they would upon a governess
who had been raised to their station, out of remembrance
for the past. Her mother was annoyed at her timidity.
She ought to dance a lot, be lively and bold, like the
other girls, crack jokes, even if they were doubtful, that
the men might repeat them and give her the reputation
of being a wit. It was incredible that with the bringing
up she had had, she should be so insignificant. The idea!
The daughter of a great man about whom people used
to crowd as soon as he entered the first salons in Europe!

A girl who had been educated at the school of the Sacred Heart in Paris, who spoke English, a little German, and spent the day reading when she did not have to clean a pair of gloves or make over a dress! Didn't she want to get married? Was she so well satisfied with that fourth-story apartment, that wretched cell so unworthy of their name?

Josephina smiled sadly. Get married! She never would get to that in the society they frequented. Everyone knew they were poor. The young men thronged the drawing-rooms in search of women with money. If by chance one of them did come up to her, attracted by her pale beauty, it was only to whisper to her shameful suggestions while they danced; to propose uncompromising engagements, friendly relations with a prudence modeled on the English, flirtations that had no result.

Renovales did not realize how his friendship with Josephina began. Perhaps it was the contrast between himself and the little woman who hardly came up to his shoulder and who seemed about fifteen when she was already past twenty. Her soft voice with its slight lisp came to his ears like a caress. He laughed when he thought of the possibility of embracing that graceful, slender form; it would break in pieces in his pugilist's hands, like a wax doll. Mariano sought her out in the drawing-rooms which she and her mother were accustomed to frequent, and spent all the time sitting at her side, feeling an impulse to confide in her as a brother, a desire of telling her all about herself, his past, his present work, his hopes, as if she were a room-mate. She listened to him, looking at him with her brown eyes that seemed to smile at him, nodding assent, often without having heard what he said, receiving like a caress the exuberance of that nature which seemed to overflow in waves of fire. He was different from all the men she had known.

When someone—nobody knows who—perhaps one of Josephina's friends, noticed this intimacy, to make sport of her, she spread the news. The painter and the Torrealta girl were engaged. That was when the interested parties discovered that they loved each other. It was something more than friendship that made Renovales pass through Josephina's street mornings, looking at the high windows in the hope of seeing her dainty silhouette through the panes. One night at the duchess' when they were left alone in the hallway, Renovales caught her hand and lifted it to his lips, but so timidly that they scarcely touched her glove. He was afraid after his rudeness, felt ashamed of his violence; he thought he was hurting the delicate, slender girl; but she let her hand stay in his, and at the same time bowed her head and began to cry.

"How good you are, Mariano!"

She felt the most intense gratitude, when she realized that she was loved for the first time; loved truly, by a man of some distinction, who fled from the women of fortune to seek a humble, neglected girl like her. All the treasures of affection which had been accumulating in the isolation of her humiliating life overflowed. How she could love the man who loved her, taking her out of that parasite's existence, lifting her by his strength and affection to the level of those who scorned her!

The noble widow of Torrealta gave a cry of indignation when she learned of the engagement of the painter and her daughter. "The blacksmith's son!" "The illustrious diplomat of imperishable memory!" But as if this protest of her pride opened her eyes, she thought of the years her daughter had spent going from one drawing-room to another, without anyone paying any attention to her. What dunces men were! She thought, too, that a celebrated painter was a personage; she remembered the articles devoted to Renovales because of his last picture, and, above all, a thing that had the most effect on her, she knew by hearsay of the great fortune that artists amassed abroad, the hundreds of thousands of francs paid for a canvas that could be carried under your arm. Why might not Renovales be one of the fortunate?

She began to annoy her countless relatives with requests for advice. The girl had no father and they must take his place. Some answered indifferently. "The painter! Hump! Not bad!" evidencing by their coldness that it was all the same to them if she married a tax-collector. Others insulted her unwittingly by showing their approval. "Renovales? An artist with a great future before him. What more do you want? You ought to be thankful he has taken a fancy to her." But the advice that decided her was that of her famous cousin, the Marquis of Tarfe, a man to whom she looked upon as the most distinguished citizen in the country, without doubt because of his office as permanent head of the Foreign Service, for every two years he was made Minister of Foreign Affairs.

"It looks very good to me," said the nobleman, hastily, for they were waiting for him in the Senate. "It is a modern marriage and we must keep up with the times. I am a conservative, but liberal, very liberal and very modern. I will protect the children. I like the marriage. Art joining its prestige with a historic family! The popular blood that rises through its merits and is mingled with that of the ancient nobility!"

And the Marquis of Tarfe, whose marquisate did not go back half a century, with these rhetorical figures of an orator in the Senate and his promises of protection, convinced the haughty widow. She was the one who spoke to Renovales, to relieve him of an explanation that would be trying because of the timidity he felt in this society that was not his own.

"I know all about it, Mariano, my dear, and you have my consent."

But she did not like long engagements. When did he intend to get married? Renovales was more eager for it than the mother. Josephina was different from other women who hardly aroused his desire. His chastity, which had been like that of a rough laborer, developed into a feverish desire to make that charming doll his own as soon as possible. Besides, his pride was flattered by this union. His fiancée was poor; her only dowry was a few ragged clothes, but she belonged to a noble family, ministers, generals—all of noble descent. They could weigh by the ton the coronets and coats-of-arms of those countless relatives who did not pay much attention to Josephina and her mother, but who would soon be his family. What would Señor Antón think, hammering iron in the suburbs of his town? What would his comrades in Rome say, whose lot consisted in living with the *ciociare* who served as their models, and marrying them afterward out of fear for the stiletto of the venerable Calabrian who insisted on providing a legitimate father for his grandsons!

The papers had much to say about the wedding, repeating with slight variations the very phrases of the Marquis of Tarfe, "Art uniting with nobility." Renovales wanted to leave for Rome with Josephina as soon as the marriage was celebrated. He had made all the arrangements for his new life there, investing in it all the money he had received from the State for his picture and the product of several pictures for the Senate for which he received commissions through his illustrious relative-to-be.

A friend in Rome (the jolly Cotoner) had hired for him an apartment in the Via Margutta and had furnished it in accordance with his artistic taste. Doña Emilia would remain in Madrid with one of her sons, who had been promoted to a position in the Foreign Office. Everybody, even the mother, was in the young couple's way. And Doña Emilia wiped away an invisible tear with the tip of her glove. Besides, she did not care to go back to the countries where she had been *somebody;* she preferred to stay in Madrid; there people knew her at least.

The wedding was an event. Not a soul in the huge family was absent; all feared the annoying questions of the illustrious widow who kept a list of relatives to the sixth remove.

Señor Antón arrived two days before, in a new suit with knee-breeches and a broad plush hat, looking somewhat confused at the smiles of those people who regarded him as a quaint type. Crestfallen and trembling in the presence of the two women, with a countryman's respect, he called his daughter-in-law "Señorita."

"No, papa, call me 'daughter.' Say Josephina to me."

But in spite of Josephina's simplicity and the tender gratitude he felt when he saw her look at his son with such loving eyes, he did not venture to take the liberty of speaking to her as his child and made the greatest efforts to avoid this danger, always speaking to her in the third person.

Doña Emilia, with her gold glasses and her majestic bearing, caused him even greater emotion. He always called her "Señora marquesa," for in his simplicity he could not admit that that lady was not at least a marchioness. The widow, somewhat disarmed by the good man's homage, admitted that he was a "rube" of some natural talent, a fact that made her tolerate the ridiculous note of his knee breeches.

In the chapel of the Marquis of Tarfe's palace, after looking dumbfounded at the great throng of nobility that had gathered for his son's wedding, the old man, standing in the doorway, began to cry:

"Now I can die, O Lord. Now I can die!"

And he repeated his sad desire, without noticing the laughter of the servants, as if, after a life of toil, happiness were the inevitable forerunner of death.

The bride and groom started on their trip the same day. Señor Antón for the first time kissed his daughter-in-law on the forehead, moistening it with his tears, and went home to his village, still repeating his longing for death, as though nothing were left in the world for him to hope for.

Renovales and his wife reached Rome after several stops on the way. Their short stay in various cities of the Riviera, the days in Pisa and Florence, though delightful, as keeping the memory of their first intimacy, seemed unspeakably vulgar, when they were installed in their little house in Rome. There the real honeymoon began, by their own fireside, free from all intrusion, far from the confusion of hotels.

Josephina, accustomed to a life of secret privation, to the misery of that fourth-floor apartment in which she and her mother lived as though they were camping out, keeping all their show for the street, admired the coquettish charm, the smart daintiness of the house in the Via Margutta. Mariano's friend, who had charge of the furnishing of the house, a certain Pepe Cotoner, who hardly ever touched his brushes and who devoted all his artistic enthusiasm to his worship of Renovales, had certainly done things well.

Josephina clapped her hands in childish joy when she saw the bedroom, admiring its sumptuous Venetian furniture, with its wonderful inlaid pearl and ebony, a princely luxury that the painter would have to pay for in instalments.

Oh! The first night of their stay in Rome! How well Renovales remembered it! Josephina, lying on the monumental bed, made for the wife of a Doge, shook with the delight of rest, stretching her limbs before she hid them under the fine sheets, showing herself with the abandon of a woman who no longer has any secrets to keep. The pink toes of her plump little feet moved as if they were calling Renovales.

Standing beside the bed, he looked at her seriously, with his brows contracted, dominated by a desire that he hesitated to express. He wanted to see her, to admire her; he did not know her yet, after those nights in the hotels when they could hear strange voices on the other side of the thin walls.

It was not the caprice of a lover, it was the desire of a painter, the demand of an artist. His eyes were hungry for beauty.

She resisted, blushing, a trifle angry at this demand which offended her deepest prejudices.

"Don't be foolish, Mariano, dear. Come to bed; don't talk nonsense."

But he persisted obstinately in his desire. She must overcome her bourgeois scruples, art scoffed at such modesty, human beauty was meant to be shown in all its radiant majesty and not to be kept hidden, despised and cursed.

He did not want to paint her; he did not dare to ask for that; but he did want to see her, to see her and admire her, not with a coarse desire, but with religious adoration.

And his hands, restrained by the fears of hurting her, gently pulled her weak arms that were crossed on her breast in the endeavor to resist his advances. She laughed: "You silly thing. You're tickling me—you're hurting me." But little by little, conquered by his persistency, her feminine pride flattered by this worship of her body, she gave in to him, allowed herself to be treated like a child, with soft remonstrances as if she were undergoing torture, but without resisting any longer.

Her body, free from veils, shone with the whiteness of pearl. Josephina closed her eyes as if she wanted to flee from the shame of her nakedness. On the smooth sheet, her graceful form was outlined in a slightly rosy tone, intoxicating the eyes of the artist.

Josephina's face was not much to look at, but her body! If he could only overcome her scruples some time and paint her!

Renovales kneeled down beside the bed in a transport of admiration.

"I worship you, Josephina. You are as fair as Venus. No, not Venus. She is cold and calm, like a goddess, and you are a woman. You are like—what are you like? Yes, now I see the likeness. You are Goya's little *Maja*, with her delicate grace, her fascinating daintiness. You are the *Maja Desnuda!*

III

Renovales' life was changed. In love with his wife, fearing that she might lack some comfort, and thinking with anxiety of the Torrealta widow, who might complain that the daughter of the "illustrious diplomat of imperishable memory" was not happy because she had lowered herself to the extent of marrying a painter, he worked incessantly to maintain with his brush the comforts with which he had surrounded Josephina.

He, who had had so much scorn for industrial art, painting for money, as did his comrades, followed their example, but with the energy that he showed in all his undertakings. In some of the studios there were cries of protest against this tireless competitor who lowered prices scandalously. He had sold his brush for a year to one of those Jewish dealers who exported paintings at so much a picture, and under agreement not to paint for any other dealer. Renovales worked from morning till night changing subjects when it was demanded by what he called his *impresario*. "Enough *ciociari*, now for some Moors." Afterwards the Moors lost their market-value and the turn of the musketeers came, fencing a valiant duel; then pink shepherdesses in the style of Watteau or ladies in powdered wigs embarking in a golden gondola to the sound of lutes. To give freshness to his stock, he would interpolate a sacristy scene with much show of embroidered chasubles and golden incensaries, or an occasional bacchanalian, imitating from memory, without models, Titians' voluptuous forms and amber flesh. When the list was ended, the *ciociari* were once more in style

and could be begun again. The painter with his extraordinary facility of execution produced two or three pictures a week, and the *impresario,* to encourage him in his
work, often visited him afternoons, following the movements of his brush with the enthusiasm of a man who
appreciated art at so much a foot and so much an hour.
The news he brought was of a sort to infuse new zest.

The last bacchanal painted by Renovales was in a
fashionable bar in New York. His pageant of the
Abruzzi was in one of the noblest castles in Russia.
Another picture, representing a dance of countesses dis-
guised as shepherdesses in a field of violets, was in the
possession of a Jewish baron, a banker in Frankfort.
The dealer rubbed his hands, as he spoke to the painter
with a patronizing air. His name was becoming famous,
thanks to him, and he would not stop until he had won
him a world-wide reputation. Already his agents were
asking him to send nothing but the works of Signor
Renovales, for they were the best sellers. But Mariano
answered him with a sudden outburst of bitterness. All
those canvases were mere rot. If that was art, he would
prefer to break stone on the high roads.

But his rebellion against this debasement of his art
disappeared when he saw his Josephina in the house
whose ornamentation he was constantly improving, con-
verting it into a jewel case worthy of his love. She was
happy in her home, with a splendid carriage in which
to drive every afternoon and perfect freedom to spend
money on her clothes and jewelry. Renovales' wife
lacked nothing; she had at her disposal, as adviser and
errand-boy, Cotoner, who spent the night in a garret that
served him as a studio in one of the cheap districts and
the rest of the day with the young couple. She was mistress of the money; she had never seen so many bank-
notes at once. When Renovales handed her the pile of

lires which the impresario gave him she said with a little laugh of joy, "Money, money!" and ran and hid it away with the serious expression of a diligent, economical housewife—only to take it out the next day and squander it with a childish carelessness. What a wonderful thing painting was! Her illustrious father (in spite of all that her mother said) had never made so much money in all his travels through the world, going from cotillon to cotillon as the representative of his king.

While Renovales was in the studio, she had been to drive in the Pincio, bowing from her landau to the countless wives of ambassadors who were stationed at Rome, to aristocratic travelers stopping in the city, to whom she had been introduced in some drawing-room, and to all the crowd of diplomatic attachés who live about the double court of the Vatican and the Quirinal.

The painter was introduced by his wife into an official society of the most rigid formality. The niece of the Marquis of Tarfe, perpetual foreign minister, was received with open arms by the high society of Rome, the most exclusive in Europe. At every reception at the two Spanish embassies, "the famous painter Renovales and his charming wife" were present and these invitations had spread to the embassies of other countries. Almost every night there was some function. Since there were two diplomatic centers, one at the court of the Italian king, the other at the Vatican, the receptions and evening parties were frequent in this isolated society that gathered every night, sufficient for its own enjoyment.

When Renovales got home at dark, tired out with his work, he would find Josephina, already half dressed, waiting for him, and Cotoner helped him to put on his evening clothes.

"The cross!" exclaimed Josephina, when she saw him

with his dress-coat on. "Why, man alive, how did you happen to forget your cross? You know that they all wear something there."

Cotoner went for the insignia, a great cross the Spanish government had given him for his picture, and the artist, with the ribbon across his shirt-front and a brilliant circle on his coat, started out with his wife to spend the evening among diplomats, distinguished travelers and cardinals' nephews.

The other painters were furious with envy when they learned how often the Spanish ambassador and his wife, the consul and prominent people connected with the Vatican visited his studio. They denied his talent, attributing these distinctions to Josephina's position. They called him a courtier and a flatterer, alleging that he had married to better his position. One of his most constant visitors was Father Recovero, the representative of a monastic order that was powerful in Spain, a sort of cowled ambassador who enjoyed great influence with the Pope. When he was not in Renovales' studio, the latter was sure that he was at his house, doing some favor for Josephina who felt proud of her friendship with this influential friar, so jovial and scrupulously correct in spite of his coarse clothes. Renovales' wife always had some favor to ask of him, her friends in Madrid were unceasing in their requests.

The Torrealta widow contributed to this by her constant chatter among her acquaintances about the high position her daughter occupied in Rome. According to her, Mariano was making millions; Josephina was reported to be a great friend of the Pope, her house was full of Cardinals and if the Pope did not visit her it was only because the poor thing was a prisoner in the Vatican. And so the painter's wife had to keep sending to Madrid some rosary that had been passed over St. Peter's tomb

pr reliques taken from the Catacombs. She urged
Father Recovero to negotiate difficult marriage dispensa-
tions and interested herself in behalf of the petitions of
pious ladies, friends of her mother. The great festivals
of the Roman Church filled her with enthusiasm because
of their theatrical interest and she was very grateful to
the generous friar who never forgot to reserve her a
good place. There never was a reception of pilgrims in
Saint Peter's with a triumphal march of the Pope carried on a platform amid feather fans, at which Josephina was not present. At other times the good Father
made the mysterious announcement that on the next
day Pallestri, the famous male soprano of the papal
chapel, was going to sing; the Spanish lady got up early,
leaving her husband still in bed, to hear the sweet voice of
the pontifical eunuch whose beardless face appeared
in shop windows among the portraits of dancers and
fashionable tenors.

Renovales laughed good-naturedly at the countless occupations and futile entertainments of his wife. Poor
irl, she must enjoy herself; that was what he was
vorking for. He was sorry enough that he could go
with her only in her evening diversions. During the
day he entrusted her to his faithful Cotoner who attended her like an old family servant, carrying her
bundles when she went shopping, performing the duties
of butler and sometimes of chef.

Renovales had made his acquaintance when he came
to Rome. He was his best friend. Ten years his senior,
ior, Cotoner showed the worship of a pupil and the affections of an older brother for the young artist. Everyone in Rome knew him, laughing at his pictures on the
rare occasions when he painted, and appreciated his
accommodating nature that to some extent dignified
his parasite's existence. Short, rotund, bald-headed,

with projecting ears and the ugliness of a good-natured, merry satyr, Signor Cotoner, when summer came, always found refuge in the castle of some cardinal in the Roman Campagna. During the winter he was a familiar sight in the Corso, wrapped in his greenish mackintosh, the sleeves of which waved like a bat's wings. He had begun in his own province as a landscape painter but he wanted to paint figures, to equal the masters, and so he landed in Rome in the company of the bishop of his diocese who looked on him as an honor to the church. He never moved from the city. His progress was remarkable. He knew the names and histories of all the artists, no one could compare with him in his ability to live economically in Rome and to find where things were cheapest. If a Spaniard went through the great city, he never missed visiting him. The children of celebrated painters looked on him as a sort of nurse, for he had put them all to sleep in his arms. The great triumph of his life was having figured in the cavalcade of the Quixote as Sancho Panza. He always painted the same picture, portraits of the Pope in three different sizes, piling them up in the attic that served him for a studio and bedroom. His friends, the cardinals whom he visited frequently, took pity on "Poor Signor Cotoner" and for a few lire bought a picture of the Pontiff horribly ugly, to present it to some village church where it would arouse great admiration since it came from Rome and was by a painter who was a friend of His Eminence.

These purchases were a ray of joy for Cotoner, who came to Renovales' studio with his head up and wearing a smile of affected modesty.

"I have made a sale, my boy. A pope; a large one, two meter size."

And with a sudden burst of confidence in his talent,

he talked of the future. Other men desired medals, triumphs in the exhibitions; he was more modest. He would be satisfied if he could guess who would be Pope when the present Pope died, in order to be able to paint up pictures, of him by the dozen ahead of time. What a triumph to put the goods on the market the day after the Conclave! A perfect fortune! And well acquainted with all the cardinals, he passed the Sacred College in mental review with the persistency of a gambler in a lottery, hesitating between the half dozen who aspired to the tiara. He lived like a parasite among the high functionaries of the Church, but he was indifferent to religion, as if this association with them had taken away all his belief. The old man clad in white and the other red gentlemen inspired respect in him because they were rich and served indirectly his wretched portrait business. His admiration was wholly devoted to Renovales. In the studio of other artists he received their irritating jests with his usual calm smile of affability, but they could not speak ill of Renovales nor discuss his ability. To his mind, Renovales could produce nothing but masterpieces and in his blind admiration he even went so far as to rave naïvely over the easel pictures he painted for his impresario.

Sometimes Josephina unexpectedly appeared in her husband's studio and chatted with him while he painted, praising the canvases that had a pretty subject. She preferred to find him alone in these visits, painting from his fancy without any other model than some clothes placed on a manikin. She felt a sort of aversion to models, and Renovales tried in vain to convince her of the necessity of using them. He had talent to paint beautiful things without resorting to the assistance of those ordinary old men and above all, of those women with their disheveled hair, their flashing eyes and their wolfish teeth, who, in the solitude and silence of the studio, actually terrified her. Renovales laughed. What nonsense! Jealous little girl! As if he were capable of thinking of anything but art with a palette in his hand!

One afternoon, when Josephina suddenly came into the studio she saw on the model's platform a naked woman, lying in some furs, showing the curves of her yellow back. The wife compressed her lips and pretended not to see her, listened to Renovales with a distracted air, as he explained this innovation. He was painting a bacchanal and it was impossible for him to proceed without a model. It was a case of necessity, flesh could not be done from memory. The model, at ease before the painter, felt ashamed of her nakedness in the presence of that fashionable lady, and after wrapping herself up in the furs, hid behind a screen and hastily dressed herself.

Renovales recovered his serenity when he reached home, seeing that his wife received him with her customary eagerness, as if she had forgotten her displeasure of the afternoon. She laughed at Cotoner's stories; after dinner they went to the theater and when bedtime came, the painter had forgotten about the surprise in the studio. He was falling asleep when he was alarmed by a painful, prolonged sigh, as if some one were stifling beside him. When he lit the light he saw Josephina with both fists in her eyes, crying, her breast heaving with sobs, and kicking in a childish fit of temper till the bed-clothes were rolled in a ball and the exquisite puff fell to the floor.

"I won't, I won't," she moaned with an accent of protest.

The painter had jumped out of bed, full of anxiety, going from one side to the other without knowing what to do, trying to pull her hands away from her eyes, giving in, in spite of his strength, to Josephina's efforts to free herself from him.

"But what's the matter? What is it you won't do? What's happened to you?"

And she continued to cry, tossing about in the bed, kicking in a nervous fury.

"Let me alone! I don't like you; don't touch me. I won't let you, no, sir, I won't let you. I'm going away. I'm going home to my mother."

Renovales, terrified at the fury of the little woman who was always so gentle, did not know what to do to calm her. He ran through the bedroom and the adjoining dressing room in his night shirt, that showed his athletic muscles; he offered her water, going so far as to pick up the bottles of perfumes in his confusion as if they could serve him as sedatives, and finally he knelt down, trying to kiss the clenched little hands that thrust him away, catching at his hair and beard.

"Let me alone. I tell you to let me alone. I know you don't love me. I'm going away."

The painter was surprised and afraid of the nervousness in this beloved little doll; he did not dare to touch her for fear of hurting her. As soon as the sun rose she would leave that house forever. Her husband did not love her. No one but her mother cared for her. He was making her a laughing stock before people. And all these incoherent complaints that did not explain the motive for her anger, continued for a long time until the artist guessed the cause. Was it the model, the naked woman? Yes, that was it; she would not consent to it, that in a studio that was practically her house, low women should show themselves immodestly to her husband's eyes. And as she protested against such abominations, her twitching fingers tore the front of her night dress, showing the hidden charms that filled Renovales with such enthusiasm.

The painter, tired out by this scene, enervated by the cries and tears of his wife, could not help laughing when he discovered the motive of her irritation.

"Ah! So it's all on account of the model. Be quiet, girl, no woman shall come into the studio."

And he promised everything Josephina wished, in order to be over with it as soon as possible. When it was dark once more, she was still sighing, but now it was in her husband's strong arms with her head resting on his breast, lisping like a grieved child that tries to justify the past fit of temper. It did not cost Mariano anything to do her this favor. She loved him dearly, so dearly, and she would love him still more if he respected her prejudices. He might call her bourgeois, a common ordinary soul, but that was what she wanted to be, just as she always had been. Besides, what was the need of painting naked women? Couldn't he do other things? She urged him to paint children in smocks and sandals, curly haired and chubby, like the child Jesus; old peasant women with wrinkled, copper-colored faces, bald-headed ancients with long beards; character studies, but no young women, understand? No naked beauties! Renovales said "yes" to everything, drawing close to him that beloved form still trembling with its past rage. They clung to each other with a sort of anxiety, desirous of forgetting what had happened, and the night ended peacefully for Renovales in the happiness of reconciliation.

When summer came they rented a little villa at Castel-Gandolfo. Cotoner had gone to Rivoli in the train of a cardinal and the married couple lived in the country accompanied only by a couple of maids and a man-servant, who took care of Renovales' painting kit.

Josephina was perfectly contented in this retirement, far from Rome, talking with her husband at all hours, free from the anxiety that filled her, when he was working in his studio. For a month Renovales remained in placid idleness. His art seemed forgotten; the boxes of paints, the easels, all the artistic luggage brought from Rome, remained packed up and forgotten in a shed in the garden. Afternoons they took long walks, returning home at nightfall slowly, with their arms around each other's waists, watching the strip of pale gold in the western sky, breaking the rural silence with one of the sweet, passionate romances that came from Naples. Now that they were alone in the intimacy of a life without cares or friendships, the enthusiastic love of the first days of their married life reawakened. But the "demon of painting" was not long in spreading over him his invisible wings, which seemed to scatter an irresistible enchantment. He became bored at the long hours in the bright sun, yawned in his wicker chair, smoking pipe after pipe, not knowing what to talk about. Josephina, on her part, tried to drive away the ennui by reading some English novel of aristocratic life, tiresome and moral, to which she had taken a great liking in her school girl days.

Renovales began to work again. His servant brought out his artist's kit and he took up his palette as enthusiastically as a beginner, and painted for himself with a religious fervor as if he thought to purify himself from that base submission to the commissions of a dealer.

He studied Nature directly; painted delightful bits of landscapes, tanned and repulsive heads that breathed the selfish brutality of the peasant. But this artistic activity did not seem to satisfy him. His life of increased intimacy with Josephina aroused in him mysterious longings that he hardly dared to formulate.

Mornings when his wife, fresh and rosy from her bath, appeared before him almost naked, he looked at her with greedy eyes.

"Oh, if you were only willing! If you didn't have that foolish prejudice of yours!"

And his exclamations made her smile, for her feminine vanity was flattered by this worship. Renovales regretted that his artistic talent had to go in search of beautiful things when the supreme, definitive work was at his side. He told her about Rubens, the great master, who surrounded Elène Froment with the luxury of a princess, and of her who felt no objection to freeing her fresh, mythological beauty from veils in order to serve as a model for her husband. Renovales praised the Flemish woman. Artists formed a family by themselves; morality and the popular prejudices were meant for other people. They lived under the jurisdiction of Beauty, regarding as natural what other people looked on as a sin.

Josephina protested against her husband's wishes with a playful indignation but she allowed him to admire her. Her abandon increased every day. Mornings, when she got up, she remained undressed longer, prolonging her toilette while the artist walked around her, praising her various beauties. "That is Rubens, pure and simple, that's Titian's color. Look, little girl, lift up your arms, like this. Oh, you are the *Maja*, Goya's little *Maja*." And she submitted to him with a gracious pout, as if she relished the expression of worship and disappointment which her husband wore at possessing her as a woman and not possessing her as a model.

One afternoon when a scorching wind seemed to stifle the countryside with its breath, Josephina capitulated. They were in their room, with the windows closed, trying to escape the terrible sirocco by shutting it out and putting on thin clothes. She did not want to see her husband with such a gloomy face nor listen to his complaints. As long as he was crazy and was set on his whim, she did not dare to oppose him. He could paint her; but only a study, not a picture. When he was tired of reproducing her flesh on the canvas they would destroy it,—just as if he had done nothing.

The painter said "yes" to everything, eager to have his brush in hand as soon as possible, before the beauty he craved. For three days he worked with a mad fever, with his eyes unnaturally wide open, as if he meant to devour the graceful outlines with his sight. Josephina, accustomed now to being naked, posed with unconscious abandon, with that feminine shamelessness which hesitates only at the first step. Oppressed by the heat, she slept while her husband kept on painting.

When the work was finished, Josephina could not help admiring it. "How clever you are! But am I really like that, so pretty?" Mariano showed his satisfaction. It was his masterpiece, his best. Perhaps in all his life he might never find another moment like that, of prodigious mental intensity, what people commonly call inspiration. She continued to admire herself in the canvas, just as she did some mornings in the great mirror in the bedroom. She praised the various parts of her beauty with frank immodesty. Dazzled by the beauty of her body she did not notice the face, that seemed unimportant, lost in soft veils. When her eyes fell on it she showed a sort of disappointment.

"It doesn't look much like me! It isn't my face!"

The artist smiled. It was not she; he had tried to disguise her face, nothing but her face. It was a mask, a concession to social conventions. As it was, no one would recognize her and his work, his great work, might appear and receive the admiration of the world.

"Because, we aren't going to destroy it," Renovales continued with a tremble in his voice, "that would be a crime. Never in my life will I be able to do anything like it again. We won't destroy it, will we, little girl?"

The little girl remained silent for a good while with her gaze fixed on the picture. Renovales' eager eyes saw a cloud slowly rise over her face, like a shadow on a white wall. The painter felt as though the floor were sinking under his feet; the storm was coming. Josephina turned pale, two tears slipped slowly down her cheeks, two others took their places to fall with them and then more and more.

"I won't! I won't!"

It was the same hoarse, nervous, despotic cry that had set his hair on end with anxiety and fear that night in Rome. The little woman looked with hatred at the naked body that radiated its pearly light from the depths of the canvas. She seemed to feel the terror of a sleep-walker who suddenly awakens in the midst of a square surrounded by a thousand curious, eager eyes and in her fright does not know what to do nor where to flee. How could she have assented to such a disgraceful thing?

"I won't have it!" she cried angrily. "Destroy it, Mariano, destroy it."

But Mariano seemed on the point of weeping too. Destroy it! Who could demand such a foolish thing? That figure was not she; no one would recognize her. What was the use of depriving him of a signal triumph? But his wife did not listen to him. She was rolling on the floor with the same convulsions and moans as on the night of the stormy scene, her hands were clenched like a crook, her feet kicked like a dying lamb's and her mouth, painfully distorted, kept crying hoarsely:

"I won't have it! I won't have it! Destroy it!"

She complained of her lot with a violence that wounded Renovales. She, a respectable woman, submitted to that degradation as if she were a street walker. If she had only known! How was she going to imagine that her husband would make such abominable proposals to her!

Renovales, offended at these insults, at these lashes which her shrill, piercing voice dealt his artistic talent, left his wife, let her roll on the floor and with clenched fists, went from one end of the room to the other, looking at the ceiling, muttering all the oaths, Spanish and Italian, that were in current use in his studio.

Suddenly he stood still, rooted to the floor by terror and surprise. Josephina, still naked, had jumped on the picture with the quickness of a wild cat. With the first stroke of her finger nails, she scratched the canvas from top to bottom, mingling the colors that were still soft, tearing off the thin shell of the dry parts. Then she caught up the little knife from the paint box and—rip! the canvas gave a long moan, parted under the thrust of that white arm which seemed to have a bluish cast in the violence of her wrath.

He did not move. For a moment he felt indignant, tempted to throw himself on her but he lapsed into a childish weakness, ready to cry, to take refuge in a corner, to hide his weak, aching head. She, blind with wrath, continued to vent her fury on the picture, tangling her feet in the wood of the frame, tearing off pieces of canvas, walking back and forth with her prey like a wild beast. The artist had leaned his head against the wall, his strong breast shook with cowardly sobs.

To the almost fatherly grief at the loss of his work was added the bitterness of disappointment. For the first time he foresaw what his life was going to be. What a mistake he had made in marrying that girl who admired his art as a profession, as a means of making money, and who was trying to mold him to the prejudices and scruples of the circle in which she was born! He loved her in spite of this and he was certain that she did not love him less, but, still, perhaps it would have been better to remain alone, free for his art and, in case a companion was necessary, to find a fair maid of all work with all the splendor and intellectual humility of a beautiful animal that would admire and obey her master blindly.

Three days passed in which the painter and his wife hardly spoke to each other. They looked at each other askance, humbled and broken by this domestic trouble. But the solitude in which they lived, the necessity of remaining together made the reconciliation imperative. She was the first to speak, as if she were terrified by the sadness and dejection of that huge giant who wandered about as peevish as a sick man. She threw her arms around him, kissed his forehead, made a thousand gracious efforts to bring a faint smile to his face. "Who loved him? His Josephina. His *Maja* but not his *Maja Desnuda;* that was over forever. He must never think of those horrible things. A decent painter does not think of them. What would all her friends say? There were many pretty things to paint in the world. They must live in each other's love, without his displeasing her with his hateful whims. His affection for the nude was a shameful remnant of his Bohemian days.

And Renovales, won over by his wife's petting, made peace,—tried to forget his work and smiled with the resignation of a slave who loves his chain because it assures him peace and life.

They returned to Rome at the beginning of the fall. Renovales began his work for the contractor, but after a few months the latter seemed dissatisfied. Not that Signor Mariano was losing power, not at all, but his agents complained of a certain monotony in the subjects of his works. The dealer advised him to travel; he might stay awhile in Umbria, painting peasants in ascetic landscapes, or old churches; he might—and this was the best thing to do—move to Venice. How much Signor Mariano could accomplish in those canals! And it was thus that the idea of leaving Rome first came to the painter.

Josephina did not object. That daily round of receptions in the countless embassies and legations was beginning to bore her. Now that the charm of the first impressions had disappeared, Josephina noticed that the great ladies treated her with an annoying condescension as if she had descended from her rank in marrying an artist. Besides, the younger men in the embassies, the attachés of different nationalities, some light, some dark, who sought relief from their celibacy without going outside diplomatic society, were disgracefully impudent as they danced with her or went through the figures of a cotillion, as if they considered her an easy conquest, seeing her married to an artist who could not display an ugly uniform in the drawing rooms. They made cynical declarations to her in English or German and she had to keep her temper, smiling and biting her lips, close to Renovales, who did not understand a word and showed his satisfaction at the attentions of which his wife was the object on the part of the fashionable youths whose manners he tried to imitate.

The trip was decided on. They would go to Venice!

Their friend Cotoner said "Good-by," he was sorry to part from them but his place was in Rome. The Pope was ailing just at that time and the painter, in the hope of his death, was preparing canvases of all sizes, striving to guess who would be his successor.

As he went back in his memories, Renovales always thought of his life in Venice with a sort of pleasant homesickness. It was the best period of his life. The enchanting city of the lagoons,—bathed in golden light, lulled by the lapping of the water, fascinated him from the first moment, making him forget his love for the human form. For some time his enthusiasm for the nude was calmed. He worshiped the old palaces, the solitary canals, the lagoon with its green, motionless water, the soul of a majestic past, which seemed to breathe in the solemn old age of the dead, eternally smiling city.

They lived in the Foscarini palace, a huge building with red walls and casements of white stone that opened on a little alley of water adjoining the Grand Canal. It was the former abode of merchants, navigators and conquerors of the Isles of the East who in times gone by had worn on their heads the golden horn of the Doges. The modern spirit, utilitarian and irreverent, had converted the palace into a tenement, dividing gilded drawing rooms with ugly partitions, establishing kitchens in the filigreed arcades of the seignorial court, filling the marble galleries to which the centuries gave the amber-like transparency of old ivory, with clothes hung out to dry and replacing the gaps in the superb mosaic with cheap square tiles.

Renovales and his wife occupied the apartment nearest the Grand Canal. Mornings, Josephina saw from a bay window the rapid silent approach of her husband's gondola. The gondolier, accustomed to the service of artists, shouted to the painter, till Renovales came down with his box of water-colors and the boat started immediately through the narrow, winding canals, moving the silvered comb of its prow from one side to the other as if it were feeling the way. What mornings of placid silence in the sleeping water of an alley, between two palaces whose boldly projecting roofs kept the surface of the little canal in perpetual shadow! The gondolier slept stretched out in one of the curving ends of his boat and Renovales, sitting beside the black canopy, painted his Venetian water-colors, a new type that his impresario in Rome received with the greatest enthusiasm. His deftness enabled him to produce these works with as much facility as if they were mechanical copies. In the maze of canals he had one of his own which he called his "estate" on account of the money it netted him. He had painted again and again its dead, silent waters which all day long were never rippled except by his gondola; two old palaces with broken blinds, the doors covered with the crust of years, stairways rotted with mold and in the background a little arch of light, a marble bridge and under it the life, the movement, the sun of a broad, busy canal. The neglected little alley came to life every week under Renovales' brush—he could paint it with his eyes shut—and the business initiative of the Roman Jew scattered it through the world.

The afternoons Mariano passed with his wife. Sometimes they went in a gondola to the promenade of the Lido and sitting on the sandy beach, watched the angry surface of the open Adriatic, that stretched its tossing white caps to the horizon, like a flock of snowy sheep hurrying in the rush of a panic.

Other afternoons they walked in the Square of Saint Mark, under the arcades of its three rows of palaces where they could see in the background, by the last rays of the sun, the pale gold of the basilica gleaming, as if in its walls and domes there were crystallized all the wealth of the ancient Republic.

Renovales, with his wife on his arm, walked calmly as if the majesty of the place impelled him to a sort of noble bearing. The august silence was not disturbed by the deafening hubbub of other great capitals; no rattling of carts or footsteps of horses or hucksters' cries. The Square, with its white marble pavement, was a huge drawing room through which the visitors passed as if they were making a call. The musicians of the Venice band were gathered in the center with their hats surmounted by black waving plumes. The blasts of the Wagnerian brasses, galloping in the mad ride of the Valkyries, made the marble columns shake and seemed to give life to the four golden horses that reared over space with silent whinnies on the cornice of St. Mark's.

The dark-feathered doves of Venice scattered in playful spirals, somewhat frightened at the music, finally settled, like rain, on the tables of the café. Then, taking flight again, they blackened the roof of the palaces and once more swooped down like a mantle of metallic luster on the groups of English tourists in green veils and round hats, who called them in order to offer them grain.

Josephina, with childish eagerness, left her husband in order to buy a cone full of grain, and spreading it out in her gloved hands she gathered the wards of St. Mark around her; they rested on the flowers of her head, fluttering like fantastic crests, they hopped on her shoulders, or lined up on her outstretched arms, they clung desperately to her slight hips, trying to walk around her waist, and others, more daring, as if possessed of human mischievousness, scratched her breast, reached out their beaks striving to caress her ruddy, half-opened lips through the veil. She laughed, trembling at the tickling of the animated cloud that rubbed against her body. Her husband watched her, laughing too, and certain that no one but she would understand him, he called to her in Spanish.

"My, but you are beautiful! I wish I could paint your picture! If it weren't for the people, I would kiss you."

Venice was the scene of her happiest days. She lived quietly while her husband worked, taking odd corners of the city for his models. When he left the house, her placid calm was not disturbed by any troublesome thought. This was painting, she was sure,—and not the conditions of affairs in Rome, where he would shut himself up with shameless women who were not afraid to pose stark naked. She loved him with a renewed passion, she petted him with constant caresses. It was then that her daughter was born, their only child.

Majestic Doña Emilia could not remain in Madrid when she learned that she was going to be a grandmother. Her poor Josephina, in a foreign land, with no one to take care of her but her husband, who had some talent according to what people said, but who seemed to her rather ordinary! At her son-in-law's expense, she made the trip to Venice and there she stayed for several months, fuming against the city, which she had never visited in her diplomatic travels. The distinguished lady considered that no cities were inhabitable except the capitals that have a court. Pshaw! Venice! A shabby town that no one liked but writers of romanzas and decorators of fans, and where there were nothing higher than consuls. She liked Rome with its Pope and kings. Besides, it made her seasick to ride in the gondolas and she complained constantly of the rheumatism, blaming it to the dampness of the lagoons.

Renovales, who had feared for Josephina's life, believing that her weak, delicate constitution could not stand the shock, broke out into cries of joy when he received the little one in his arms and looked at the mother with her head resting on the pillow as if she were dead. Her white face was hardly outlined against the white of the linen. His first thought was for her, for the pale features, distorted by the recent crisis, which gradually were growing calmer with rest. Poor little girl! How she had suffered! But as he tip-toed out of the bed room in order not to disturb the heavy sleep that, after two cruel days, had overpowered the sick woman, he gave himself up to his admiration for the bit of flesh that lay in the huge flabby arms of the grandmother, wrapped in fine linen. Ah, what a dear little thing! He looked at the livid little face, the big head, thinly covered with hair, seeking for some suggestion of himself in this surge of flesh that was in motion and still without definite form. "Mamma, whom does she look like?"

Doña Emilia was surprised at his blindness. Whom should she look like? Like him, no one but him. She was large, enormous; she had seen few babies as large as this one. It did not seem possible that her poor daughter could live after giving birth to "that." They could not complain that she was not healthy; she was as ruddy as a country baby.

"She's a Renovales; she's yours, wholly yours, Mariano. We belong to a different class."

And Renovales, without noticing his mother's words, saw only that his daughter was like him, overjoyed to see how robust she was, shouting his pleasure at the health of which the grandmother spoke in a disappointed tone.

In vain did he and Doña Emilia try to dissuade Josephina from nursing the baby. The little woman, in spite of the weakness that kept her motionless in bed, wept and cried almost as she had in the crises that had so terrified Renovales.

"I won't have it," she said with that obstinacy that made her so terrible.

"I won't have a strange woman's milk for my daughter. I will nurse her, her mother."

And they had to give the baby to her.

When Josephina seemed recovered, her mother, feeling that her mission was over, went home to Madrid. She was bored to death in that silent city of Venice, night after night she thought she was dead, for she could not hear a single sound from her bed. The calm, interrupted now and then by the shouts of the gondoliers filled her with the same terror that she felt in a cemetery. She had no friends, she did not "shine"; there was nobody in that dirty hole and nobody knew her. She was always recalling her distinguished friends in Madrid where she thought she was an indispensable personage. The modesty of her granddaughter's christening left a deep impression in her mind in spite of the fact that they gave her name to the child; an insignificant little party that needed only two gondolas; she, who was the godmother, with the godfather, an old Venetian painter, who was a friend of Renovales and, besides, Renovales himself and two artists, a Frenchman and another Spaniard. The Patriarch of Venice did not officiate at the baptism, not even a bishop. And she knew so many of them at home. A mere priest, who was in a shameful hurry, had been sufficient to christen the granddaughter of the famous diplomat, in a little church, as the sun was setting. She went away repeating once more that Josephina was killing herself, that it was perfect folly for her to nurse the baby in

her delicate condition, regretting that she did not follow the example of her mother who had always in-
trusted her children to nurses.

Josephina cried bitterly when her mother went, but
Renovales said "good-by" with ill-concealed joy. *Bon
voyage!* He simply could not endure the woman, always complaining that she was being neglected when
she saw how her son-in-law was working to make her
daughter happy. The only thing he agreed with her in
was in scolding Josephina tenderly for her obstinacy
in nursing the baby. Poor little *Maja Desnuda!* Her
form had lost its bud-like daintiness in the full flower
of motherhood.

She appeared more robust, but the stoutness was accompanied by an anemic weakness. Her husband, seeing how she was losing her daintiness, loved her with
more tender compassion. Poor little girl! How good
she was! She was sacrificing herself for her daughter.

When the baby was a year old, the great crisis in
Renovales' life occurred. Desirous of taking a "bath
in art," of knowing what was going on outside of the
dungeon in which he was imprisoned, painting at so
much a piece, he left Josephina in Venice and made a
short trip to Paris to see its famous Salon. He came
back transfigured, with a new fever for work and a
determination to transform his existence which filled his
wife with astonishment and fear. He was going to
break with his *impresario,* he would no longer debase
himself with that false painting, even if he had to beg
for his living. Great things were being done in the
world, and he felt that he had the courage to be an innovator, following the steps of those modern painters
who made such a profound impression on him.

Now he hated old Italy, where artists went to study
under the protection of ignorant governments.

In reality what they found there was a market of tempting commissions where they soon grew accustomed to taking orders, to the luxurious, indifferent life of easy profit. He wanted to move to Paris. But Josephina, who listened to Renovales' fancies in silence, unable to understand them for the most part, modified this determination by her advice. She too wanted to leave Venice. The city seemed gloomy in the winter with its ceaseless rains that left the bridges slippery and the marble alleys impassable. Since they were determined to break up camp, why not go back to Madrid? Mamma was sick, she complained in all her letters at living so far from her daughter. Josephina wanted to see her, she had a presentiment that her mother was going to die. Renovales thought it over; he too wanted to go back to Spain. He felt homesick; he thought of the great stir he would cause there, teaching his new methods amid the general routine. The desire of shocking the Academicians, who had accepted him before because he had renounced his ideals, tempted him.

They went back to Madrid with little Milita, as they called her for short, abbreviating the diminutive of Emilia. Renovales brought with him as his whole capital some few thousand lire, that represented Josephina's savings and the product of his sale of part of the furniture that decorated the poorly furnished halls of the Foscarini palace.

At first it was hard. Doña Emilia died a few months after they reached Madrid. Her funeral did not come up to the dreams the illustrious widow had always fashioned. Hardly a score of her countless relatives were present. Poor old lady, if she had known how her hopes were destined to be disappointed! Renovales was almost glad of the event. With it, the only tie that bound them to society was broken. He and Josephina lived in a fifth story flat on the Calle de Alcalá, near the Plaza de Toros, with a large terrace that the artist converted into a studio. Their life was modest, secluded, humble, without friends or functions. She spent the day taking care of her daughter and the house, without help except a dull, poorly-paid maid. Oftentimes when she seemed most active, she fell into a sudden languor, complaining of strange, new ailments.

Mariano hardly ever worked at home; he painted out of doors. He despised the conventional light of the studio, the closeness of its atmosphere. He wandered through the suburbs of Madrid and the neighboring provinces in search of rough, simple types, whose faces seemed to bear the stamp of the ancient Spanish soul. He climbed the Guadarrama in the midst of winter, standing alone in the snowy fields like an Arctic explorer, to transfer to his canvas the century-old pines, twisted and black under their caps of frozen sleet.

When the Exhibition took place, Renovales' name became famous in a flash. He did not present a huge picture with a key, as he had at his first triumph. They were small canvases, studies prompted by a chance meeting; bits of nature, men and landscapes reproduced with an astonishing, brutal truth that shocked the public.

The sober fathers of painting writhed as if they had received a slap in the face, before those sketches that seemed to flame among the other dead, leaden pictures. They admitted that Renovales was a painter, but he lacked imagination, invention, his only merit was his ability to transfer to the canvas what his eyes saw. The younger men flocked to the standard of the new master; there were endless disputes, impassioned arguments, deadly hatred, and over this battle Renovales' name flitted, appearing almost daily in the newspapers, till he was almost as celebrated as a bull-fighter or an orator in the Congress.

The struggle lasted for six years, giving rise to a storm of insults and applause every time that Renovales exhibited one of his works, and meanwhile the master, discussed as he was, lived in poverty, forced to paint watercolors in the old style which he secretly sent to his dealer in Rome. But all combats have their end. The public finally accepted as unquestionable a name that they saw every day; his enemies, weakened by the unconscious effect of public opinion, grew tired, and the master like all innovators, as soon as the first success of the scandal was over, began to limit his daring, pruning and softening his original brutality. The dreaded painter became fashionable. The easy, instantaneous success he had won at the beginning of his career was renewed, but more solidly and more definitely, like a conquest made by rough, hard paths when there is a struggle at every step.

Money, the fickle page, came back to him, holding the train of glory. He sold pictures at prices unheard of in Spain and they grew fabulously as they were repeated by his admirers. Some American millionaires, surprised that a Spanish painter should be mentioned abroad and that the principal reviews in Europe should reproduce his works, bought canvases as objects of great luxury. The master, embittered by the poverty of his years of struggle, suddenly felt a longing for money, an overpowering greed that his friends had never known in him. His wife seemed to grow more sickly every day; her daughter was growing up and he wanted his Milita to have the education and the luxuries of a princess. They now had a respectable house of their own, but he wanted something better for them.

His business instinct, which everyone recognized in him when he was not blinded by some artistic prejudice, strove to make his brush an instrument of great profits.

Pictures were bound to disappear, according to the master. Modern rooms, small and soberly decorated, were not fitted for the large canvases that ornamented the walls of drawing rooms in the old days. Besides, the reception rooms of the present, like the rooms in a doll's house, were good merely for pretty pictures marked by stereotyped mannerisms. Scenes taken from nature were out of place in this background. The only way to make money then was to paint portraits and Renovales forgot his distinction as an innovator in order to win at any cost fame as a portrait painter of society people. He painted members of the royal family in all sorts of postures, not omitting any of their important occupations; on foot, and on horseback, with a general's plumes or a gray hunting jacket, killing pigeons or riding in an automobile. He portrayed the beauties of the oldest families, concealing imperceptibly, with clever dissimulation, the ravages of time, giving firmness to the flabby flesh with his brush, holding up the heavy eyelids and cheeks that sagged with fatigue and the poison of rouge. After successes at court, the rich considered a portrait by Renovales as an indispensable decoration for their drawing rooms. They sought him because his signature cost thousands of dollars; to possess a canvas by him was an evidence of opulence, quite as necessary as an automobile of the best make.

Renovales was as rich as a painter can be. It was at that time that he built what envious people called his "pantheon"; a magnificent mansion behind the iron grating of the Retiro.

He had a violent desire to build a home after his own heart and image, like those mollusks that build a shell with the substance of their bodies so that it may serve both as a dwelling and a defense. There awakened in him that longing for show, for pompous, swaggering, amusing originality that lies dormant in the mind of every artist. At first he planned a reproduction of Rubens' palace in Antwerp, open *loggie* for studios, leafy gardens covered with flowers at all seasons, and in the paths, gazelles, giraffes, birds of bright plumage, like flying flowers, and other exotic animals which this great painter used as models in his desire to copy Nature in all its magnificence.

But he was forced to give up this dream, on account of the nature of the building sites in Madrid, a few thousand feet of barren, chalky soil, bounded by a wretched fence and as dry as only Castile can be. Since this Rubenesque ostentation was not possible, he took refuge in Classicism and in a little garden he erected a sort of Greek temple that should serve at once as a dwelling and a studio. On the triangular pediment rose three tripods like torch-holders, that gave the house the appearance of a commemorative tomb. But in order that those who stopped outside the grating might make no mistake, the master had garlands of laurel, palettes surrounded with crowns, carved on the stone façade, and in the midst of this display of simple modesty a short inscription in gold letters of average size—"Renovales." Exactly like a store. Inside, in two studios where no one ever painted and which led to the real working studio, the finished pictures were exhibited on easels covered with antique textures, and callers gazed with wonder at the collection of properties fit for a theater,—suits of armor, tapestries, old standards hanging from the ceiling, show-cases full of ancient knickknacks, deep couches with canopies of oriental stuffs supported by lances, century old coffers and open secretaries shining with the pale gold of their rows of drawers.

These studios where no one studied were like the luxurious line of waiting rooms in the house of a doctor who charges twenty dollars for a consultation, or like the anterooms, furnished in dark leather with venerable pictures, of a famous lawyer, who never opens his mouth without carrying off a large portion of his client's fortune. People who waited in these two studios spacious as the nave of a church, with the silent majesty which comes with the lapse of years, were brought to the necessary frame of mind to make them submit to the enormous prices the master demanded.

Renovales had "made good" and he could rest calmly, as his admirers said. And still the master was gloomy; his nature, embittered by his years of silent suffering, broke out in violent fits of temper.

The slightest attack by some insignificant enemy was enough to send him into a rage. His pupils thought it was due to the fact that he was getting old. His struggles had so aged him that with his heavy beard and his round shoulders he looked ten years older than he was.

In this white temple, on the pediment of which his name shone in letters of glorious gold, he was not so happy as in the modest houses in Italy or the little garret near the Plaza de Toros. All that was left of the Josephina of the first months of his married life was a distant shadow. The *"Maja Desnuda"* of the happy nights in Rome and Venice was nothing but a memory. On her return to Spain the false stoutness of motherhood had disappeared.

She grew thin, as if some hidden fire were devouring her; the flesh that had covered her body with graceful curves melted away in the flames that burned within her. The sharp angles and dark hollows of her skeleton began to show beneath her pale, flabby flesh. Poor *"Maja Desnuda"!* Her husband pitied her, attributing her decline to the struggles and cares she had suffered when they first returned to Madrid.

For her sake, he was eager to conquer, to become rich, that he might provide her with the comforts he had dreamed of. Her illness seemed to be mental; it was neurasthenia, melancholia. The poor woman had suffered without doubt at being condemned to a pauper's existence, in Madrid, where she had once lived in comparative splendor, this time in a wretched house, struggling with poverty, forced to perform the most menial tasks. She complained of strange pains, her legs lost their strength, she sank into a chair where she would stay motionless for hours at a time, weeping without knowing why. Her digestion was poor; for weeks her stomach refused all nourishment. At night she would toss about in bed, unable to sleep and at daybreak she was up flitting about the house with a feverish activity, turning things upside down, finding fault with the servant, with her husband, with herself, until suddenly she would collapse from the height of her excitement and begin to cry.

These domestic trials broke the painter's spirit, but he bore them patiently. Now a gentle sympathy was added to his former love, when he saw her so weak, without any remnant of her former charm except her eyes, sunk in their bluish sockets, bright with the mysterious fire of fever. Poor little girl! Her struggles brought her to such a pass. Her weakness filled Renovales with a sort of remorse. Her lot was that of the soldier who sacrifices himself for his general's glory. He had conquered, but he left behind him the woman he loved, fallen in the struggle because she was the weaker.

He admired, too, her maternal self-sacrifice. The baby, Milita, who attracted attention because of her whiteness and ruddiness, had the strength that her mother lacked. The greediness of this strong, enslaving creature had absorbed all of the mother's life.

When the artist was rich and installed his family in the new house, he thought that Josephina was going to get well. The doctors were confident of a rapid improvement. The first day that they walked through the parlors and studios of the new house, taking note of the furniture and the valuables, old and new, with a glance of satisfaction, Renovales put him arm around the waist of the weak little doll, bending his head over her, caressing her forehead with his bearded lips.

Everything was hers, the house and its sumptuous decorations, hers too was the money that was left and that he would continue to make. She was the owner, the absolute mistress, she could spend all she wanted to, he would stand for everything. She could wear stylish clothes, have carriages, make her former friends green with envy, be proud of being the wife of a famous painter, much more proud than others who had landed a ducal crown by marriage. Was she satisfied?

She said "Yes," nodding her assent weakly, and she even stood on tip-toe to kiss the lips that seemed to caress her through a cloud of hair, but her expression was sad and her listless movements were like a withered flower's, as if there was no joy on earth that could lift her out of this dejection.

After a few days, when the first impress of the change in her mode of life was over, the old outbreaks that had so often disturbed their former dwelling began again in the luxurious palace.

Renovales found her in the dining-room with her head in her hands, crying, but unwilling to explain the cause of her tears. When he tried to take her in his arms, caressing her like a child, the little woman became as agitated as if she had received an insult.

"Let me go!" she cried with a hostile look. "Don't touch me. Go away!"

At other times he looked all over the house for her in vain, questioning Milita who, accustomed to her mother's outbreaks and made selfish by her girlish strength, paid little attention to her and kept on playing with her dolls.

"I don't know, papa; she's probably crying up stairs," she would answer naïvely.

And in some corner of the upper story, in the bedroom, beside the bed or among the clothes in the wardrobe, the husband would find her, sitting on the floor with her chin in her hands, her eyes fixed on the wall as if she were looking at something invisible and mysterious that only she could see. She was not crying, her eyes were dry and enlarged with an expression of terror, and her husband tried in vain to attract her attention. She remained motionless, cold, indifferent to his caresses, as if he were a stranger, as if there were a hopeless gap between them.

"I want to die," she said in a serious, tense tone. "I am of no use in the world; I want to rest."

The deadly resignation would change a moment later into furious antagonism. Renovales could never tell how the quarrel began. The most insignificant word on his part, the expression of his face, silence even, was all that was needed to bring on the storm. Josephina began to speak with a taunting accent that made her words cut like cold steel. She found fault with the painter for what he did and what he did not do, for his most trifling habits, for what he painted, and presently, extending the radius of her insults to include the whole

world, she broke out into denunciations of the distinguished people who formed her husband's clientele and
brought him such profits. He might be satisfied with
painting the portraits of those people, disreputable society men and women. Her mother, who was in close
touch with that society, had told her many stories about
them. The women she knew still better; almost all of
them had been her companions at boarding-school or her
friends. They had married to make sport of their husbands; they all had a past, they were worse than the
women who walked the streets at night. This house
with all its façade of laurels and its gold letters was
a brothel. One of these fine days she would come into
the studio and throw them into the street to have their
pictures painted somewhere else.

"For God's sake, Josephina," Renovales murmured
with a troubled voice, "don't talk like that. Don't think
of such outrageous things. I don't see how you can
talk that way. Milita will hear us."

Now that her nervous anger was exhausted, Josephina
would burst into tears and Renovales would have to
leave the table and take her to bed, where she lay, crying out for the hundredth time that she wanted to die.

This life was even more intolerable because he was
faithful to his wife, because his love, mingled with habit
and routine, kept him firmly devoted to her.

At the end of the afternoon, several of his friends
used to gather in his studio, among them the jolly Cotoner who had moved to Madrid. When the twilight
crept in through the huge window and made them all
prone to friendly confidences, Renovales always made
the same statement.

"As a boy I had my good times just like anyone else,
but since I was married I have never had anything to

do with any woman except my own wife. I am proud to say so."

And the big man drew himself up to his full height and stroked his beard, as proud of his faithfulness to his wife as other men are of their good fortune in love.

When they talked about beautiful women in his presence, or looked at portraits of great foreign beauties, the master did not conceal his approval.

"Very beautiful! Very pretty to paint!"

His enthusiasm over beauty never went beyond the limits of art. There was only one woman in the world for him, his wife; the others were models.

He, who carried in his mind a perfect orgy of flesh, who worshiped the nude with religious fervor, reserved all his manly homage for his wife who grew constantly more sickly, more gloomy, and waited with the patience of a lover for a moment of calm, a ray of sunlight among the incessant storms.

The doctors, who admitted their inability to cure the nervous disorder that was consuming the wife, had hopes of a sudden change and recommended to the husband that he should be extremely kind to her. This only increased his patient gentleness. They attributed the nervous trouble to the birth and nursing of the child, that had broken her weak health; they suspected, too, the existence of some unknown cause that kept the sick woman in constant excitement.

Renovales, who studied his wife closely in his eagerness to recover peace in his house, soon discovered the true cause of her illness.

Milita was growing up; already she was a woman. She was fourteen years old and wore long skirts, and her healthy beauty was beginning to attract the glances of men.

"One of these days they'll carry her off," said the

master laughing. And his wife, when she heard him talking about marriage, making conjectures on his future son-in-law, closed her eyes and said in a tense voice, that revealed her insuperable obstinacy:

"She shall marry anyone she wants to,—except a painter. I would rather see her dead than that."

It was then Renovales divined his wife's true illness. It was jealousy, a terrific, deadly, ruinous jealousy; it was the sadness of realizing that she was sickly. She was certain of her husband; she knew his declarations of faithfulness to her. But when the painter spoke of his artistic interests in her presence, he did not hide his worship of beauty, his religious cult of form. Even if he was silent, she penetrated his thoughts; she read in him that fervor which dated from his youth and had grown greater as the years went by. When she looked at the statues of sovereign nakedness that decorated the studios, when she glanced through the albums of pictures where the light of flesh shone brightly amid the shadows of the engraving, she compared them mentally with her own form emaciated by illness.

Renovales' eyes that seemed to worship every beauty of form were the same eyes that saw her in all her ugliness. That man could never love her. His faithfulness was pity, perhaps habit, unconscious virtue. She could not believe that it was love. This illusion might be possible with another man, but he was an artist. By day he worshiped beauty; at night he was brought face to face with ugliness, with physical wretchedness.

She was constantly tormented by jealousy, that embittered her mind and consumed her life, a jealousy that was inconsolable for the very reason that it had no real foundation.

The consciousness of her ugliness brought with it a sadness, an insatiable envy of everyone, a desire to die but to kill the world first, that she might drag it down with her in her fall.

Her husband's caresses irritated her like an insult. Maybe he thought he loved her, maybe his advances were in good faith, but she read his thoughts and she found there her irresistible enemy, the rival that over-shadowed her with her beauty. And there was no remedy for this. She was married to a man who, as long as he lived, would be faithful to his religion of beauty. How well she remembered the days when she had refused to allow her husband to paint her youthful body! If youth and beauty would but come back to her, she would recklessly cast off all her veils, would stand in the middle of the studio as arrogantly as a bacchante, crying,

"Paint! Satisfy yourself with my flesh, and whenever you think of your eternal beloved, whom you call Beauty, fancy that you see her with my face, that she has my body!"

It was a terrible misfortune to be the wife of an artist. She would never marry her daughter to a painter; she would rather see her dead. Men who carry with them the demon of form, cannot live in peace and happiness except with a companion who is eternally young, eternally fair.

Her husband's fidelity made her desperate. That chaste artist was always musing over the memory of naked beauties, fancying pictures he did not dare to paint for fear of her. With her sick woman's penetration, she seemed to read this longing in her husband's face. She would have preferred certain infidelity, to see him in love with another woman, mad with passion. He might return from such a wandering outside the bonds of matrimony, wearied and humble, begging her forgiveness; but from the other, he would never return.

When Renovales discovered the cause of her sadness, he tenderly undertook to cure his wife's mental disorder. He avoided speaking of his artistic interests in her presence; he discovered terrible defects in the fair ladies who sought him as a portrait painter; he praised Josephina's spiritual beauty; he painted pictures of her, putting her features on the canvas, but beautifying them with subtle skill.

She smiled, with that eternal condescension that a woman has for the most stupendous, most shameful deceits, as long as they flatter her.

"It's you," said Renovales, "your face, your charm, your air of distinction. I really don't think I have made you as beautiful as you are."

She continued to smile, but soon her look grew hard, her lips tightened and the shadow spread little by little across her face.

She fixed her eyes on the painter's as if she were scrutinizing his thoughts.

It was a lie. Her husband was flattering her; he thought he loved her, but only his flesh was faithful. The invincible enemy, the eternal beloved, was mistress of his mind.

Tortured by this mental unfaithfulness and by the rage which her helplessness produced, she would gradually fall into one of the nervous storms that broke out in a shower of tears and a thunder of insults and recriminations.

Renovales' life was a hell at the very time when he possessed the glory and wealth which he had dreamed of so many years, building on them his hope of happiness.

IV

It was three o'clock in the afternoon when the painter went home after his luncheon with the Hungarian.

As he entered the dining-room, before going to the studio, he saw two women with their hats and veils on who looked as if they were getting ready to go out. One of them, as tall as the painter, threw her arms around his neck.

"Papa, dear, we waited for you until nearly two o'clock. Did you have a good luncheon?"

And she kissed him noisily, rubbing her fresh, rosy cheeks against the master's gray beard.

Renovales smiled good naturedly under this shower of caresses. Ah, his Milita! She was the only joy in that gloomy, showy house. It was she who sweetened that atmosphere of tedious strife which seemed to emanate from the sick woman. He looked at his daughter with an air of comic gallantry.

"Very pretty; yes, I swear you are very pretty to-day. You are a perfect Rubens, my dear, a brunette Rubens. And where are we going to show off?"

He looked with a father's pride at that strong, rosy body, in which the transition to womanhood was marked by a sort of passing delicacy—the result of her rapid growth—and a dark circle around her eyes. Her soft, mysterious glance was that of a woman who is beginning to understand the meaning of life. She dressed with a sort of exotic elegance; her clothes had a masculine appearance; her mannish collar and tie were in keeping with the rigid energy of her movements, with her widesoled English boots, and the violent swing of her legs that opened her skirts like a compass when she walked, more intent on speed and a heavy step than on a graceful carriage. The master admired her healthy beauty. What a splendid specimen! The race would not die out with her. She was like him, wholly like him; if he had been a woman, he would have been like his Milita.

She kept on talking, without taking her arms from her father's shoulders, with her eyes, tremulous like molten gold, fixed on the master.

She was going for her daily walk with "Miss," a two hours' tramp through the Castellana and the Retiro, without stopping a moment to sit down, taking a peripatetic lesson in English on the way. For the first time Renovales turned around to speak to "Miss," a stout woman with a red, wrinkled face who, when she smiled, showed a set of teeth that shone like yellow dominoes. In the studio Renovales and his friends often laughed at "Miss's" appearance and eccentricities, at her red wig that was placed on her head as carelessly as a hat, at her terrible false teeth, at her bonnets that she made herself out of chance bits of ribbon and discarded ornaments, of her chronic lack of appetite, that forced her to live on beer, which kept her in a continual state of confusion, which was revealed in her exaggerated curtsies. Soft and heavy from drink, she was alarmed at the approach of the hour of the walk, a daily torment for her, as she tried painfully to keep up with Milita's long strides. Seeing the painter looking at her, she turned even redder and made three profound curtsies.

"Oh, Mr. Renovales, oh, sir!"

And she did not call him "Lord," because the master greeting her with a nod, forgot her presence and began to talk again with his daughter.

Milita was eager to hear about her father's luncheon

with Tekli. And so he had had some Chianti? Selfish man! When he knew how much she liked it! He ought to have let them know sooner that he would not be home. Fortunately Cotoner was at the house and mamma had made him stay, so that they would not have to lunch alone. Their old friend had gone to the kitchen and prepared one of those dishes he had learned to make in the days when he was a landscape-painter. Milita observed that all landscape-painters knew something about cooking. Their outdoor life, the necessities of their wandering existence among country inns and huts, defying poverty, gave them a liking for this art.

They had had a very pleasant luncheon; mamma had laughed at Cotoner's jokes, who was always in good humor, but during the dessert, when Soldevilla, Renovales' favorite pupil, came, she had felt indisposed and had disappeared to hide her eyes swimming with tears and her breast that heaved with sobs.

"She's probably upstairs," said the girl with a sort of indifference, accustomed to these outbreaks. "Good-by, papa, dear, a kiss. Cotoner and Soldevilla are waiting for you in the studio. Another kiss. Let me bite you."

And after fixing her little teeth gently in one of the master's cheeks, she ran out, followed by Miss, who was already puffing in anticipation at the thought of the tiresome walk.

Renovales remained motionless as if he hesitated to shake off the atmosphere of affection in which his daughter enveloped him. Milita was his, wholly his. She loved her mother, but her affection was cold in comparison with the ardent passion she felt for him—that vague, instinctive preference girls feel for their fathers and which is, as it were, a forecast of the worship the man they love will later inspire in them.

For a moment he thought of looking for Josephina to

console her, but after a brief reflection, he gave up the
idea. It probably was nothing; his daughter was not disturbed; a sudden fit such as she usually had. If he went
upstairs he would run the risk of an unpleasant scene
that would spoil the afternoon, rob him of his desire to
work and banish the youthful light-heartedness that filled
him after his luncheon with Tekli.

He turned his steps towards the last studio, the only
one that deserved the name, for it was there he worked,
and he saw Cotoner sitting in a huge armchair, the seat
of which sagged under his corpulent frame, with his
elbows resting on the oaken arms, his waistcoat unbuttoned to relieve his well-filled paunch, his head sunk between his shoulders, his face red and sweating, his eyes
half closed with the sweet joy of digestion in that comfortable atmosphere heated by a huge stove.

Cotoner was getting old; his mustache was white and
his head was bald, but his face was as rosy and shining
as a child's. He breathed the placidness of a respectable
old bachelor whose only love is for good living and who
appreciates the digestive sleepiness of the boaconstrictor
as the greatest of happiness.   ·

He was tired of living in Rome. Commissions were
scarce. The Popes lived longer than the Biblical patri-
archs. The chromo portraits of the Pontiff had simply
forced him out of business. Besides, he was old and the
young painters who came to Rome did not know him;
they were poor fellows who looked on him as a clown,
and never laid aside their seriousness except to make
sport of him. His time had passed. The echoes of
Mariano's triumphs at home had come to his ears, had
determined him to move to Madrid. Life was the same
everywhere. He had friends in Madrid, too. And here
he had continued the life he had led in Rome, without
any effort, feeling a kind of longing for glory in that

narrow personality which had made him a mere day-laborer in art, as if his relations with Renovales imposed on him the duty of seeking a place near his in the world of painting.

He had gone back to landscapes, never winning any greater success than the simple admirations of wash-women and brickmakers who gathered around his easel in the suburbs of Madrid, whispering to each other that the gentleman who wore on his lapel the variegated button of his numerous Papal Orders, must be a famous old "buck," one of the great painters the papers talked about. Renovales had secured for him two honorable mentions at the Exhibitions and after this victory, shared with all the young chaps who were just beginning, Cotoner settled down in the rut, to rest forever, counting that the mission of his life was fulfilled.

Life in Madrid was no more difficult for him than in Rome. He slept at the house of a priest whom he had known in Italy, and had accompanied on his tours as Papal representative. This chaplain, who was employed in the office of the Rota, considered it a great honor to entertain the artist, recalling his friendly relations with the cardinals and believing that he was in correspondence with the Pope himself.

They had agreed on a sum which he was to pay for his lodging, but the priest did not seem to be in any hurry for payment; he would soon give him a commission for a painting for some nuns for whom he was confessor.

The eating problem offered still less difficulty for Cotoner. He had the days of the week divided among various rich families noted for their piety, whom he had met in Rome during the great Spanish pilgrimages. They were wealthy miners from Bilbao, gentlemen farmers from Andalusia, old marchionesses who thought about God a great deal, but continued to live their comfortable life to which they gave a serious tone by the respectable color of devotion.

The painter felt closely attached to this little group; they were serious, religious and they ate well. Everyone called him "good Cotoner." The ladies smiled with gratitude when he presented them with a rosary or some other article of devotion brought from Rome. If they expressed the desire of obtaining some dispensation from the Vatican, he would offer to write to "his friend the cardinal." The husbands, glad to entertain an artist so cheaply, consulted him about the plan for a new chapel or the designs for an altar, and on their saint's day they would receive with a condescending mien some present from Cotoner—a "little daub," a landscape painted on a piece of wood, that often needed an explanation before they could understand what it was meant for.

At dinners he was a constant source of amusement for these people of solid principles and measured words, with his stories of the strange doings of the "Monsignori" or the "Eminences" he used to know in Rome. They listened to these jokes with a sort of unction, however dubious they were, seeing that they came from such respectable personages.

When the round of invitations was interrupted by illness or absence, and Cotoner lacked a place to dine, he stayed at Renovales' house without waiting for an invitation. The master wanted him to live with them, but he did not accept. He was very fond of the family; Milita played with him as if he were an old dog, Josephina felt a sort of affection for him, because his presence reminded her of the good old days in Rome. But Cotoner, in spite of this, seemed to be somewhat reluctant, divining the storms that darkened the master's life. He preferred his free existence, to which he adapted himself with the ease of a parasite. After dinner was over, he would listen to the weighty discussions between learned priests and serious old church-goers, nodding his approval, and an hour later he would be jesting impiously in some café or other with painters, actors and journalists. He knew everybody; he only needed to speak to an artist twice and he would call him by his first name and swear that he loved and admired him from the bottom of his heart. When Renovales came into the studio, he shook off his drowsiness and stretched out his short legs so that he could touch the floor and get out of the chair.

"Did they tell you, Mariano? A magnificent dish! I made them an Andalusian pot-pourri! They were tickled to death over it!"

He was enthusiastic over his culinary achievement as if all his merits were summed up in this skill. Afterwards, while Renovales was handing his coat and hat to the servant who followed him, Cotoner with the curiosity of an intimate friend who wants to know all the details of his idol's life, questioned him about his luncheon with the foreigner.

Renovales lay down on a divan deep as a niche, between two bookcases and lined with piles of cushions. As they spoke of Tekli, they recalled friends in Rome, painters of different nationalities who twenty years before had walked with their heads high, following the star of hope as if they were hypnotized. Renovales, in his pride in his strength, incapable of hypocritical modesty, declared that he was the only one who had succeeded. Poor Tekli was a professor; his copy of Velásquez amounted to nothing more than the work of a patient cart horse in art.

"Do you think so?" asked Cotoner doubtfully. "Is his work so poor?"

His selfishness kept him from saying a word against

anyone; he had no faith in criticism, he believed blindly in praise; thereby preserving his reputation as a good fellow, which gave him the entrée everywhere and made his life easy. The figure of the Hungarian was fixed in his memory and made him think of a series of luncheons before he left Madrid.

"Good afternoon, master."

It was Soldevilla who came out from behind a screen with his hands clasped behind his back under the tail of his short sack coat, his head in the air, tortured by the excessive height of his stiff, shining collar, throwing out his chest so as to show off better his velvet waistcoat. His thinness and his small stature were made up for by the length of his blond mustache that curled around his pink little nose as if it were trying to reach the straight, scraggly bangs on his forehead. This Soldevilla was Renovales' favorite pupil—"his weakness" Cotoner called him. The master had fought a great battle to win him the fellowship at Rome; afterward he had given him the prize at several exhibitions.

He looked on him almost as a son, attracted perhaps by the contrast between his own rough strength and the weakness of that artistic dandy, always proper, always amiable, who consulted this master about everything, even if afterwards he did not pay much attention to his advice. When he criticized his fellow painters, he did it with a venomous suavity, with a feminine finesse. Renovales laughed at his appearance and his habits and Cotoner joined in. He was like china, always shining; you could not find the least speck of dust on him; you were sure he slept in a cupboard. These present-day painters! The two old artists recalled the disorder of their youth, their Bohemian carelessness, with long beards and huge hats, all their odd extravagances to distinguish them from the rest of men, forming a world by themselves. They felt out of humor with these painters of the last batch—proper, prudent, incapable of doing anything absurd, copying the fashions of the idle and presenting the appearance of State functionaries, clerks, who wielded the brush.

His greeting over, Soldevilla fairly overwhelmed the master with his effusive praise. He had been admiring the portrait of the Countess of Alberca.

"A perfect marvel, master. The best thing you have painted, and it's only half done, too."

This praise aroused Renovales. He got up, shoved aside the screen and pulled out an easel that held a large canvas, until it was opposite the light that came in through the wide window.

On a gray background stood a woman dressed in white, with that majesty of beauty that is accustomed to admiration. The aigrette of feathers and diamonds seemed to tremble on her tawny yellow curls, the curve of her breasts was outlined through the lace of her low-necked gown, her gloves reached above her elbows, in one of her hands she held a costly fan, in the other, a dark cloak, lined with flame-colored satin, that slipped from her bare shoulders, on the point of falling. The lower part of the figure was merely outlined in charcoal on the white canvas. The head, almost finished, seemed to look at the three men with its proud eyes, cold, but with a false coldness that bespoke a hidden passion within, a dead volcano that might come to life at any moment.

She was a tall, stately woman, with a charming, well-proportioned figure, who seemed to keep the freshness of youth, thanks to the healthy, comfortable life she led. The corners of her eyes were narrowed with a tired fold.

Cotoner looked at her from his seat with chaste calmness, commenting tranquilly on her beauty, feeling above temptation.

"It's she, you've caught her, Mariano. She has been a great woman."

Renovales appeared offended at this comment.

"She is," he said with a sort of hostility. "She is still."

Cotoner could not argue with his idol and he hastened to correct himself.

"She is a charming woman, very attractive, yes sir, and very stylish. They say she is talented and cannot bear to let men who worship her suffer. She has certainly enjoyed life."

Renovales began to bristle again, as if these words cut him.

"Nonsense! lies, calumnies!" he said angrily. "Inventions of some young fellows who spread these disgraceful reports because they were rejected."

Cotoner began to explain away what he had said. He did not know anything, he had heard it. The ladies at whose houses he dined spoke ill of the Alberca woman, but perhaps it was merely woman's gossip. There was a moment of silence and Renovales, as if he wanted to change the subject of conversation, turned to Soldevilla.

"And you, aren't you painting any longer? I always find you here in working hours."

He smiled somewhat knowingly as he said this, while the youth blushed and tried to make excuses. He was working hard, but every day he felt the need of dropping into his master's studio for a minute before he went to his own.

It was a habit he had formed when he was a beginner, in that period, the best in his life, when he studied beside the great painter in a studio far less sumptuous than this.

"And Milita? Did you see her?" continued Renovales with a good-natured smile that had not lost its playfulness. "Didn't she 'kid' you, for wearing that dazzling new tie?"

Soldevilla smiled too. He had been in the dining-room with Doña Josephina and Milita and the latter had made fun of him as usual. But she did not mean anything; the master knew that Milita and he treated each other like brother and sister.

More than once when she was a little tot and he a lad, he had acted as her horse, trotting around the old studio with the little scamp on his back, pulling his hair and pounding him with her tiny fists.

"She's very cute," interrupted Cotoner. "She is the most attractive, the best girl I know."

"And the unequaled López de Sosa?" asked the master, once more in a playful tone. "Didn't that 'chauffeur' that drives us crazy with his automobiles come to-day?"

Soldevilla's smile disappeared. He grew pale and his eyes flashed spitefully. No, he had not seen the gentleman. According to the ladies, he was busy repairing an automobile that had broken down on the Pardo road. And as if the recollection of this friend of the family was trying for him and he wished to avoid any further allusions to him, he said "good-by" to the master. He was going to work; he must take advantage of the two hours of sunlight that were left. But before he went out he stopped to say another word in praise of the portrait of the countess.

The two friends remained alone for a long while in silence. Renovales, buried in the shadow of that niche of Persian stuffs with which his divan was canopied, gazed at the picture.

"Is she going to come to-day?" asked Cotoner, pointing to the canvas.

Renovales shrugged his shoulders. To-day or the next

day; it was impossible to do any serious work with that
woman.

He expected her that afternoon; but he would not feel
surprised if she failed to keep her appointment.   For
nearly a month he had been unable to get in two days
in succession.   She was always engaged; she was president of societies for the education and emancipation of
woman; she was constantly planning festivals and raf-
fles; the activity of a tired woman of society, the fluttering of a wild bird that made her want to be everywhere
at the same time, without the will to withdraw when once
she was started in the current of feminine excitement.
Suddenly the painter whose eyes were fixed on the portrait gave a cry of enthusiasm.

"What a woman, Pepe! What a woman to paint!"

His eyes seemed to lay bare the beauty that stood on
the canvas in all its aristocratic grandeur.   They strove
to penetrate the mystery of that covering of lace and
silk, to see the color and the lines of the form that was
hardly revealed through the gown.   This mental recon-
struction was helped by the bare shoulders and the
curve of her breasts that seemed to tremble at the edge
of her dress, separated by a line of soft shadow.

"That's just what I told your wife," said the Bohemian
naïvely.   "If you paint beautiful women, like the countess, it is merely for the sake of painting them and not
that you would think of seeing in them anything more
than a model."

"Aha! So my wife has been talking to you about that!"

Cotoner hastened to set his mind at ease, fearing his
digestion might be disturbed.   A mere trifle, nervousness
on the part of poor Josephina, who saw the dark side of
everything in her illness.

She had referred during the luncheon to the Alberca
woman and her portrait.   She did not seem to be very

fond of her, in spite of the fact that she had been her companion in boarding-school. She felt as other women did; the countess was an enemy, who inspired them with fear. But he had calmed her and finally succeeded in making her smile faintly. There was no use in talking about that any longer.

But Renovales did not share his friend's optimism. He was well aware of his wife's state of mind; he understood now the motive that had made her flee from the table, to take refuge upstairs and to weep and long for death. She hated Concha as she did all the women who entered his studio. But this impression of sadness did not last very long in the painter; he was used to his wife's susceptibility. Besides, the consciousness of his faithfulness calmed him. His conscience was clean, and Josephina might believe what she would. It would only be one more injustice and he was resigned to endure his slavery without complaint.

In order to forget his trouble, he began to talk about painting. The recollection of his conversation with Tekli enlivened him, for Tekli had been traveling all over Europe and was well acquainted with what the most famous masters were thinking and painting.

"I'm getting old, Cotoner. Did you think I didn't know it? No, don't protest. I know that I am not old; forty-three years. I mean that I have lost my gait and cannot get started. It's a long time since I have done anything new; I always strike the same note. You know that some people, envious of my reputation are always throwing that defect in my face, like a vile insult."

And the painter, with the selfishness of great artists who always think that they are neglected and the world begrudges them their glory, complained at the slavery that was imposed upon him by his good fortune. Making money! What a calamity for art! If the world were governed by his common sense, artists with talent would be supported by the State, which would generously provide for all their needs and whims. There would be no need of bothering about making a living. "Paint what you want to, and as you please." Then great things would be done and art would advance with giant strides, not constrained to debase itself by flattering public vulgarity and the ignorance of the rich. But now, to be a celebrated painter it was necessary to make money and this could not be done except by portraits, opening a shop, painting the first one that appeared, without the right of choice. Accursed painting! In writing, poverty was a merit. It stood for truth and honesty. But the painter must be rich, his talent was judged by his profits. The fame of his pictures was connected with the idea of thousands of dollars. When people talked about his work they always said, "He's making such and such a sum of money," and to keep up this wealth, the indispensable companion of his glory, he had to paint by the job, cringing before the vulgar throng that pays.

Renovales walked excitedly around the portrait. Sometimes this laborer's work was tolerable, when he was painting beautiful women and men whose faces had the light of intelligence. But the vulgar politicians, the rich men that looked like porters, the stout dames with dead faces that he had to paint! When he let his love for truth overcome him and copied the model as he saw it, he won another enemy, who paid the bill grumblingly and went away to tell everyone that Renovales was not so great as people thought. To avoid this he lied in his painting, having recourse to the methods employed by other mediocre artists and this base procedure tormented his conscience, as if he were robbing his inferiors who deserved respect for the very reason that they were less endowed for artistic production than he.

"Besides, that is not painting, the whole of painting. We think we are artists because we can reproduce a face, and the face is only a part of the body. We tremble with fear at the thought of the nude. We have forgotten it. We speak of it with respect and fear, as we would of something religious, worthy of worship, but something we never see close at hand. A large part of our talent is the talent of a dry-goods clerk. Cloth, nothing but cloth; garments. The body must be carefully wrapped up or we flee from it as from a danger."

He ceased his nervous walking to and fro and stopped in front of the picture, fixing his gaze on it.

"Imagine, Pepe," he said in an undertone, looking first instinctively toward the door, with that eternal fear of being heard by his wife in the midst of his artistic raptures. "Imagine, if that woman would undress; if I could paint her as she certainly is."

Cotoner burst into laughter with a look like a knavish friar.

"Wonderful, Mariano, a masterpiece. But she won't. I'm sure she would refuse to undress, though I admit she isn't always particular."

Renovales shook his fists in protest.

"And why won't they? What a rut! What vulgarity!"

In his artistic selfishness he fancied that the world had been created without any other purpose than supporting painters, the rest of humanity was made to serve them as models, and he was shocked at this incomprehensible modesty. Ah, where could they find now the beauties of Greece, the calm models of sculptors, the pale Venetian ladies painted by Titian, the graceful Flemish women of Rubens, and the dainty, sprightly beauties of Goya? Beauty was eclipsed forever behind the veils of hypocrisy and false modesty. Women had one lover to-day, another to-morrow and still they blushed at recalling the woman of other times, far more pure than they, who did not hesitate to reveal to the public admiration the perfect work of God, the chastity of the nude.

Renovales lay down on the divan again, and in the twilight he talked confidentially with Cotoner in a subdued voice, sometimes looking toward the door as if he feared being overheard.

For some time he had been dreaming of a masterpiece. He had it in his imagination complete even to the least details. He saw it, closing his eyes, just at it would be, if he ever succeeded in painting it. It was Phryne, the famous beauty of Athens, appearing naked before the crowd of pilgrims on the beach of Delphi. All the suffering humanity of Greece walked on the shore of the sea toward the famous temple, seeking divine intervention for the relief of their ills, cripples with distorted limbs, repulsive lepers, men swollen with dropsy, pale, suffering women, trembling old men, youths disfigured in hideous expressions, withered arms like bare bones, shapeless elephant legs, all the phases of a perverted Nature, the piteous, desperate expressions of human pain. When they see on the beach Phryne, the glory of Greece, whose beauty was a national pride, the pilgrims stop and gaze upon her, turning their backs to the temple, that outlines its marble columns in the background of the parched mountains; and the beautiful woman, filled with pity by this procession of suffering, desires to brighten their sadness, to cast a handful of health and beauty among their wretched furrows, and tears off her veils, giving them the royal alms of her nakedness. The white, radiant body is outlined on the dark blue of the sea. The wind scatters her hair like golden serpents on her ivory shoulders; the waves that die at her feet, toss upon her stars of foam that make her skin tremble with the caress from her amber neck down to her rosy feet. The wet sand, polished

and bright as a mirror, reproduces the sovereign nakedness, inverted and confused in serpentine lines that take
on the shimmer of the rainbow as they disappear. And
the pilgrims, on their knees, in the ecstasy of worship,
stretch out their arms toward the mortal goddess, believing that Beauty and eternal Health have come to
meet them.

Renovales sat up and grasped Cotoner's arm as he described his future picture, and his friend nodded his approval gravely, impressed by the description.

"Very fine! Sublime, Mariano!"

But the master became dejected again after this flash
of enthusiasm.

The task was very difficult. He would have to go and
take up quarters on the shore of the Mediterranean, on
some secluded beach at Valencia or in Catalonia; he
would have to build a cabin on the very edge of the sand
where the water breaks with its bright reflections, and
take woman after woman there, a hundred if it was
necessary, in order to study the whiteness of their skin
against the blue of the sea and sky, until he found the
divine body of the Phryne he had dreamed.

"Very difficult," murmured Renovales. "I tell you it
is very difficult. There are so many obstacles to struggle
against."

Cotoner leaned forward with a confidential expression.

"And besides, there's the mistress," he said in a quiet
voice, looking at the door with a sort of fear. "I don't
believe Josephina would be very much pleased with this
picture and its pack of models."

The master lowered his head.

"If you only knew, Pepe! If you could see the life I
lead every day!"

"I know what it is," Cotoner hastened to say, "or
rather, I can imagine. Don't tell me anything."

And in his haste to avoid the sad confidences of his friend, there was a great deal of selfishness, the desire not to disturb his peaceful calm with other men's sorrows that excite only a distant interest.

Renovales spoke after a long silence. He often wondered whether an artist ought to be married or single. Other men, of weak, hesitating character needed the support of a comrade, the atmosphere of a family.

He recalled with relish the first few months of his married life; but since then it had weighed on him like a chain. He did not deny the existence of love; he needed the sweet company of a woman in order to live, but with intermissions, without the endless imprisonment of common life. Artists like himself ought to be free, he was sure of it.

"Oh, Pepe, if I had only stayed like you, master of my time and my work, without having to think what my family will say if they see me painting this or that, what great things I should have done!"

The old man, who had failed in all his tasks, was going to say something when the door of the studio opened and Renovales' servant came in, a little man with fat red cheeks and a high voice which, according to Cotoner, sounded like the messenger of a monastery.

"The countess."

Cotoner jumped out of his armchair. Those models didn't like to see people in the studio. How could he get out? Renovales helped him to find his hat, coat and cane, which with his usual carelessness he had left in different corners of the studio.

The master pushed him out of a door that led into the garden. Then, when he was alone, he ran to an old Venetian mirror, and looked at himself for a moment in its deep, bluish surface, smoothing his curly gray hair with his fingers.

V

SHE came in with a great rustling of silks and laces, her least step accompanied by the *frou-frou* of her skirts, scattering various perfumes, like the breath of an exotic garden.

"Good afternoon, *mon cher maître.*"

As she looked at him through her tortoise-shell lorgnette, hanging from a gold chain, the gray amber of her eyes took on an insolent stare through the glasses, a strange expression, half caressing, half mocking.

He must pardon her for being so late. She was sorry for her lack of attention, but she was the busiest woman in Madrid. The things she had done since luncheon! Signing and examining papers with the secretary of the "Women's League," a conference with the carpenter and the foreman (two rough fellows who fairly devoured her with their eyes), who had charge of putting up the booths for the great fair for the benefit of destitute working women; a call on the president of the Cabinet, a somewhat dissolute old gentleman, in spite of his gravity, who received her with the airs of an old-fashioned gallant, kissing her hand, as they used to in a minuet.

"We have lost the afternoon, haven't we, *maître?* There's hardly sun enough to work by now. Besides, I didn't bring my maid to help me."

She pointed with her lorgnette to the door of an alcove that served as a dressing-room for the models and where she kept the evening gown and the flame-colored cloak in which he was painting her.

Renovales, after looking furtively at the entrance of

the studio, assumed an arrogant air of swaggering gallantry, such as he used to have in his youth in Rome,
free and obstreperous.

"You needn't give up on that account. If you will let
me, I'll act as maid for you."

The countess began to laugh loudly, throwing back her
head and shoulders, showing her white throat that shook
with merriment.

"Oh, what a good joke! And how daring the master is
getting. You don't know anything about such things,
Renovales. All you can do is paint. You are not in
practice."

And in her accent of subtle irony, there was something
like pity for the artist, removed from mundane things,
whose conjugal virtue everyone knew. This seemed to
offend him for he spoke to the countess very sharply as
he picked up the palette and prepared the colors. There
was no need of changing her dress; he would make use
of what little daylight remained to work on the head.

Concha took off her hat and then, before the same
Venetian mirror in which the painter had looked at himself, began to touch up her hair. Her arms curved
around her golden head, while Renovales contemplated
the grace of her back, seeing at the same time her face
and breast in the glass. She hummed as she arranged
her hair, with her eyes fixed on their own reflection, not
letting anything distract her in this important operation.

That brilliant, striking golden hair was probably
bleached. The painter was sure of it, but it did not seem
less beautiful to him on that account. The beauties of
Venice in the olden times used to dye their hair.

The countess sat down in an armchair, a short distance from the easel. She felt tired and as long as he
was not going to paint anything but her face, he would
not be so cruel as to make her stand, as he did on days of

real sittings. Renovales answered with monosyllables and shrugs of his shoulders. That was all right—for what they were going to do. An afternoon lost. He would limit himself to working on her hair and her forehead. She might take it easy, looking anywhere she wanted to.

The master did not feel any desire to work either. A dull anger disturbed him; he was irritated by the ironical accent of the countess who saw in him a man different from other men, a strange being who was incapable of acting like the insipid young men who formed her court and many of whom, according to common gossip, were her lovers. A strange woman, provoking and cold! He felt like falling on her, in his rage at her offence, and beating her with the same scorn that he would a low woman, to make her feel his manly superiority.

Of all the ladies whose pictures he had painted, none had disturbed his artistic calm as she had. He felt attracted by her mad jesting, by her almost childish levity, and at the same time he hated her for the pitying air with which she treated him. For her he was a good fellow, but very commonplace, who by some rare caprice of Nature possessed the gift of painting well.

Renovales returned this scorn by insulting her mentally. That Countess of Alberca was a fine one. No wonder people talked about her. Perhaps when she appeared in his studio, always in a hurry and out of breath, she came from a private interview with some one of those young bloods that hung around her, attracted by her still fresh, alluring maturity.

But if Concha spoke to him with her easy freedom, telling him of the sadness she said she felt and allowing herself to confide in him, as if they were united by a long standing friendship, that was enough to make the master change his thoughts immediately. She was a superior woman of ideals, condemned to live in a depressing aristocratic atmosphere. All the gossip about her was a calumny, a lie forged by envious people. She ought to be the companion of a superior man, of an artist.

Renovales knew her history; he was proud of the friendly confidence she had had in him. She was the only daughter of a distinguished gentleman, a solemn jurist, and a violent Conservative, a minister in the most reactionary cabinets of the reign of Isabel II. She had been educated at the same school as Josephina, who in spite of the fact that Concha was four years her senior, retained a vivid recollection of her lively companion. "For mischief and deviltry you can't beat Conchita Salazar." It was thus that Renovales heard her name for the first time. Then when the artist and his wife had moved from Venice to Madrid, he learned that she had changed her name to that of the Countess of Alberca by marrying a man who might have been her father.

He was an old courtier who performed his duties as a grandee of Spain with great conscientiousness, proud of his slavery to the royal family. His ambition was to belong to all the honorable orders of Europe and as soon as he was named to one of them, he had his picture painted, covered with scarfs and crosses, wearing the uniform of one of the traditional military Orders. His wife laughed to see him, so little, bald and solemn, with high boots, a dangling sword, his breast covered with trinkets, a white plumed helmet resting in his lap.

During the life of isolation and privation with which Renovales struggled so courageously, the papers brought to the artist's wretched house the echoes of the triumphs of the "fair Countess of Alberca." Her name appeared in the first line of every account of an aristocratic function. Besides, they called her "enlightened," and talked about her literary culture, her classic education which she owed to her "illustrious father," now dead. And with this public news there reached the artist on the whispering wings of Madrid gossip other tales that represented the Countess of Alberca as consoling herself merrily for the mistake she had made in marrying an old man.

At Court, they had taken her name from the lists, as a result of this reputation. Her husband took part at all the royal functions, for he did not have a chance every day to show off his load of honorary hardware, but she stayed at home, loathing these ceremonious affairs. Renovales had often heard her declare, dressed luxuriously and wearing costly jewels in her ears and on her breast, that she laughed at his set, that she was on the inside, she was an anarchist! And he laughed as he heard her, just as all men laughed at what they called the "ways" of the Alberca woman.

When Renovales won success and, as a famous master, returned to those drawing rooms through which he had passed in his youth, he felt the attraction of the countess who in her character as a "woman of intellect," insisted on gathering celebrated men about her. Josephina did not accompany him in this return to society. She felt ill; contact with the same people in the same places tired her; she lacked the strength to undertake even the trips her doctors urged upon her.

The countess enrolled the painter in her following, appearing offended when he failed to present himself at her house on the afternoons on which she received her friends. What ingratitude to show to such a fervent admirer! How she liked to exhibit him before her friends, as if he were a new jewel! "The painter Renovales, the famous master."

At one of these afternoon receptions, the count spoke to Renovales with the serious air of a man who is crushed beneath his worldly honors.

"Concha wants a portrait done by you, and I like to please her in every way. You can say when to begin. She is afraid to propose it to you and has commissioned me to do it. I know that your work is better than that of other painters. Paint her well, so that she may be pleased."

And noticing that Renovales seemed rather offended at his patronizing familiarity, he added as if he were doing him another favor,

"If you have success with Concha, you may paint my picture afterward. I am only waiting for the Grand Chrysanthemum of Japan. At the Government offices they tell me the titles will come one of these days."

Renovales began the countess's portrait. The task was prolonged by that rattle-brained woman who always came late, alleging that she had been busy. Many days the artist did not take a stroke with his brush; they spent the time chatting. At other times the master listened in silence while she with her ceaseless volubility made fun of her friends and related their secret defects, their most intimate habits, their mysterious amours, with a kind of relish, as if all women were her enemies. In the midst of one of these confidential talks, she stopped and said with a shy expression and an ironical accent:

"But I am probably shocking you, Mariano. You, who are a good husband, a staunch family-man."

Renovales felt tempted to choke her. She was making fun of him; she looked on him as a man different from the rest of men, a sort of monk of painting. Eager to wound her, to return the blow, he interrupted once brutally in the midst of her merciless gossip.

"Well, they talk about you, too, Concha. They say things that wouldn't be very pleasing to the count."

He expected an outburst of anger, a protest, and all that resounded in the silence of the studio was a merry,

reckless laugh that lasted a long time, stopping occa-
sionally, only to begin again. Then she grew pensive,
with the gentle sadness of women who are "misunder-
stood." She was very unhappy. She could tell him
everything because he was a good friend. She had married when she was still a child; a terrible mistake. There
was something else in the world besides the glare of fortune, the splendor of luxury and that count's coronet,
which had stirred her school-girl's mind.

"We have the right to a little love, and if not love, to a
little joy. Don't you think so, Mariano?"

Of course he thought so. And he declared it in such
a way, looking at Concha with alarming eyes, that she
finally laughed at his frankness and threatened him with
her finger.

"Take care, master. Don't forget that Josephina is
my friend and if you go astray, I'll tell her everything."

Renovales was irritated at her disposition, always restless and capricious as a bird's, quite as likely to sit down
beside him in warm intimacy as to flit away with tormenting banter.

Sometimes she was aggressive, teasing the artist from
her very first words, as had just happened that afternoon.

They were silent for a long time—he, painting with
an absent-minded air, she watching the movement of the
brush, buried in an armchair in the sweet calm of rest.

But the Alberca woman was incapable of remaining
silent long. Little by little her usual chatter began, paying no attention to the painter's silence, talking to relieve
the convent-like stillness of the studio with her words
and laughter.

The painter heard the story of her labors as president
of the "Women's League," of the great things she meant
to do in the holy undertaking for the emancipation of the
sex. And, in passing, led on by her desire of ridiculing

all women, she gaily made sport of her co-workers in the great project; unknown literary women, school teachers, whose lives were embittered by their ugliness, painters of flowers and doves, a throng of poor women with extravagant hats and clothes that looked as though they were hung on a bean-pole; feminine Bohemians, rebellious and rabid against their lot, who were proud to have her as their leader and who made it a point to call her "Countess" in sonorous tones at every other word, in order to flatter themselves with the distinction of this friendship. The Alberca woman was greatly amused at her following of admirers; she laughed at their intolerance and their proposals.

"Yes, I know what it is," said Renovales breaking his long silence. "You want to annihilate us, to reign over man, whom you hate."

The countess laughed at the recollection of the fierce feminism of some of her acolytes. As most of them were homely, they hated feminine beauty as a sign of weakness. They wanted the woman of the future to be without hips, without breasts, straight, bony, muscular, fitted for all sorts of manual labor, free from the slavery of love and reproduction. "Down with feminine fat!"

"What a frightful idea! Don't you think so, Mariano?" she continued. "Woman, straight in front and straight behind, with her hair cut short and her hands hardened, competing with men in all sorts of struggles! And they call that emancipation! I know what men are; if they saw us looking like that, in a few days they would be beating us."

No, she was not one of them. She wanted to see a woman triumph, but by increasing still more her charm and her fascination. If they took away her beauty what would she have left? She wanted her to be man's equal in intelligence, his superior by the magic of her beauty.

"I don't hate men, Mariano, I am very much a woman, and I like them. What's the use of denying it?"

"I know it, Concha, I know it," said the painter, with a malicious meaning.

"What do you know? Lies, gossip that people tell about me because I am not a hypocrite and am not always wearing a gloomy expression."

And led on by that desire for sympathy that all women of questionable reputation experience, she spoke once more of her unpleasant situation. Renovales knew the count, a good man in spite of his hobbies, who thought of nothing but his honorary trinkets. She did everything for him, watched out for his comfort, but he was nothing to her. She lacked the most important thing—heart-love.

As she spoke she looked up, with a longing idealism that would have made anyone but Renovales smile.

"In this situation," she said slowly, looking into space, "it isn't strange that a woman seeks happiness where she can find it. But I am very unhappy, Mariano; I don't know what love is. I have never loved."

Ah, she would have been happy, if she had married a man who was her superior. To be the companion of a great artist, of a scholar, would have meant happiness for her. The men who gathered around her in her drawing-rooms were younger and stronger than the poor count, but mentally they were even weaker than he. There was no such thing as virtue in the world, she admitted that; she did not dare to lie to a friend like the painter. She had had her diversions, her whims, just as many other women who passed as impregnable models of virtue, but she always came out of these misdoings with a feeling of disenchantment and disgust. She knew that love was a reality for other women, but she had never succeeded in finding it.

Renovales had stopped painting. The sunlight no longer came in through the wide window. The panes took on a violet opaqueness. Twilight filled the studio, and in the shadows there shone dimly like dying sparks, here the corner of a picture frame, beyond the old gold of an embroidered banner, in the corners the pummel of a sword, the pearl inlay of a cabinet.

The painter sat down beside the countess, sinking into the perfumed atmosphere which surrounded her with a sort of nimbus of keen voluptuousness.

He, too, was unhappy. He said it sincerely, believing honestly in the lady's melancholy despair. Something was lacking in his life; he was alone in the world. And as he saw an expression of surprise on Concha's face, he pounded his chest energetically.

Yes, alone. He knew what she was going to say. He had his wife, his daughter. About Milita he did not want to talk; he worshiped her; she was his joy. When he felt tired out with work, it gave him a sweet sense of rest to put his arms around her neck. But he was still too young to be satisfied with this joy of a father's love. He longed for something more and he could not find it in the companion of his life, always ill, with her nerves constantly on edge. Besides, she did not understand him. She never would understand him; she was a burden who was crushing his talent.

Their union was based merely on friendship, on mutual consideration for the suffering they had undergone together. He, too, had been deceived in taking for love what was only an impulse of youthful attraction. He needed a true passion; to live close to a soul that was akin to his, to love a woman who was his superior, who could understand him and encourage him in his bold projects, who could sacrifice her commonplace prejudices to the demands of art.

He spoke vehemently, with his eyes fixed on Concha's eyes that shone with light from the window.

But Renovales was interrupted by a cruel, ironical laugh, while the countess pushed back her chair, as if to avoid the artist who slowly leaned forward toward her.

"Look out, you're slipping, Mariano! I see it coming. A little more and you would have made me a confession. Heavens! These men! You can't talk to them like a good friend, show them any confidence without their beginning to talk love on the spot. If I would let you, in less than a minute you would tell me that I am your ideal, that you worship me."

Renovales, who had moved away from her, recovering his sternness, felt cut by that mocking laugh and said in a quiet tone:

"And what if it were true? What if I loved you?"

The laugh of the countess rang out again, but forced, false, with a tone that seemed to tear the artist's breast.

"Just what I expected! The confession I spoke of! That's the third one I've received to-day. But isn't it possible to talk with a man of anything but love?"

She was already on her feet, looking around for her hat, for she could not remember where she had left it.

"I'm going, *cher maître*. It isn't safe to stay here. I'll try to come earlier next time so that the twilight won't catch us. It's a treacherous hour; the moment of the greatest follies."

The painter objected to her leaving. Her carriage had not yet come. She could wait a few minutes longer. He promised to be quiet, not to talk to her, as long as it seemed to displease her.

The countess remained, but she would not sit down in the chair. She walked around the studio for a few moments and finally opened the organ that stood near the window.

"Let's have a little music; that will quiet us. You, Mariano, sit still as a mouse in your chair and don't come near me. Be a good boy now."

Her fingers rested on the keys; her feet moved the pedals and the *Largo* of Handel, grave, mystic, dreamy, swelled softly through the studio. The melody filled the wide room, already wrapped in shadows, it made its way through the tapestries, prolonging its winged whisper through the other two studios, as though it were the song of an organ played by invisible hands in a deserted cathedral at the mysterious hour of dusk.

Concha felt stirred with feminine sentimentality, that superficial, whimsical, sensitiveness that made her friends look on her as a great artist. The music filled her with tenderness; she strove to keep back the tears that came to her eyes,—why, she could not tell.

Suddenly she stopped playing and looked around anxiously. The painter was behind her, she fancied she felt his breath on her neck. She wanted to protest, to make him draw back with one of her cruel laughs, but she could not.

"Mariano," she murmured, "go sit down, be a good boy and mind me. If you don't I'll be cross."

But she did not move; after turning half way around on the stool, she remained facing the window with one elbow resting on the keys.

They were silent for a long time; she in this position, he watching her face that now was only a white spot in the deepening shadow.

The panes of the window took on a bluish opaqueness. The branches of the garden cut them like sinuous, shifting lines of ink. In the deep calm of the studio the creaking of the furniture could be heard, that breathing of wood, of dust, of objects in the silence and shadow.

Both of them seem to be captivated by the mystery of the hour, as if the death of day acted as an anæsthetic on their minds. They felt lulled in a vague, sweet dream.

She trembled with pleasure.

"Mariano, go away," she said slowly, as if it cost her an effort. "This is so pleasant, I feel as if I were in a bath, a bath that penetrates to my very soul. But it isn't right. Turn on the lights, master. Light! Light! This isn't proper."

Mariano did not listen to her. He had bent over her, taking her hand that was cold, unfeeling, as if it did not notice the pressure of his.

Then, with a sudden start, he kissed it, almost bit it.

The countess seemed to awake and stood up, proudly, angrily.

"That's childish, Mariano. It isn't fair."

But in a moment she laughed with her cruel laugh, as if she pitied the confusion that Renovales showed when he saw her anger. "You are pardoned, master. A kiss on the hand means nothing. It is the conventional thing. Many men kiss my hand."

And this indifference was a bitter torment for the artist, who considered that his kiss was a sign of possession.

The countess continued to search in the darkness, repeating in an irritated voice:

"Light, turn on the light. Where in the world is the button?"

The light was turned on without Mariano's moving, before she found the button she was looking for. Three clusters of electric lights flashed out on the ceiling of the studio, and their crowns of white needles, brought out of the shadows the golden picture frames, the bril-

liant tapestries, the shining arms, the showy furniture
and the bright-colored paintings.

They both blinked, blinded by the sudden brightness.

"Good evening," said a honeyed voice from the doorway.

"Josephina!"

The countess ran toward her, embracing her effusively, kissing her bright red, emaciated cheeks.

"How dark you were," continued Josephina with a
smile that Renovales knew well.

Concha fairly stunned her with her flow of chatter.
The illustrious master had refused to light up, he
liked the twilight. An artist's whim! They had been
talking about their dear Josephina, while she was waiting for her carriage to come. And as she said this, she
kept kissing the little woman, drawing back a little to
look at her better, repeating impetuously:

"My, how pretty you are to-day. You look better
than you did three days ago."

Josephina continued to smile. She thanked her. Her
carriage was waiting at the door. The servant had told
her when she came downstairs, attracted by the distant sound of the organ.

The countess seemed to be in a hurry to leave. She
suddenly remembered a host of things she had to do,
she enumerated the people who were waiting for her
at home. Josephina helped her to put on her hat and
veil and even then the countess gave her several good-
by kisses through the veil.

"God-by, *ma chère.* Good-by, *mignonne.* Do you
remember our school days? How happy we were there!
Good-by, *maître.*"

She stopped at the door to kiss Josephina once more.

And finally, before she disappeared, she exclaimed in
the querulous tone of a victim who wants sympathy:

"I envy you, *chèrie*. You, at least, are happy. You have found a husband who worships you. Master, take lots of care of her. Be good to her so that she may get well and pretty. Take care of her or we shall quarrel."

VI

RENOVALES had finished reading the evening papers in bed as was his custom, and before putting out the light he looked at his wife.

She was awake. Above the fold of the sheet he saw her eyes, unusually wide open, fixed on him with a hostile stare, and the little tails of her hair, that stuck out under the lace of her night-cap straight and sedate.

"Aren't you asleep?" the painter asked in an affectionate tone, in which there was some anxiety.

"No."

And after this hard monosyllable, she turned over in the bed with her back to him.

Renovales remained in the darkness, with his eyes open, somewhat disturbed, almost afraid of that body, hidden under the same sheet, lying a short distance from him, which avoided touching him, shrinking with manifest repulsion.

Poor little girl! Renovales' better nature felt tormented with a painful remorse. His conscience was a cruel beast that had awakened, angry and implacable, tearing him with scornful teeth. The events of the afternoon meant nothing, a moment of thoughtlessness, of weakness. Surely the countess would not remember it and he, for his part, was determined not to slip again.

A pretty situation for a father of a family, for a man whose youth was past, compromising himself in a love affair, getting melancholy in the twilight, kissing a white hand like an enamored troubadour! Good God! How his friends would have laughed to see him in that posture! He must purge himself of that romanticism which sometimes mastered him. Every man must follow his fate, accepting life as he found it. He was born to be virtuous, he must put up with the relative peace of his domestic life, must accept its limited pleasures as a compensation for the suffering his wife's illness caused him. He would be content with the feasts of his thought, with the revels in beauty at the banquets served by his fancy. He would keep his flesh faithful though it amounted to perpetual privation. Poor Josephina! His remorse at a moment of weakness which he considered a crime, impelled him to draw closer to her, as if he sought in her warmth and contact a mute forgiveness.

Her body, burning with a slow fever, drew away as it felt his touch, it shriveled like those timid molluscs that shrink and hide at the least touch. She was awake. He could not hear her breathing; she seemed dead in the profound darkness, but he fancied her with her eyes open, a scowl on her forehead and he felt the fear of a man who has a presentiment of danger in the mystery of the darkness.

Renovales too remained motionless, taking care not to touch again that form which silently repelled him. The sincerity of his repentance brought him a sort of consolation. Never again would he forget his wife, his daughter, his respectability.

He would give up forever the longings of youth, that recklessness, that thirst for enjoying all the pleasures of life. His lot was cast; he would continue to be what he always had been. He would paint portraits and everything that was given to him as a commission; he would please the public; he would make more money, he would adapt his art to meet his wife's jealous de-

mands, that she might live in peace; he would scoff at
that phantom of human ambition which men call glory.
Glory! A lottery, where the only chance for a prize
depended on the tastes of people still to be born! Who
knew what the artistic inclinations of the future would
be? Perhaps it would appreciate what he was now producing with such loathing; perhaps it would laugh scornfully at what he wanted to paint. The only thing
of importance was to live in peace, as long as he could
be surrounded by happiness. His daughter would
marry. Perhaps her husband would be his favorite
pupil, that Soldevilla, so polite, so courteous, who was
mad over the mischievous Milita. If it was not he, it
would be López de Sosa, a crazy fellow, in love with
his automobiles, who pleased Josephina more than the
pupil because he had not committed the sin of showing
talent and devoting himself to painting. He would have
grandchildren, his beard would grow white, he would
have the majesty of an Eternal Father and Josephina,
cared for by him, restored to health by an atmosphere
of affection, would grow old too, freed from her nervous troubles.

The painter felt allured by this picture of patriarchal
happiness. He would go out of the world without having tasted the best fruits which life offers, but still with
the peace of a soul that does not know the great heat
of passion.

Lulled by these illusions, the artist was sinking into
sleep. He saw in the darkness, the image of his calm
old age, with rosy wrinkles and silvery hair, at his side
a sprightly little old lady, healthy and attractive, with
wavy hair, and around them a group of children, many
children, some of them with their fingers in their noses,
others rolling on their backs on the floor, like playful
kittens, the older ones with pencils in their hands, mak-

ing caricatures of the old couple and all shouting in a chorus of loving cries: "Grandpa, dear! Pretty grandma!"

In his sleepy fancy, the picture grew indistinct and was blotted out. He no longer saw the figures, but the loving cry continued to sound in his ears, dying away in the distance.

Then it began to increase again, drew slowly nearer, but it was a complaint, a howl like that of the victim that feels the sacrificer's knife at its throat.

The artist, terrified by this moan, thought that some dark animal, some monster of the night was tossing beside him, brushing him with its tentacles, pushing him with the bony points of its joints.

He awoke and with his brain still cloudy with sleep, the first sensation he experienced was a tremble of fear and surprise, reaching from his head to his feet. The invisible monster was beside him, dying, kicking violently, sticking him with its angular body. The howl tore the darkness like a death rattle.

Renovales, aroused by his fear, awoke completely. That cry came from Josephina. His wife was tossing about in the bed, shrieking while she gasped for breath.

The electric button snapped and the white, hard light of the lamp showed the little woman in the disorder of her nervous outbreak; her weak limbs painfully convulsed, her eyes, staring, dull with an uncanny vacancy; her mouth contracted, dripping with foam.

The husband, dazed at this awakening, tried to take her in his arms, to hold her gently against him, as if his warmth might restore her calm.

"Let me—alone," she cried brokenly. "Let go of me. I hate you!"

And though she asked him to let go of her, she was the one who clung to him, digging her fingers into his throat, as if she wanted to strangle him. Renovales, insensible to this clutch which made little impression on his strong neck, murmured with sad kindness:

"Squeeze! Don't be afraid of hurting me. Relieve your feelings!"

Her hands, tired out with this useless pressure on that muscular flesh, relaxed their grasp with a sort of dejection. The outbreak lasted for some time, but tears came and she lay exhausted, inert, without any other signs of life than the heaving of her breast and a constant stream of tears.

Renovales had jumped out of bed, moving about the room in his night clothing, searching on all sides, without knowing what he was looking for, murmuring loving words to calm his wife.

She stopped crying, struggling to enunciate each syllable between her sobs. She spoke with her head buried in her arms. The painter stopped to listen to her, astounded at the coarse words that came from her lips, as if the grief that stirred her soul had set afloat all the shameful, filthy words she had heard in the streets that were hidden in the depth of her memory.

"The ——!" (And here she uttered the classic word, naturally, as if she had spoken thus all her life.) "The shameless woman! The ——!"

And she continued to volley a string of interjections which shocked her husband to hear them coming from those lips.

"But whom are you talking about? Who is it?"

She, as if she were only waiting for his question, sat up in bed, got onto her knees, looking at him fixedly, shaking her head on her delicate neck, so that the short, straight locks of hair whirled around it.

"Whom do you suppose? The Alberca woman. That

peacock! Look surprised! You don't know what I mean! Poor thing!"

Renovales expected this, but when he heard it, he assumed an injured expression, fortified by his determination to reform and by the certainty that he was telling the truth. He raised his hand to his heart in a tragic attitude, throwing back his shock of hair, not noticing the absurdity of his appearance that was reflected in the bedroom mirror.

"Josephina, I swear by all that I love most in the world that your suspicions are not true. I have had nothing to do with Concha. I swear it by our daughter!"

The little woman became more irritated.

"Don't swear, don't lie, don't name my daughter. You deceiver! You hypocrite! You are all alike!"

Did he think she was a fool? She knew everything that was going on around her. He was a rake, a false husband, she had discovered it a few months after their marriage; a Bohemian without any other education than the low associations of his class. And the woman was as bad; the worst in Madrid. There was a reason why people laughed at the count everywhere. Mariano and Concha understood each other; birds of a feather; they made fun of her in her own house, in the dark of the studio.

"She is your mistress," she said with cold anger. "Come now, admit it. Repeat all those shameless things about the rights of love and joy that you talk about to your friends in the studio, those infamous hypocrisies to justify your scorn for the family, for marriage, for everything. Have the courage of your convictions."

But Renovales, overwhelmed by this fierce outpouring of words that fell on him like a rain of blows, could only repeat, with his hand on his heart and the expression of noble resignation of a man who suffers an injustice:

"I am innocent. I swear it. Your suspicions are absolutely groundless."

And walking around to the other side of the bed, he tried again to take Josephina in his arms, thinking he could calm her, now that she seemed less furious and that her angry words were broken by tears.

It was a useless effort. The delicate form slipped out of his hands, repelling them with a feeling of horror and repugnance.

"Let me alone. Don't touch me. I loathe you."

Her husband was mistaken if he thought that she was Concha's enemy. Pshaw! She knew what women were. She even admitted (since he was so insistent in his protestations of innocence) that there was nothing between them. But if so, it was due solely to Concha—she had plenty of admirers and, besides, her old time friendship would impel her not to embitter Josephina's life. Concha was the one who had resisted and not he.

"I know you. You know that I can guess your thoughts, that I read in your face. You are faithful because you are a coward, because you have lacked an opportunity. But your mind is loaded with foul ideas; I detest your spirit."

And before he could protest, his wife attacked him anew, pouring out in one breath all the observations she had made, weighing his words and deeds with the subtlety of a diseased imagination.

She threw in his face the expression of rapture in his eyes when he saw beautiful women sit down before his easel to have their portraits painted; his praise of the throat of one, the shoulders of another; the almost religious unction with which he examined the photographs and engravings of naked beauties, painted by other artists whom he would like to imitate in his licentious impulses.

"If I should leave you! If I should disappear! Your studio would be a brothel, no decent person could enter it; you would always have some woman stripped in there, painting some disgraceful picture of her."

And in the tremble of her irritated voice there was revealed the anger, the bitter disappointment she had experienced in the constant contact with this cult of beauty, that paid no attention to her, who was aged before her time, sickly, with the ugliness of physical misery, whom each one of these enthusiastic homages wounded like a reproach, marking the abyss between her sad condition and the ideal that filled the mind of her husband.

"Do you think I don't know what you are thinking about. I laugh at your fidelity. A lie! Hypocrisy! As you get older, a mad desire is mastering you. If you could, if you had the courage, you would run after these creatures of beautiful flesh that you praise so highly. You are commonplace. There's nothing in you but coarseness and materialism. Form! Flesh! And they call that artistic? I'd have done better to marry a shoemaker, one of those honest, simple men that takes his poor little wife to dinner in a restaurant on Sunday and worships her, not knowing any other."

Renovales began to feel irritated at this attack that was no longer based on his actions but on his thoughts. That was worse than the Inquisition. She had spied on him constantly; always on the watch, she picked up his least words and expressions, she penetrated his thoughts, making his inclinations and enthusiasms a subject for jealousy.

"Stop, Josephina. That's despicable. I won't be able to think, to produce. You spy on me and pursue me even in my art."

She shrugged her shoulders scornfully. His art! She scoffed at it.

And she began again to insult painting, repenting that she had joined her lot to an artist's. Men like him ought not to marry respectable women, what people call "homebodies." Their fate was to remain single or to join with unscrupulous women who were in love with their own form and were capable of exhibiting it in the street, taking pride in their nakedness.

"I used to love you; did you know it?" she said coldly. "I used to love you, but I no longer love you. What's the use? I know that even if you swore to me on your knees, you would never be faithful to me. You might be tied to my apron strings but your thoughts would go wandering off to caress those beauties you worship. You've got a perfect harem in your head. I think I am living alone with you and when I look at you, the house is peopled with women that surround me, that fill everything and mock at me; all fair, like children of the devil all naked, like temptations. Let me alone, Mariano, don't come near me. I don't want to see you. Put out the light."

And seeing that the artist did not obey her command, she pressed the button herself. The cracking of her bones could be heard as she wrapped herself up in the bedclothes.

Renovales was left in utter darkness, and feeling his way, he got into bed too. He no longer implored, he remained silent, angry. The tender compassion that made him put up with his wife's nervous attacks had disappeared. What more did she expect of him? How far was it going to go? He lived the life of a recluse, restraining his healthy passion, keeping a chaste fidelity out of habit and respect, seeking an outlet in the ardent vagaries of his fancy, and even that was a crime!

With the acumen of a sick woman, she saw within him, divining his ideas, following their course, tearing off the veil behind which he concealed those feasts of fancy with which he passed his solitary hours. This persecution reached even his brain. He could not patiently endure the jealousy of that woman who was embittered by the loss of her youthful freshness.

She began her weeping again in the darkness. She sobbed convulsively, tossing the clothes with the heaving of her breast.

His anger made him insensible and hard.

"Groan, you poor wretch," he thought with a sort of relish. "Weep till you ruin yourself. I won't be the one to say a word."

Josephina, tired out by his silence, interjected words amid her sobs. People made fun of her. She was a constant laughing-stock. How his friends who hung on his words, and the ladies who visited him in his studio, laughed when they heard him enthusiastically praising beauty in the presence of his sickly, broken-down wife! What did she amount to in that house, that terrible pantheon, that home of sorrow? A poor housekeeper who watched out for the artist's comforts. And he thought that he was fulfilling his duty by not keeping a mistress, by staying at home, but still abusing her with his words that made her an object of derision. If her mother were only alive! If her brothers were not so selfish, wandering about the world from embassy to embassy, satisfied with life, paying no attention to her letters filled with complaints, thinking she was insane because she was not contented with a distinguished husband and with wealth!

Renovales, in the darkness, lifted his hands to his forehead in despair, infuriated at the sing-song of her unjust words.

"Her mother!" he thought. "It's lucky that intolerable old dame is under the sod forever. Her brothers!
A crowd of rakes that are always asking me for something whenever they get a chance. Heavens! Give
me the patience to stand this woman, the calm resignation to keep a cool head and not to forget that I am a
man!"

He scorned her mentally in order to maintain his indifference in this way. Bah! A woman! and a sick
one! Every man carries his cross and his was Josephina.

But she, as if she penetrated his thoughts, stopped
crying and spoke to him slowly in a voice that shook with
cruel irony.

"You need not expect anything from the Alberca woman," she said suddenly with feminine incoherence. "I
warn you that she has worshipers by the dozen, young
and stylish, too, something that counts more with wom-
en than talent."

"What difference does that make to me?" Renovales'
voice roared in the darkness with an outbreak of wrath.

"I'm telling you, so that you won't fool yourself.
Master, you are going to suffer a failure. You are very
old, my good man, the years are going by. So old and
so ugly that if you had looked the way you do when I
met you, I should never have been your wife in spite of
all your glory."

After this thrust, satisfied and calm, she seemed to
go to sleep.

The master remained motionless, lying on his back
with his head resting on his arms and his eyes wide
open, seeing in the darkness a host of red spots that
spread out in ceaseless rotation, forming floating, fiery
rings. His wrath had set his nerves on edge; the final
thrust made sleep impossible. He felt restless, wide-

awake after this cruel shock to his pride. He thought that in his bed, close to him, he had his worst enemy. He hated that frail form that he could touch with the slightest movement, as if it contained the rancor of all the adversaries he had met in life.

Old! Contemptible! Inferior to those young bloods that swarmed around the Alberca woman; he, a man known all over Europe, and in whose presence all the young ladies that painted fans and water-colors of birds and flowers, grew pale with emotion, looking at him with worshiping eyes!

"I will soon show you, you poor woman," he thought, while a cruel laugh shook silently in the darkness. "You'll soon see whether glory means anything and people find me as old as you believe."

With boyish joy, he recalled the twilight scene, the kiss on the countess's hand, her gentle abandon, that mingling of resistance and pleasure which opened the way for him to go farther. He enjoyed these memories with a relish of vengeance.

Afterwards, his body, as he moved, touched Josephina, who seemed to be asleep, and he felt a sort of repugnance as if he had rubbed against a hostile creature.

She was his enemy; she had distorted and ruined his life as an artist, she had saddened his life as a man. Now he believed that he might have produced the most remarkable works, if he had not known that little woman who crushed him with her weight. Her silent censure, her prying eyes, that narrow, petty morality of a well-educated girl, blocked his course and made him turn out of his way. Her fits of temper, her nervous attacks, made him lose his bearings, belittling him, robbing him of his strength for work. Must he always live like this? The thought of the long years before him filled him with horror, the long road that life offered him,

monotonous, dusty, rough, without a shadow or a resting place, a painful journey lacking enthusiasm and ar-
dor, pulling at the chain of duty, at the end of which
dragged the enemy, always fretful, always unjust, with
the selfish cruelty of disease, spying on him with searching eyes in the hours when his mind was off its guard,
while he slept, violating his secrecy, forcing his immo-
bility, robbing him of his most intimate ideas, only to
parade them before his eyes later with the insolence of
a successful thief. And that was what his life was to
be! God! No, it was better to die.

Then in the black recesses of his brain there rose,
like a blue spark of infernal gleam, a thought, a desire,
that made a chill of terror and surprise run over his
body.

"If she would only die!"

Why not? Always ill, always sad, she seemed to
darken his mind with the wings that beat ominously. He
had a right to liberty, to break the chain, because he was
the stronger. He had spent his life in the struggle for
glory, and glory was a delusion, if it brought only cold
respect from his fellows, if it could not be exchanged
for something more positive. Many years of intense
existence were left; he could still exult in a host of pleasures, he could still live, like some artists whom he admired, intoxicated with worldly joys, working in mad
freedom.

"Oh, if she would only die!"

He recalled books he had read, in which other imaginary people had desired another's death that they might
be able to satisfy more fully their appetites and passions.

Suddenly he felt as though he were awakening from
a bad dream, as though he were throwing off an overwhelming nightmare. Poor Josephina! His thought
filled him with horror, he felt the infernal desire burn-

ing his conscience, like a hot iron that throws off a shower of sparks when touched. It was not tenderness that made him turn again towards his companion; not that; his old animosity remained. But he thought of her years of sacrifice, of the privations she had suffered, following him in the struggle with misery, without a complaint, without a protest, in the pains of motherhood, in the nursing of her daughter, that Milita who seemed to have stolen all the strength of her body and perhaps was the cause of her decline. How terrible to wish for her death! He hoped that she would live. He would bear everything with the patience of duty. She die? Never, he would rather die himself.

But in vain did he struggle to forget the thought. The atrocious, monstrous desire, once awakened, resisted, refused to recede, to hide, to die in the windings of his brain whence it had arisen. In vain did he repent his villainy, or feel ashamed of his cruel idea, striving to crush it forever. It seemed as though a second personality had arisen within him, rebellious to his commands, opposed to his conscience, hard and indifferent to his sympathetic scruples, and this personality, this power, continued to sing in his ear with a merry accent, as if it promised him all the pleasures of life.

"If she would only die! Eh, master? If she would only die!"

PART II

I

At the coming of spring López de Sosa, "the intrepid sportsman," as Cotoner called him, appeared at Renovales' house every afternoon.

Outside the entrance gate stood his eighty-horsepower automobile, his latest acquisition, of which he was intensely proud, a huge green car, that started and backed under the hand of the chauffeur while its owner was crossing the garden of the painter's house.

Renovales saw him enter the studio, in a blue suit with a shining visor over his eyes, affecting the resolute bearing of a sailor or an explorer.

"Good afternoon, Don Mariano, I have come for the ladies."

And Milita came down stairs in a long gray coat, with a white cap, around which she wound a long blue veil. After her came her mother clad in the same fashion, small and insignificant beside the girl, who seemed to overwhelm her with her health and grace.

Renovales approved of these trips. Josephina's legs were troubling her; a sudden weakness sometimes kept her in her chair for days at a time. Finding any sort of movement difficult, she liked to ride motionless in that car that fairly ate up space, reaching distant suburbs of Madrid without the least effort, as if she had not moved from the house.

"Have a good time," said the painter with a sort of joy at the prospect of being left alone, completely alone, without the disturbance of feeling his wife's hostility near him. "I entrust them to you, Rafaelito; be careful, now."

And Rafaelito assumed an expression of protest, as if he were shocked that anyone could doubt his skill. There was no danger with him.

"Aren't you coming, Don Mariano? Lay down your brushes for a while. We're only going to the Pardo."

The painter declined; he had a great deal to do. He knew what it was, and he did not like to go so fast. There was no pleasure in swallowing space with your eyes almost closed, unable to see anything but a hazy blur of the scenery, amid clouds of dust and crushed stone. He preferred to look at the landscape calmly, without haste, with the reflective quiet of the student. Besides he was out of place in things that did not belong to his time; he was getting old and these frightful novelties did not agree with him.

"Good-by, papa."

Milita, lifting her veil, put out her red, tempting lips, showing her bright teeth as she smiled. After this kiss came the other, formal and cold, exchanged with the indifference of habit, without any novelty except that Josephina's mouth drew back from his, as if she wanted to avoid any contact with him.

They went out, the mother leaning on Rafaelito's arm with a sort of languor, as if she could hardly drag her weak body,—her pale face unrelieved by the least sign of blood.

When Renovales found himself alone in the studio he would feel as happy as a schoolboy on a holiday. He worked with a lighter touch, he roared out old songs, delighting to listen to the echoes that his voice awakened in the high-studded rooms. Often when Cotoner came in, he would surprise him by the serene shamelessness

with which he sang some one of the licentious songs he
had learned in Rome, and the painter of the Popes,
smiling like a faun, joined in the chorus, applauding at
the end these ribald verses of the studio.

Tekli, the Hungarian, who sometimes spent an afternoon with him, had departed for his native land with his
copy of *Las Meninas,* but not before lifting Renovales'
hands several times to his heart, with extravagant terms
of affection and calling him "noble master." The portrait of the Countess of Alberca was no longer in the
studio; in a glittering frame it hung on the walls of the
illustrious lady's drawing-room, where it received the
worship of her admirers.

Sometimes of an afternoon when the ladies had left
the studio and the dull mumble of the car and the tooting of the horn had died away, the master and his friend
would talk of López de Sosa. A good fellow, somewhat
foolish, but well-meaning; this was the judgment of
Renovales and his old friend. He was proud of hi⁻
mustache that gave him a certain likeness to the Ge.
man emperor, and when he sat down, he took care to
show his hands, by placing them prominently on his
knees, in order that everyone might appreciate their vigorous hugeness, the prominent veins, and the strong fingers, all this with the naïve satisfaction of a ditch-dig-
ger. His conversation always turned on feats of
strength and before the two artists he strutted as if he
belonged to another race, talking of his prowess as a
fencer, of his triumphs in the bouts, of the weights he
could lift with the slightest effort, of the number of
chairs he could jump over without touching one of them.
Often he interrupted the two painters when they
were eulogizing the great masters of art, to tell them of
the latest victory of some celebrated driver in the con-
test for a coveted cup. He knew by heart the names

of all the European champions who had won the immortal laurel, in running, jumping, killing pigeons, box-
ing or fencing.

Renovales had seen him come into the studio one afternoon, trembling with excitement, his eyes flashing,
and showing a telegram.

"Don Mariano, I have a Mercedes; they have just
announced its shipment."

The painter looked blank. Who was that personage with the woman's name? And Rafaelito smiled with
pity.

"The best make, a Mercedes, better than a Panhard;
everyone knows that. Made in Germany; sixty thousand francs. There isn't another one in Madrid."

"Well, congratulations."

And the artist shrugged his shoulders and went on
painting.

López de Sosa was wealthy. His father, a former
manufacturer of canned goods, had left him a fortune
that he administered prudently, never gambling, nor
keeping mistresses (he had no time for such follies)
but finding all his amusement in sports that strengthen
the body. He had a coach-house of his own, where he
kept his carriages and his automobiles which he showed
to his friends with the satisfaction of an artist. It was
his museum. Besides, he owned several teams of horses,
for modern fads did not make him forget his former
tastes, and he took as much pride in his past glories as
a horseman as he did in his skill as a driver of cars. At
rare intervals, on the days of an important bull-fight or
when some sensational races were being run in the Hippodrome, he won a triumph on the box by driving
six cabs, covered with tassels and bells, that seemed to
proclaim the glory and wealth of their owner with their
noisy course.

He was proud of his virtuous life; free from foolishness or petty love affairs, wholly devoted to sports
and show. His income was less than his expenses.
The numerous personnel of his stable-garage, his horses,
gasoline and tailors' bills ate up even a part of the
principal. But López de Sosa was undisturbed in this
ruinous course,—for he was conscious of the danger,
in spite of his extravagance. It was a mere youthful
folly, he would cut down his expenses when he married. He devoted his evenings to reading, for he could
not sleep quietly, unless he went through his classics
(sporting-papers, automobile catalogs, etc.), and every
month he made new acquisitions abroad, spending thousands of francs and, complaining, like a serious business man, of the rise in the Exchange, of the exorbi-
tant customs charges, of the stupidity of the Government that so shackled the development of the country.
The price of every automobile was greatly increased on
crossing the frontier. And after that, politicians expected progress and regeneration!

He had been educated by the Jesuits at the University of Deusto and had his degree in law. But that had
not made him over-pious. He was liberal, he lived the
modern spirit; he had no use for fanaticism nor hypocrisy. He had said good-by to the good Fathers as
soon as his own father, who was a great admirer of
them, had died. But he still preserved a certain respect
for them because they had been his teachers and he
knew that they were great scholars. But modern life
was different. He read with perfect freedom, he read
a great deal; he had in his house a library composed
of at least a hundred French novels. He purchased all
the volumes that came from Paris with a woman's picture on the cover and in which, under pretext of de-
scribing Greek, Roman, or Egyptian customs, the au-

thor placed a large number of youths and maidens without any other decorations of civilization than the
fillets and the caps that covered their heads.

He insisted on freedom, perfect freedom, but for
him, men were divided into two castes, decent people
and those who were not. Among the first figured en
masse all the young fellows of the Gran Peña, the old
men of the Casino, together with some people whose
names appeared in the papers, a certain evidence of their
merit. The rest was the rabble, despicable and vulgar
in the streets of the cities, repulsive and displeasing on
the road, whom he insulted with all of the coarseness of
ill-breeding and threatened to kill when a child ran in
front of his car with the vicious purpose of letting itself be crushed under the wheels, to stir up trouble with
a decent person, or when some workingman, pretending he could not hear the warnings of his horn, would
not get out of the way and was run over—as if a man
who makes two pesetas a day were superior to machines that cost thousands of francs! What could you
do with such ignorant, commonplace people! And
some wretches were still talking about the rights of
man and revolutions!

Cotoner, who expended incredible care in keeping
his single suit presentable for calls and dinners, ques-
tionel López de Sosa with astonishment in regard to the
progress of his wardrobe.

"How many ties have you now, Rafael?"

"About seven hundred." He had counted them recently. And ashamed that he did not yet own the
longed-for thousand, he spoke of fitting himself out on
his next trip to London when the principal British au-
tomobilists were to contend for the cup. He received
his boots from Paris, but they were made by a Swiss
boot-maker, the same one who provided the foot-gear

of Edward of England; he counted his trousers by the
dozen, and never wore one pair more than eight or ten
times; his linen was given to his valet almost before it
was used, his hats all came from London. He had eight
frock-coats made every year, that often grew old without ever being worn, of different colors to suit the cir-
cumstances and the hours when he must wear them.
One in particular, dead black with long skirts, gloomy
and austere, copied from the foreign illustrations that
represented duels, was his uniform on solemn occasions, which he wore when some friend looked him up
at the Peña, to get his assistance in representing him
with his customary skill in affairs of honor.

His tailor admired his talent, his masterly command
in choosing cloth and deciding on the cut among the
countless designs. Result, he spent something like five
thousand dollars a year on his clothes, and said ingen-
uously to the two artists,

"How much less can a decent person spend if he wants
to be presentable?"

López de Sosa visited Renovales' house as a friend
after the latter had painted his portrait. In spite of his
automobiles, his clothes, and the fact that he chose his
associates among people who bore noble titles, he could
not succeed in getting a foothold in society. He knew
that behind his back people nicknamed him, "Pickled
Herring," alluding to his father's trade, and that the
young ladies, who counted him as a friend, rebelled at
the idea of marrying the "Canned-goods Boy," which
was another of his names. The friendship of Renovales
was a source of pride.

He had requested him to make his portrait, paying him without haggling, in order that he might appear at the Exhibition, quite as good a way as any other
of introducing his insignificance among the famous men

who were painted by the artist. After that he was on
intimate terms with the master, talking everywhere
about "his friend, Renovales!" with a sort of familiarity, as if he were a comrade who could not live without him. This raised him greatly in the estimation of
his acquaintances. Besides, he had felt a real admiration for the master ever since one afternoon when tired
out with the account of his prowess as a fencer, Renovales had laid aside his brushes and taking down two
old foils, had had several bouts with him. What a man
he was! And how he remembered the points he had
learned in Rome!

In his frequent visits to the artist's house, he finally
felt attracted toward Milita; he saw in her the woman
he wanted to marry. Lacking more sonorous titles, it
was something to be the son-in-law of Renovales. Besides, the painter enjoyed the reputation of being
wealthy, he spoke of his enormous profits, and he still
had many years before him, to add to his fortune, all of
which would be his daughter's.

López de Sosa began to pay court to Milita, calling
on his great resources, appearing every day in a different suit, coming every afternoon, sometimes in a
carriage drawn by a dashing pair, sometimes in one of
his cars. The fashionable youth won the favor of her
mother,—an important part. This was the kind of a
husband for her daughter. No painter! And in vain
did Soldevilla put on his brightest ties and show off
shocking waist-coats; his rival crushed him and, what
was worse, the master's wife, who formerly used to
have a sort of motherly concern for him and called him
by his first name, for she had known him as a boy, now
received him coldly, as if she wished to discourage his
suit for Milita.

The girl fluctuated between her two admirers with a

mocking smile. One seemed to interest her as much as the other. She drove the painter, the companion of her childhood, to despair, at times abusing him with her jests, at others attracting him with her effusive intimacy, as in the days when they played together; and at the same time she praised López de Sosa's stylishness, laughed with him, and Soldevilla even suspected that they wrote letters to each other as if they were engaged.

Renovales rejoiced at the cleverness with which his daughter kept the two young men uncertain and eager about her. She was a terror, a boy in skirts, more manly than either of her worshipers.

"I know her, Pepe," he said to Cotoner. "We must let her do what she wants to. The day she decides in favor of one or the other we'll have to marry her at once. She isn't one of the girls to wait. If we don't marry her soon and to her taste, she's likely to elope with her fiancé."

The father excused Milita's impatience. Poor girl! Think what she saw in her home! Her mother always ill, terrifying her with her tears, her cries and her nervous attacks; her father working in his studio, and her only companion the unsympathetic "Miss." He owed his thanks to López de Sosa for taking them outdoors on these dizzy rides from which Josephina returned greatly quieted.

Renovales preferred his pupil. He was almost his son, he had fought many a hard battle to give him fellowships and prizes. He was a trifle displeased at some of his slight infidelities, for as soon as he had won some renown, he bragged about his independence, praising everything that the master thought condemnable behind his back. But even so, the idea of his marrying his daughter pleased him; a painter as a son-in-law; his grandchildren painters, the blood of Renovales

perpetuated in a dynasty of artists who would fill history
with their glory.

"But, oh, Pepe! I'm afraid the girl will choose the
other. After all, she's a woman. And women appreciate only what they see, gallantry and youth."

And the master's words betrayed a certain bitterness,
as though he were thinking of something very different
from what he was saying.

Then he began to discuss the merits of López de Sosa,
as if he were already a member of the family.

"A good boy, isn't he, Pepe? A little stupid for us,
unable to talk for ten minutes without making us yawn,
a fine fellow, but not our kind."

There was scorn in Renovales' voice as he spoke of
the vigorous healthy young men of the present, with
their brains absolutely free from culture, who had just
assaulted life, invading every phase of it. What people!
Gymnastics, fencing, kicking a huge bull, swinging a
mallet on horseback, wild flights in an automobile; from
the royal family down to the last middle-class scion
everyone rushed into this life of childish joy, as if a
man's mission consisted merely in hardening his muscles, sweating and delighting in the shifting chances of
a game. Activity fled from the brain to the extremi-
ties of the body. They were strong, but their minds lay
fallow, wrapped in a haze of childish credulity. Modern men seemed to stop growing at the age of fourteen;
they never went beyond, content with the joys of movement and strength. Many of these big fellows were ignorant of women, or almost so, at the age when in other
times they were turning back, satiated with love. Busy
running without direction or end, they had no time nor
quiet to think about women. Love was about to go
on a strike, unable to resist the competition of sports.
The young men lived by themselves, finding in athletic

exercise a satisfaction that left them without any desire or curiosity for the other pleasures of life. They were big boys with strong fists; they could fight with a bull and yet the approach of a woman filled them with terror. All the sap of their life was used up in violent exercise. Intelligence seemed to have concentrated in their hands, leaving their heads empty. What was going to become of this new people? Perhaps it would form a healthier, stronger human race, but without love or passion, without any other association than the blind impulse of reproduction.

"We are a different sort, eh, Pepe?" said Renovales with a sly wink. "When we were boys we didn't care for our bodies so well, but we had better times. We weren't so pure, but we were interested in something higher than automobiles and prize cups; we had ideals."

Then he began to talk again of the young man who expected to become one of his family and made sport of his mentality.

"If Milita decides on him, I won't object. The important thing in such matters is that they should be congenial to each other. He's a good boy; I could almost give him my blessing. But I suspect that when the sensation of novelty has worn off, he will go back to his fads and poor Milita will be jealous of those machines that are eating up the greater part of his fortune."

Sometimes, before the light died out in the afternoon, Renovales excused his model, if he had one, and laying aside his brushes went out of the studio. When he came back, he would have on his coat and hat.

"Pepe, let's take a walk."

Cotoner knew where this walk would land them.

They followed the iron fence of the Retiro and went down the Calle de Alcalá, walking slowly among the groups of strollers, some of whom turned round behind them to point out the master. "That taller one is Renovales, the painter." In a few minutes, Mariano hastened his step with nervous impatience, he stopped talking and Cotoner followed him with an ill-humored expression, humming between his teeth. When they reached the Cibeles, the old painter knew that their walk was nearly over.

"I'll see you to-morrow, Pepe, I'm going this way. I've got to see the countess."

One day, he did not limit himself to this brief leave-taking. After he had gone a few steps, he came back toward his companion and said hesitatingly:

"Listen, if Josephina asks you where I went, don't say anything. I know that you are prudent but she is always worried. I tell you this so as to avoid any trouble. The two women don't get along together very well. Some woman's quarrel!"

II

At the opening of spring, when Madrid was beginning to think good weather had really come, and people were impatiently getting out their summer clothes, there was an unexpected and treacherous return of winter that clouded the sky and covered with a coat of snow the muddy ground and the gardens where the first flowers of spring were beginning to sprout.

There was a fire once more in the fireplace in the drawing-room of the Countess of Alberca, where all the gentlemen who formed her coterie gathered to keep warm on days when she was "at home," not having a meeting to preside over or calls to make.

When Renovales came one afternoon, he spoke enthusiastically of the view of Moncloa, covered with snow. He had just been there, a beautiful sight, the woods, buried in wintry silence, surprised by the white shroud when they were beginning to crack with the swelling of the sap. It was a pity that the camera craze filled the woods with so many people who went back and forth with their outfits, sullying the purity of the snow.

The countess was as interested as a child. She wanted to see that, she would go the next day. Her friends tried in vain to dissuade her, telling her the weather would probably change presently. To-morrow the sun would come out, the snow would melt; these unexpected storms were characteristic of the fickle climate of Madrid.

"It makes no difference," said Concha obstinately,

"I've got the idea into my head. It's years since I have seen it. My life is such a busy one."

She would go to see the thaw in the morning; no, not in the morning. She got up late and had to receive all those Women's Rights ladies that came to consult her. In the afternoon, she would go after luncheon. It was too bad that Renovales worked at that time and could not go with her. He could appreciate landscapes so well with his artist's eyes and had often spoken to her of the sunset from the palace of Moncloa, a sight almost equal to the one you can see in Rome from the Pinzio at dusk. The painter smiled gallantly. He would try to be at Moncloa the next day; they would meet.

The countess seemed to take sudden fright at this promise and glanced at Doctor Monteverde. But she was disappointed in her hope of being censured for her fickleness and unfaithfulness, for the doctor remained indifferent.

Lucky doctor! How Renovales hated him. He was a young man, as fair and as fragile as a porcelain figure, a combination of such striking beauties that his face was almost a caricature. His hair, parted in two waves over his pale forehead, was black, very black and shining with bluish reflections, his eyes, as soft as velvet, showed the read spot of the lachrymal on the polished ivory of the cornea, veritable odalisque eyes, his bright red lips showed under his bristly mustache, his complexion was as pale as a camellia, and his teeth flashed like pearl. Concha looked at him with ecstatic devotion, talked with her eyes on him, consulting him with her glance, lamenting inwardly his lack of mastery, eager to be his slave, to be corrected by him in all the caprices of her giddy character.

Renovales scorned him, questioning his manhood,

making the most atrocious comments on him in his rough fashion.

He was a doctor of science and was waiting for a chair at Madrid to be declared vacant, that he might become a candidate for it. The Countess of Alberca had him under her high protection, talking about him enthusiastically to all the important gentlemen who exercised any influence in University circles. She would break out into the most extravagant praise of the doctor in Renovales' presence. He was a scholar and what made her admire him was the fact that all his learning did not keep him from dressing well and being as fair as an angel.

"For pretty teeth, look at Monteverde's," she would say, looking at him in the crowded room, through her lorgnette.

At other times, following the course of her ideas, she would interrupt the conversation, without noticing the irrelevancy of her words.

"But did you notice the doctor's hands? They're more delicate than mine! They look like a woman's hands."

The painter was indignant at these demonstrations of Concha's that often occurred in her husband's presence.

The calm of that honorable gentleman astounded him. Was the man blind? And the count with fatherly good humor always said the same thing.

"That Concha! Did you ever hear such frankness! Don't mind her, Monteverde, it's my wife's way, childishness."

The doctor would smile, flattered at the atmosphere of worship with which the countess surrounded him.

He had written a book on the natural origin of animal organism, of which the fair countess spoke enthusiastically. The painter observed this change in her tastes with surprise and envy. No more music, nor verses, nor plastic arts which had formerly occupied her flighty attention, that was attracted by everything that shines or makes a noise. Now she looked on the arts as pretty, insignificant toys that were fit to amuse only the childhood of the human race. Times were changing, people must be serious. Science, nothing but science; she was the protectress, the good friend, the adviser of a scholar. And Renovales found famous books on the tables and chairs, feverishly run through and laid aside because she grew tired of them or could not understand them after the first impulse of curiosity.

Her coterie, almost wholly composed of old gentlemen attracted by the beauty of the countess, and in love with her though without hope, smiled to hear her talking so weightily about science. Men who were prominent in politics admired her frankly. How many things that woman knew! Many that they did not know themselves. The others, well-known physicians, professors, lawyers, who had not studied anything for years, approved complacently. For a woman it was not at all bad. And she, lifting her glasses to her eyes from time to time to relish the doctor's beauty, talked with a pedantic slowness about protoplasms, and the reproduction of the cells, the cannibalisms of the phagocytes, catarine, anthropoid and pithecoid apes, discoplacentary mammals and the Pithecanthropos, treating the mysteries of life with friendly confidence, repeating strange scientific words, as if they were the names of society folks, who had dined with her the evening before.

The handsome Doctor Monteverde, according to her, was head and shoulders above all the scholars of universal reputation.

Their books made her tired, she could not make anything out of them, in spite of the fact that the doctor admired them greatly. To make up for this, she had read Monteverde's book over and over, and she recommended this wonderful work to her lady friends, who in matters of reading never went beyond the novels in popular magazines.

"He is a scholar," said the countess one afternoon while talking alone with Renovales. "He's just beginning now, but I will push him ahead and he will turn out to be a genius. He has extraordinary talent. I wish you had read his book. Are you acquainted with Darwin? You aren't, are you? Well, he is greater than Darwin, much greater."

"I can believe that," said the painter. "Your Monteverde is as pretty as a baby and Darwin was an ugly old fellow."

The countess hesitated whether to get serious or to laugh, and finally she shook her lorgnette at him.

"Keep still, you horrid man. After all, you're a painter. You can't understand tender friendships, pure relations, fraternity based on study."

How bitterly the painter laughed at this purity and fraternity! His eyes were good and Concha, for her part, was no model of prudence in hiding her feelings. Monteverde was her lover, just as formerly a musician had been, at a period when the countess talked of nothing but Beethoven and Wagner, as if they were callers, and long before that a pretty little duke, who gave private amateur bull-fights at which he slaughtered the innocent oxen after greeting lovingly the Alberca woman, who, wrapped in a white mantilla, and decorated with pinks, leaned out of the box in the grandstand. Her relations with the doctor were almost common talk. That was amply proved by the fury with which the gentlemen of her coterie pulled him to pieces, declaring that he was an idiot and that his book was a Harlequin's coat, a series of excerpts from other men, poorly basted together, with the daring of ignorance. They, too, were stung by envy, in their senile, silent love, by the triumph of that stripling who carried off their idol, whom they had worshiped with a contemplative devotion that gave new life to their old age.

Renovales was angry with himself. He tried in vain to overcome the habit that made him turn his steps every afternoon toward the countess's house.

"I'll never go there again," he would say when he was back in his studio. "A pretty part you're playing, Mariano! Acting as a chorus to a love duet, in the company of all these senile imbeciles. A fine aim in life, this countess of yours!"

But the next day he would go back, thinking with a sort of hope of Monteverde's pretentious superiority, and the disdainful air with which he received his fair adorer's worship. Concha would soon get tired of this mustached doll and turn her eyes on him, a man.

The painter observed the transformation of his nature. He was a different man, and he made every effort to keep his family from noticing this change. He recognized mentally that he was in love, with the satisfaction of a mature man who sees in this a sign of youth the budding of a second life. He had felt impelled toward Concha by the desire of breaking the monotony of his existence, of imitating other men, of tasting the acidity of infidelity, in a brief escape from the stern imposing walls that shut in the desert of married life which was every day covered with more brambles and tares. Her resistance exasperated him, increasing his desire. He was not exactly sure how he felt; perhaps it was merely a physical attraction and added to that the wound to his pride, the bitterness of being repelled when he came down from the heights of virtue, where he had held his position with savage pride, believing that all the joys of the earth were waiting for him, dazzled by his glory and that he had only to hold out his arms and they would run to him.

He felt humiliated by his failure; a dumb rage filled him when he compared his gray hair and his eyes, surrounded by growing wrinkles, with that pretty boy of science who seemed to drive the countess insane. Women! Their intellectual interest, their exaggerated admiration of fame! A lie! They worshiped talent only when it was well presented in a young and beautiful covering.

Impelled by his obstinacy, Renovales was determined to overcome the resistance. He recalled, without the least remorse, the scene with his wife in the bedroom, and her scornful words that foretold his failure with the countess. Josephina's disdain was only another spur to urge him to continue his course.

Concha kept him off and led him on at the same time. There was no doubt that the master's love flattered her vanity. She laughed at his passionate protestations, taking them in jest, always answering them in the same tone: "Be dignified, master. That isn't becoming to you. You are a great man, a genius. Let the boys be the ones to play the part of the lovesick student." But when enraged at her subtle mockery, he took a mental oath not to come back again, she seemed to guess it and she suddenly assumed an affectionate air, attracting him with an interest that made him foresee the near approach of his triumph.

If he was offended and kept silence, she was the one who talked of love, of eternal passions between two beings of lofty minds, based on the harmony of their thoughts; and she did not cease this dangerous conversation until the master, with a sudden renewal of confidence, came forward offering his love, only to be received with that kindly and still ironical smile that seemed to look on him as a child whose judgment was faulty.

And so the master lived, fluctuating between hope and despair, now favored, now repelled, but always incapable of escaping from her influence, as if a crime were haunting him. He sought opportunities to see her alone with the ingenuity of a college boy, he invented pretexts for going to her house at unusual hours, when there were no callers present, and his courage failed him when he ran into the pretty doctor and felt around himself that sensation of uneasiness which always seizes an unwelcome guest.

The vague hope of meeting the countess at Moncloa, of walking with her a whole afternoon, unmolested by that circle of insufferable people who surrounded her with their drooling worship, kept him excited all night and the next morning, as if a real rendezvous were awaiting him. Would she go? Was not her promise a mere whim that she had immediately forgotten? He sent a note to an ex-minister of State, whose portrait he was painting, to ask him not to come to the studio that afternoon, and after luncheon he got into a cab, telling the cabby to beat the horse, to go full speed, for fear of being late.

He knew that it would be hours before she came, if she did come; but a mad, unreasonable impatience filled him. He thought without knowing why that, by arriving ahead of time, he would hasten the countess's coming.

He got out in the square in front of the little palace of Moncloa. The cab disappeared in the direction of Madrid, up hill along an avenue that was lost in the distance behind an arch of dry branches.

Renovales walked up and down, alone in the little

square. The sun was shining in a patch of blue sky, among the heavy clouds. In the places which its rays did not reach, it was cold. The water ran down from the foot of the trees, after dripping from the branches and trickling down the trunks; it was melting rapidly. The wood seemed to weep with joy under the caress of the sun, that destroyed the last traces of the white shroud.

The majestic silence of Nature, abandoned to its own power, surrounded the artist. The pines were swinging with the long gusts of wind, filling space with a murmur, like the sound of distant harps. The square was hidden in the icy shadow of the trees. Up above in the front of the palace some pigeons, seeking the sun above the tops of the pines, swept around the old flag-pole and the classic busts blackened by the weather. Then, tired of flying, they settled down on the rusty iron balconies, adding to the old building a white fluttering decoration, a rustling garland of feathers. In the middle of the square a marble swan, with its neck violently stretched toward the sky, threw out a jet, whose murmur seemed to heighten the impression of icy cold which he felt in the shadow.

Renovales began to walk, crushing the frozen crust that cracked under his feet in the shady places. He leaned over the circular iron rail that surrounds a part of the square. Through the curtain of black branches, where the first buds were beginning to open, he saw the ridge that bounds the horizon; the mountains of Guadarrama, phantoms of snow that were mingled with the masses of clouds. Nearer, the mountains of Pardo stood out with their dark peaks, black with pines, and to the left stretched out the slopes of the hills of the Casa de Campo, where the first yellow touches of spring were beginning to show.

At his feet lay the fields of Moncloa, the antique little

gardens, the grove of Viveros, bordering the stream. Carriages were moving in the roads below, their varnished tops flashing in the sun like fiery mortar boards. The meadows, the foliage of the woods, everything seemed clean and bright after the recent storm. The all-pervading green tone, with its infinite variations from black to yellow, smiled at the touch of the sun after the chill of the snow. In the distance sounded the constant reports of shotguns that seemed to tear the air with the intensity that is common in still afternoons. They were hunting in the Casa de Campo. Between the colonnades of trees and the green sheets of the meadows, the water flashed in the sun, bits of ponds, glimpses of canals, pools of melted snow, like bright trembling edges of huge swords, lost in the grass.

Renovales hardly looked at the landscape; it had no message for him that afternoon. He was preoccupied with other things. He saw a smart coupé come down the avenue, and he left the belvedere to go to meet it. She was coming! But the coupé passed by him, slowly and majestically without stopping and he saw through the window an old lady wrapped in furs, with sunken eyes and distorted mouth, trembling with old age, her head bobbing with the movement of the carriage. It disappeared in the direction of the little church beside the palace and the painter was alone again.

No! She would not come! His heart began to tell him that there was no use waiting.

Some little girls, with battered shoes, and straight greasy hair that floated around their necks, began to run about the square. Renovales did not see where they came from. Perhaps they were the children of the guardian of the palace.

A guard came down the avenue with his gun hanging from his shoulder, and his horn at his side. Beyond approached a man in black, who looked like a servant, escorted by two huge dogs, two majestic bluish-gray Danes, that walked with a dignified bearing, prudent and moderate but proud of their terrifying appearance. Not a carriage could be seen. Curses!

Seated on one of the stone benches, the master finally took out the little notebook that he always carried with him. He sketched the figures of the children as they ran around the fountain. That was one way to kill time. One after the other he sketched all the girls, then he caught them in several groups, but at last they disappeared behind the palace, going down toward the Caño Gordo. Renovales, having nothing to distract him, left his seat and walked about, stamping noisily. His feet were like ice, this waiting in the cold was putting him in a terrible mood. Then he went and sat down on another bench near the servant in black, who had the two dogs at his knees. They were sitting on their hind paws, resting with as much dignity as real people, watching that gentleman with their gray eyes that winked intelligently, as he looked at them attentively and then moved his pencil on the book that rested on his knee. The painter sketched the two dogs in different postures, giving himself up to the work with such interest that he quite forgot his purpose in coming there. Oh, what splendid creatures! Renovales loved animals in which beauty was united with strength. If he had lived alone and could have consulted his own tastes, he would have converted his house into a menagerie.

The servant went away with his dogs and the artist once more was left alone. Several couples passed slowly, arm in arm, and disappeared behind the palace toward the gardens below. Then a group of school boys that left behind them, as their cassocks fluttered, that odor of

healthy, dirty flesh that is peculiar to barracks and convents. And still the countess did not come!

The painter went again to rest his elbows on the balus-
trade of the belvedere. He would only wait a half an
hour longer. The afternoon was wearing away; the sun
was still high, but from time to time the landscape was
darkened. The clouds that had been confined on the
horizon had been let loose and they were rolling through
the field of the sky like a flock of sheep, assuming
fantastic shapes, rushing eagerly in tumultuous confusion as if they wished to swallow the ball of fire that
was slipping slowly over a bit of clear blue sky.

Suddenly, Renovales felt a sort of shock near his
heart. No one had touched him; it was a warning of his
nerves that for some time had been especially irritable.
She was near, was coming he was sure. And turning
around, he saw her, still a long way off, coming down
the avenue, in black with a fur coat, her hands in a little
muff and a veil over her eyes. Her tall, graceful silhouette was outlined against the yellow ground as she
passed the trees. Her carriage was returning up the hill,
perhaps to wait for her at the top near the School of
Agriculture.

As she met him in the center of the square she held
out, her gloved hand, warm from the muff, and they
turned toward the belvedere, chatting.

"I'm in a furious mood, disgusted to death. I didn't
expect to come; I forgot all about it, upon my word.
But as I was coming out of the President's house I
thought of you. I was sure I would find you here. And
so I have come to have you drive away my ill humor."

Through the veil, Renovales saw her eyes that flashed
hostilely and her dainty lips angrily tightened.

She spoke quickly, eager to vent the wrath that was
swelling her heart, without paying any attention to what

was around her, as if she were in her own drawing room where everything was familiar.

She had been to see the Prime-Minister to recommend her "affair" to his attention; a desire of the count's on the fulfillment of which his happiness depended. Poor Paco (her husband) dreamed of the Golden Fleece. That was the only thing that was lacking to crown the tower of crosses, keys and ribbons that he was raising about his person, from his belly to his neck, till not an inch of his body was without this glorious covering. The Golden Fleece and then death! Why should they not do this favor for Paco, such a good man, who would not hurt a fly? What would it cost them to grant him this toy and make him happy?

"There aren't any friends any longer, Mariano," said the countess bitterly. "The Prime-Minister is a fool who forgets his old friendships now that he is head of the government. I who have seen him sighing around me like a comic opera tenor, making love to me (yes, I tell the truth to you) and ready to commit suicide because I scorned his vulgarity and foolishness! This afternoon, the same old story; lots of holding my hand, lots of making eyes, 'dear Concha,' 'sweet Concha' and other sugary expressions, just such as he sings in Congress like an old canary. Sum total, the Fleece is impossible, he is very sorry, but at Court they are unwilling."

And the countess, as if she saw for the first time where she was, turned her eyes angrily toward the dark hills of the Casa de Campo, where shots could still be heard.

"And they wonder that people think this way or that! I am an anarchist, do you hear, Mariano? Every day I feel more revolutionary. Don't laugh, for it is no jest. Poor Paco, who is a lamb of God, is horrified to hear me. 'Woman, think what we are! We must be on good terms with the royal house.' But I rise in rebellion; I know them; a crowd of reprobates. Why shouldn't my Paco have the Fleece, if the poor man needs it. I tell you, master, this cowardly, meek country makes me raging mad. We ought to have what France had in '93. If I were alone, without all these trifles of name and position, I would do to-day something that would stir people. I'd throw a bomb, no, not a bomb; I'd get a revolver and——"

"Fire!" shouted the painter, bursting into a laugh.

Concha drew back indignantly.

"Don't joke, master. I'll go away. I'll slap you. This is more serious than you think. This afternoon is no time for jokes."

But her fickle nature contradicted the seriousness that she pretended to give her words, for she smiled slightly, as if pleased at some memory.

"It wasn't wholly a failure," she said after a long pause. "My hands aren't empty. The prime-minister didn't want to make me his enemy and so he offered me a compensation, since the 'Lamb' affair was impossible. A deputy's chair at the next election."

Renovales' eyes opened in astonishment. "For whom do you want that? To whom is that going to be given?"

"To whom?" mimicked Concha with mock astonishment. "To whom! To whom do you suppose, you simpleton! Not for you, you don't know anything about that or anything else, except your brushes. For Monteverde, for the doctor, who will do great things."

The artist's noisy laugh resounded in the silence of the square.

"Darwin a deputy of the majority! Darwin saying 'Aye' and 'No.'"

And after these exclamations his laugh of mock astonishment continued.

"Laugh, you old bear! Open that mouth wider; wag your apostolic beard! How funny you are! And what's strange about that? But don't laugh any longer; you make me nervous. I'll go away, if you keep on like this."

They remained silent for a long while. The countess was not long in forgetting her troubles; her bird-like brain never retained any one impression for long. She looked around her with disdainful eyes, eager to mortify the painter. Was that what Renovales raved over so? Was there nothing more?

They began to walk slowly, going down to the terraced gardens behind the palace. They descended the moss-covered slopes that were streaked with the black flint of the flights of stairs.

The silence was deathlike. The water murmured as it flowed from the trunks of the trees, forming little streams that trickled down hill, almost invisible in the grass. In some shady spots there still remained piles of snow, like bundles of white wool. The shrill cries of the birds sounded like the scratching of a diamond on glass. At the edge of the stairways, the pedestals of black, crumbling stone recalled the statues and urns they had once supported. The little gardens, cut in geometric figures, stretched out the Greek square of their carpet of foliage on each level of the terrace. In the squares, the fountains spurted in pools surrounded by rusted railings, or flowed down triple layers with a ceaseless murmur. Water everywhere,—in the air, in the ground, whispering, icy, adding to the cold impression of the landscape, where the sun seemed a red blotch of color devoid of heat.

They passed under arches of vines, between huge

dying trees covered to the top with winding rings of ivy that clung to the venerable trunks, veneered with a green and yellow crust. The paths were bounded on one side by the slope of the hill, from the top of which came the invisible tinkling of a bell, and where from time to time there appeared on the blue background of the sky the massive outline of a slowly moving cow. On the other, a rustic railing of branches painted white bounded the path and, beyond it, in the valley, lay the dark flower beds with their melancholy solitude and their fountains that wept day and night in an atmosphere of old age and abandon. The closely matted brambles stretched from tree to tree along the slopes. The slender cypresses, the tall pines with their straight trunks, formed a thick colonnade, a lattice through which the sunlight flitted, a false unearthly light, that striped the ground with bands of gold and bars of shadow.

The painter praised the spot enthusiastically. It was the only corner for artists that could be found in Madrid. It was there that the great Don Francisco had worked. It seemed as though at some turn in the path they would run into Goya, sitting before his easel, scowling ill-naturedly at some dainty duchess who was serving as his model.

Modern clothes seemed out of keeping with this background. Renovales declared that the correct apparel for such a landscape was a bright coat, a powdered wig, silk stockings, walking beside a Directoire gown.

The countess smiled as she listened to the painter. She looked about with great curiosity; that was not a bad walk; she guessed it was the first time she ever saw it. Very pretty! But she was not fond of the country.

To her mind the best landscape was the silks of a drawing room and, as for trees, she preferred the scenery at the Opera to the accompaniment of music.

"The country bores me, master. It makes me so sad. If you leave Nature alone to itself it is very commonplace."

They entered a little square in the center of which was a pool, on the level of the ground, with stone posts that marked where there had once been a railing. The water, swollen by the melting snow, was overflowing the stone curb, and reached out in a thin sheet as it started down hill. The countess stopped, afraid of wetting her feet. The painter went ahead, putting his feet in the driest places, taking her hand to guide her, and she followed him, laughing at the obstacle and picking up her skirts.

As they continued their way down another path, Renovales kept that soft little hand in his, feeling its warmth through the glove. She let him hold it, as if she did not notice his touch, but still with a faint expression of mischievousness on her lips and in her eyes. The master seemed undecided, embarrassed, as if he did not know how to begin.

"Always the same?" he asked weakly. "Haven't you a little charity for me to-day?"

The countess broke out in a merry laugh.

"There it comes. I was expecting it; that's why I hesitated to come. In the carriage I said to myself several times: 'My dear, you're making a mistake in going to Moncloa; you will be bored to death; you may expect declaration number one thousand.'"

Then she assumed a tone of mock indignation.

"But, master, can't you talk about anything else? Are we women condemned to be unable to talk with a man without his feeling obliged to pour out a proposal?"

Renovales protested. She might say that to other men, but not to him, for he was in love with her. He swore it; he would say it on his knees, to make her believe it. Madly in love with her! But she mimicked him grotesquely, raising one hand to her breast and laughing cruelly.

"Yes, I know, the old story. There's no use in your repeating it; I know it by heart. A volcano in my breast, impossible to live without you—if you do not love me, I will kill myself. They all say the same thing. I never saw such a lack of originality. Master, for goodness sake, do not be so commonplace! A man like you saying such things!"

Renovales was crushed by her mocking mimicry. But Concha, as if she took pity on him, hastened to add, in an affectionate tone:

"Why should you have to be in love with me? Do you think I shall esteem you less if I relieve you from an obligation that all men who surround me feel under? I like you, master; I need to see you; I should be very sorry if we quarreled. I like you as a friend; the best of all, the first. I like you because you are good; a great big boy; a bearded baby who doesn't know even the least bit about the world, but who is very, *very* talented. I've wanted for a long time to see you alone, to talk with you quite freely, to tell you this. I like you as I like no one else. When I am with you, I feel a confidence such as no other man inspires in me. Good friends, brother and sister, if you will. But don't put on such a gloomy face! Look pleasant, please! Give one of your laughs that cheer my soul, master!"

But the master remained sullen, looking at the ground, running the fingers of his hand through his thick beard.

"All that's a lie, Concha," he said rudely. "The truth is that you are in love, you're mad over that worthless Monteverde."

The countess smiled, as if the rudeness of these words flattered her.

"Well, yes, Mariano. We like each other; I believe I

love him as I never loved any man. I have never told anyone; you are the first one to hear it from me, because you are my friend, because somehow or other I tell you everything. We like each other or, rather, I like him much more than he does me. There is something like gratitude in my love. I don't deceive myself, Mariano! Thirty-six years! I venture to confess my age to you. However, I am still presentable; I keep my youth well, but he is much younger. Years younger and I could almost be his mother."

She was silent for a moment, almost frightened at this difference between her lover's age and hers, but then she added with a sudden confidence:

"He likes me, too, I know. I am his adviser, his inspiration; he says that with me he feels a new strength for work, that he will be a great man, thanks to me. But I like him more, much more than he does me; there is almost as great a difference in our affections as there is in our ages."

"And why do you not love me?" said the master tearfully. "I worship you, the tables would be turned. I would be the one to surround you with constant idolatry, and you would let me worship you, caress you, as I would an idol, my head bowed at its feet."

Concha laughed again, mocking the artist's hoarse voice, his passionate expression, and his eager eyes.

"Why don't I love you? Master, don't be childish. There's no use in asking such things, you cannot dictate to Love. I do not like you as you want me to, because it is impossible. Be satisfied to be my best friend. You know I show a confidence in you that I do not show to Monteverde. Yes, I tell you things I would never tell him."

"But the other part!" exclaimed the painter violently.

"What I need, what I am hungry for,—you, your beauty, real love!"

"Master, contain yourself," she said with affected modesty. "How well I know you! You're going to say some of those horrid things that men always say when they rave over a woman. I'm going away so as not to hear you."

Then she added with maternal seriousness, as if she wanted to reprimand his violence:

"I am not so crazy as people think. I consider the consequences of my actions carefully. Mariano, look at yourself, think of your position. A wife, a daughter who will marry one of these days, the prospect of being a grandfather. And you still think of such follies! I could not accede to your proposal even if I loved you. How terrible! To deceive Josephina, the friend of my school-days! Poor thing, so gentle, so kind,—always ill. No, Mariano, never. A man cannot enter such compromising affairs, unless he is free. I could never feel like loving you. Friends, nothing more than friends!"

"Well, we will not be that," exclaimed Renovales impetuously. "I will leave your house forever. I will not see you any longer. I will do anything to forget you. It is an intolerable torment. My life will be calmer if I do not see you."

"You will not go away," said Concha quietly, certain of her power. "You will remain beside me just as you always have, if you really like me, and I shall have in you my best friend. Don't be a baby, master, you will see that there is something charming about our friendship that you do not understand now. I shall give you something that the rest do not know,—intimacy, confidence."

And as she said this, she put one hand on the painter's

arm and drew closer to him, searching him with her eyes in which there was a strange, mysterious light.

A horn sounded near them; there was swift rush of heavy wheels. An automobile shot past them at full speed, following the highroad. Renovales tried to make out the figures in the car, hardly larger than dolls in the distance. Perhaps it was López de Sosa, who was driving, perhaps his wife and daughter were those two little figures, wrapped in veils, who occupied the seats.

The possibility of Josephina's having passed through the background of the landscape without seeing him, without noticing that he was there, forgetful of everything, an imploring lover, overcame him with the sense of remorse.

They remained motionless for a long while in silence, leaning on the rough wooden railing, watching through the colonnade of the trees the bright, cherry-red sun, as it sank, lighting up the horizon with a blaze of fire. The leaden clouds, seeing it on the point of death, assailed it with treacherous greed.

Concha watched the sunset with the interest that a sight but seldom seen arouses.

"Look at that huge cloud, master. How black it is! It looks like a dragon; no, a hippopotamus; see its round paws, like towers. How it runs! It's going to eat the sun. It's eating it! It has swallowed it now!"

The landscape grew dark. The sun had disappeared inside of that monster that filled the horizon. Its waving back was edged with silver, and as if it could not hold the burning star; it broke below, pouring out a rain of pale rays. Then, burned by this digestion, it vanished in smoke, was torn into black tufts, and once more the red disc appeared, bathing sky and earth with gold, peopling the water of the pools with restless fiery fishes.

Renovales, leaning on the railing with one elbow be-

side the countess, breathed her subtle fragrance, felt the
warm touch of her firm body.

"Let's go back, master," she said with a suggestion of
uneasiness in her voice. "I feel cold. Besides, with a
companion like you, it's impossible to stay still."

And she hastened her step, realizing from her experience with men the danger of remaining alone with Renovales. His pale, excited face warned her that he was
likely to make some reckless, impetuous advance.

In the square of Caño Gordo they passed a couple
going slowly down the hill, very close together, not yet
daring to walk arm in arm, but ready to put their arms
around each other's waists as soon as they disappeared
in the next path. The young man carried his cloak under
his arm, as proudly as a gallant in the old comedies; she,
small and pale, without any beauty except that of youth,
was wrapped in a poor cloak and walked with her simple
eyes fixed on her companion's.

"Some student with his girl," said Renovales. "They
are happier than we are, Concha."

"We are getting old, master," she said with feigned
sadness, excluding herself from old age, loading the
whole burden of years on her companion.

Renovales turned toward her in a final outburst of protest.

"Why should I not be as happy as that boy? Haven't
I a right to it? Concha, you do not know who I am; you
forget it, accustomed as you are to treat me like a child.
I am Renovales, the painter, the famous master. I am
known all over the world."

And he spoke of his fame with brutal indelicacy, growing more and more irritated at her coldness, displaying
his renown like a mantle of light that should blind women
and make them fall at his feet. And a man like him had

to submit to being put off for that simpleton of a doctor?

The countess smiled with pity. Her eyes, too, revealed a sort of compassion. The fool! The child! How absurd men of talent were!

"Yes, you are a great man, master. That is why I am proud of your friendship. I even admit that it gives me some importance. I like you. I feel admiration for you."

"No, not admiration, Concha, love! To belong to each other! Complete love."

She continued to laugh.

"Oh, my boy; Love!"

Her eyes seemed to speak to him ironically. Love does not distinguish talents; it is ignorant and therefore boasts of its blindness. It only perceives the fragrance of youth, of life in its flower.

"We shall be friends, Mariano, friends and nothing more. You will grow accustomed to it and find our affection dear. Don't be material; it doesn't seem as if you were an artist. Idealism, master, that is what you need."

And she continued to talk to him from the heights of her pity, until they parted near the place where her carriage was waiting for her.

"Friends, Mariano, nothing more than friends, but true friends."

When Concha had gone, Renovales walked in the shadows of the twilight, gesticulating and clenching his fists, until he left Moncloa. Finding himself alone, he was again filled with wrath and insulted the countess mentally, now that he was free from the loving subjection that he suffered in her presence. How she amused herself with him! How his friends would laugh to see him helplessly submissive to that woman who had belonged to so many! His pride made him insist on conquering her, at any cost, even of humiliation and brutality. It was an affair of honor to make her his, even if it were only once, and then to take revenge by repelling her, throwing her at his feet, and saying with a sovereign air, "That is what I do to people who resist me."

But then he realized his weakness. He would always be beaten by that woman who looked at him coldly, who never lost her calm and considered him an inferior being. His dejection made him think of his family, of his sick wife, and the duties that bound him to her, and he felt the bitter joy of the man who sacrifices himself, taking up his cross.

His mind was made up. He would flee from the woman. He would not see her again.

III

'And he did not see her; he did not see her for two days. But on the third there came a letter in a long blue envelope scented with a perfume that made him tremble.

The countess complained of his absence in affectionate terms. She needed to see him, she had many things to tell him. A real love-letter which the artist hastened to hide, for fear that if any one read it, he would suspect what was not yet true.

Renovales was indignant.

"I will go to see her," he said to himself, walking up and down the studio. "But it will be only to give her a piece of my mind, and have done with her once and for all. If she thinks she is going to play with me, she is mistaken; she doesn't know that, when I want to be, I am like stone."

Poor master! While in one corner of his mind he was formulating this cruel determination to be a man of stone, in the other a sweet voice was murmuring seductively:

"Go quickly, take advantage of the opportunity. Perhaps she has repented. She is waiting for you; she is going to be yours."

And the artist hastened to the countess's anxiously. Nothing. She complained of his absence with affected sadness. She liked him so much! She needed to see him, she could not have any peace as long as she felt that he was offended with her on account of the other afternoon. And they spent nearly two hours together in the private room she used as an office, until at the end of the afternoon the serious friends of the countess began to

arrive, her coterie of mute worshipers and last of all
Monteverde with the calm of a man who has nothing to
fear.

The painter left the house. Nothing out of the ordinary
had happened except that he had twice kissed the countess's hand; the conventional caress and nothing more.
Whenever he tried to go farther, moving his lips along her
arm, she checked him imperiously.

"I shall be angry, master, and not receive you any more
alone! You are not keeping the agreement!"

Renovales protested. They had not made any agreement; but Concha managed to calm him instantly by asking about Milita, praising her beauty, inquiring for poor
Josephina, so good, so lovable, showing great concern
for her health and promising to call on her soon. And
the master was restrained, tormented by remorse, not
daring to make any new advances, until his discomfort
had disappeared.

He continued to visit the countess, as before. He felt
that he must see her; he had grown accustomed to her
enthusiastic praise of his artistic merits.

Sometimes the impetuous nature of his youthful days
awakened and he longed to rid himself of this shameful
chain. The woman had bewitched him; she sent for him
without any reason, she seemed to delight in making him
suffer, she needed him for a plaything. She spoke of
Monteverde and their love with quiet cynicism, as if the
doctor were her husband. She had to confide the secrets
of her life to some one, with that imperious naïveté that
forces the guilty to confess. Little by little she let the
master into the secret of her passion, telling him unblush-
ingly of the most intimate details of their meetings, which
were often in her own house. They took advantage of the
blindness of the count, who seemed almost stunned by his

failure to receive the Fleece; they took a morbid delight
in the danger of being surprised.

"I tell you this, Mariano, I don't know why it is I
feel as I do toward you; I like you as a brother. No, not
as a brother, rather as a confidential woman friend."

When Renovales was alone, he despised Concha's
frankness. It was just as people believed; she was very
attractive, very pretty, but absolutely lacking in scruples.
As for himself, he heaped insults on himself in the slang
of his Bohemian days, comparing himself with all the
horned animals he could think of.

"I won't go there again. It's disgraceful. A pretty
part you are playing, master!"

But he had hardly been absent two days when Marie,
the Countess's French maid, appeared with the scented
letter, or it arrived in the mail, where it stood out scandalously among the other envelopes of the master's correspondence.

"Curse that woman!" exclaimed Renovales, hastening
to hide the showy note. "What a lack of prudence.
One of these fine days, Josephina will discover these letters."

Cotoner, in his blind devotion to his idol whom he considered irresistible, supposed that the Alberca woman
was madly in love with the master and shook his head
sadly.

"This will have a bad end, Mariano. You ought to
break with her. The peace of your home! You are
piling up trouble for yourself."

The letters were always alike; endless complaints at
his short absences. *"Cher maître*, I could not sleep last
night, thinking of you," and she ended with "Your admirer and good friend, Coquillerosse," a *nom de guerre*
she had adopted for her correspondence with the artist.

She wrote in a disordered style, at unusual hours, just

as her fancy and her abnormal nervous system prompted. Sometimes she dated her letter at three in the morning, she could not sleep, got out of bed and to pass the sleepless hours filled four sheets of paper (with the facility of despair) in her fine hand, addressed to her good friend, talking to him of the count, of what her acquaintances said, telling him the latest gossip about the Court, lamenting the doctor's coldness. At other times, there were only four brief, desperate lines. "Come at once, dear Mariano. A very urgent matter."

And the master, leaving his tasks early in the morning, ran to the countess' house, where she received him still in bed in her fragrant chamber which the gentleman with honorary crosses had not entered for many years.

The painter came in in great anxiety, disturbed at the possibility of some terrible event, and Concha, tossing about between the embroidered sheets, tucking in the golden wisps of hair that escaped from her lace cap, talked and talked, as incoherently as a bird sings, as if the silence of the night had hopelessly confused her ideas. A great idea had occurred to her; during her sleep she had thought out an absolutely original scientific theory that would delight Monteverde. And she explained it earnestly to the master, who nodded his approval without understanding a word, thinking it was a pity to see such an attractive mouth uttering such follies.

At other times she would talk to him about the speech she was preparing for a fair of the Woman's Association, the *magnum opus* of her presidency; and drawing her ivory arms from under the sheet with a calmness that dazed Renovales, she would pick up from the near-by table some sheets of paper scribbled with pencil, and ask her friend to tell her who was the greatest painter in the world, for she had left a blank to fill in with this name.

After an hour of incessant chatter while the artist watched her silently with greedy eyes, he finally came to the urgent matter, the desperate summons that had made the master leave his work. It was always an affair of life or death, compromises in which her honor was at stake. Sometimes she wanted him to paint some little thing on the fan of a foreign lady who was eager to take away from Spain some souvenir of the great master. The person in question had asked her at a diplomatic soirée the night before, knowing her friendship with Renovales. Or she had sent for him to ask him for some little sketch, a daub, any one of the little things that lay in the corner of his studio for a bazaar of the Association for the Benefit of Fallen Women, whom the countess and her friends were very eager to rescue.

"Don't put on such a wry face, master, don't be stingy. You must expect to sacrifice something for friendship. Everybody thinks that I have great power over the famous artist, and they ask me favors and are constantly getting me into difficulty. They don't know you, they don't realize how perverse, how rebellious you are, you horrid man!"

And she let him kiss her hand, smiling condescendingly. But as she felt the touch of his lips and his beard on her arm she struggled to free herself, half-laughing, half-trembling.

"Let me go, Mariano! I'll scream! I'll call Marie! I won't receive you again in my bedroom. You aren't worthy of being trusted. Quiet, master, or I'll tell Josephina everything."

Sometimes when Renovales came, full of alarm at her summons, he found her pale, with dark circles under her eyes, as if she had spent the night weeping. When she saw the master her tears began to flow again. It was pique, deep pain at Monteverde's coldness. He passed whole days without seeing her; he even went so far as to say that women are a hindrance to serious study. Oh, these scholars! And she, madly devoted to him, submissive as a slave, putting up with his whimsical moods, worshiping him with that ardent passion of a woman who is older than her lover and appreciates her own inferiority!

"Oh, Renovales. Never fall in love. It is hell. You do not know the happiness you enjoy in not understanding these things."

But the master, indifferent to her tears, enraged by her confidences, walked up and down gesticulating, just as if he were in his studio, and he spoke to the countess with brutal frankness, as he would to a woman who had revealed all her secrets and weaknesses. What difference did all that make to him? Had she sent for him to tell him such stuff? She grieved with childish sighs from the bed. She was alone in the world, she was very unhappy. The master was her only friend; he was her father, her brother. To whom could she tell her troubles if not to him? And taking courage at the painter's silence who finally was moved by her tears, she recovered her boldness and expressed her wish. He must go to Monteverde, give him a good, heart-to-heart lecture, so that he would be good and not make her suffer. The doctor respected him highly; he was one of his greatest admirers; she was certain that a few words of the master would be enough to bring him back like a lamb. He must show him that she was not alone, that she had some one to defend her, that no one could make sport of her with impunity.

But before she finished her request, the painter was walking around the bed waving his arms, cursing in the violence of his excitement.

"That's the last straw! One of these days you'll be asking me to shine his boots. Are you mad, woman? What are you thinking of? You have enough accommodating people already in the count. Don't drag me into it!"

But she rolled over in bed, weeping disconsolately. She had no friends left! The master was like the others; if he would not accede to her requests, their friendship was over. All talk, oaths, and then not the least sacrifice!

Suddenly she sat up, frowning angrily with the coldness of an offended queen. She knew him at last, she had made a mistake in counting on him. And as Renovales, confused at her anger, tried to offer excuse, she interrupted him haughtily.

"Will you, or will you not? One, two——"

Yes, he would do what she wanted; he had sunk so low that it did not matter if he went a little farther. He would lecture the doctor, throwing in his face his stupidity in scorning such happiness,—he said this with all his heart, his voice trembling with envy. What else did his fair despot want? She might ask without fear. If it was necessary he would challenge the count, with all his decorations, to single combat and would kill him so that she might be free to join her little doctor.

"You joker," cried Concha, smiling at her triumph. "You are as nice as can be but you are very perverse. Come here, you horrid man."

And lifting a lock of his heavy hair with her hand, she kissed him on the forehead, laughing at the start the painter gave at her caress. He felt his legs trembling, then his arms strove to embrace the warm, scented body, that seemed to slip from him in its delicate covering.

"It was on the forehead," cried Concha in protest.

"A sister's caress, Mariano. Stop! You're hurting me!
I'll call!"

And she called, realizing her weakness, seeing that
she was on the point of being overcome in his fierce,
masterly grasp. The electric bell sounded out of the
maze of corridors and rooms and the door opened.
Marie entered in a black dress with a white apron and
a lace cap, discreet and silent. Her pale, smiling face,
accustomed to see everything, to guess everything, did
not reveal the slightest impression.

The countess stretched out her hand to Renovales,
calmly and affectionately, as if the entrance of the maid
had found her saying good-by. She was sorry that he
must go so soon, she would see him in the evening at
the Opera.

When the painter breathed the air of the street and
jostled against the people, he felt as if he were awakening from a nightmare. He loathed himself. "You're
showing off finely, master." His weakness that made
him give in to all of the countess's demands, his base
acquiescence in serving as an intermediary between her
and her lover was sickening now. But he still felt the
touch of her kiss on his forehead; he still breathed the
atmosphere of the bedroom, heavy with perfume. Optimism overcame him. The affair was not going badly.
However disagreeable the path was, it would lead to
the realization of his desire.

Many evenings Renovales went to the Opera, in obedience to Concha, who wanted to see him, and spent
whole acts in the back of her box, conversing with her.
Milita laughed at this change in the habits of her father,
who used to go to bed early, so as to be able to work
early in the morning. She was the one who, charged
with the household affairs on account of her mother's
constant illness, helped him to put on his dress-coat, and

amid caresses and laughter combed his hair and adjusted his tie.

"Papa, dear. I shouldn't know you, you're getting dissipated. When are you going to take me with you?"

The artist excused himself seriously. It was a duty of his profession; artists must go into society. And as for taking her with him—some other time. He had to go alone this time, he had to talk to a great many people at the theater.

Another change took place in him that provoked joyful comments on the part of Milita. Papa was getting young.

Under irreverent trimmings, every week his hair became shorter, his beard diminished until only a light remnant remained of that tangled growth that gave him such a ferocious appearance. He did not want to look like other men, he must preserve the exterior that stamped him as an artist, so that people might not pass by the great Renovales without recognizing him. But he managed, while keeping within this desire, to approach and mingle with the fashionably dressed young men who frequented the countess's house.

Other people too noticed this change. Students in the School of Fine Arts pointed him out from the gallery of the Opera-house or stopped on the sidewalk when they saw him at night, with a shining silk hat on his carefully trimmed hair and the expanse of shirt-front showing in his unbuttoned overcoat. The boys in their simple admiration imagined the great master thundering before his easel, as savage, fierce and intractable as Michael Angelo in his studio. And so when they saw him looking so differently, their eyes followed him enviously. "What a good time the master is having!" And they fancied the great ladies disputing over him, believing in perfect faith that no woman could resist a man who painted so well.

His enemies, established artists but who were inferior to him, growled in their conversations. "Four-flusher, prig! He wasn't satisfied with making so much money and now he's playing the sport among the aristocracy, to pick up more portraits, to get all he can out of his signature."

Cotoner, who sometimes stayed at the house in the evenings, to keep the ladies company, smiled sadly as he saw him leave, shaking his head. "It's bad. Mariano married too soon. Now that he is almost an old man, he's doing what he didn't do in his youth in his fever for work and glory." Many people were laughing at him already, divining his passion for the Alberca woman, that love without practical results, that made him live with her and Monteverde, acting as a good-natured mediator, a tolerant kindly father. When the famous master took off his mask of fierceness, he was a poor fellow about whom people talked with pity: they compared him with Hercules, dressed as a woman and spinning at the feet of his fair seducer.

He had contracted a close friendship with Monteverde as a result of meeting him so often at the countess's. He no longer seemed foolish and unattractive. Renovales found in him something of the woman he loved and therefore his company was pleasing. He experienced that calm attraction, free from jealousy, that the husband of a mistress inspires in some men. They sat together at the theater, went to walk, conversing amiably, and the doctor frequently visited the artist's studio in the afternoon. This intimacy quite disconcerted people, for they could no longer tell with certainty which one was the Alberca woman's master and which the aspirant, even going so far as to believe that by a mutual agreement they all three lived in an ideal world.

Monteverde admired the master and the latter, from his years and the superiority of his fame, assumed a paternal authority over him. He chided him when the countess complained of him.

"Women!" the doctor would say with a bored expression. "You don't know what they are, master. They are only a hindrance to obstruct a man's career. You have been successful because you haven't let them dominate you because you are strong."

And the poor strong man looked at Monteverde narrowly suspecting that he was making sport of him. He felt tempted to knock him down at the thought that the doctor scorned what he craved so keenly.

Concha was more communicative with the master. She confessed to him what she had never dared to tell the doctor.

"I tell you everything, Mariano. I cannot live without seeing you. Do you know what I think? The doctor is a sort of husband to me and you are the lover of my heart. Don't get excited; don't move or I'll call. I have spoken from my heart. I like you too much to think of the coarse things you want."

Sometimes Renovales found her excited, nervous, speaking hoarsely, working her delicate fingers as if she wanted to scratch the air. They were terrible days that stirred up the whole house. Marie ran from room to room with her silent step, pursued by the ringing of the bells; the count slipped out of doors, like a frightened school-boy. Concha was bored, felt tired of everything, hated her life. When the painter appeared she would almost throw herself in his arms.

"Take me out of here, Mariano; I'm tired of it, I'm dying. This life is killing me. My husband! He doesn't

count. My friends! Fools that flay me as soon as I leave
them. The doctor! as untrustworthy as a weathercock.
All those men in my coterie, idiots. Master, have pity
on me. Take me far away from here. You must know
some other world; artists know everything."

If she only was not such a familiar figure and if
people only did not know the master in Madrid! In
her nervous excitement she formed the wildest projects.
She wanted to go out at night arm in arm with Renovales. She in a shawl and a kerchief over her head
and he in a cape and a slouch hat. She would be his
grisette; she would imitate the carriage and stride of a
woman of the streets and they would go to the lowest
districts like two night-hawks, and they would drink,
would get into a brawl; he would defend her and they
would go and spend the night in the police station.

The painter looked shocked. What nonsense! But
she insisted on her wish.

"Laugh, master, open that great mouth of yours, you
ugly thing. What is strange about what I said? You,
with all your artist's hair and soft hats, are humdrum,
a peaceful soul that is incapable of doing anything original in order to amuse yourself."

When she thought of the couple they had seen one
afternoon at Moncloa, she grew melancholy and senti-
mental. She, too, thought it would be fun to play the
grisette, to walk arm in arm with the master as if she
were a poor dressmaker and he a clerk, to end the
trip in a picnic park, and he would give her a ride in
the green swing, while she screamed with pleasure, as
she went up and down with her skirts whirling around
her feet. That was not foolishness. Just the simplest,
most rustic pleasure!

What a pity that they were both so well known. But
what they would do, at least, was to disguise themselves

some morning and go house-hunting in some low quarter, like the Rastro, as if they were a newly married couple. No one would recognize them in that part of Madrid. Agreed, master?

And the master approved of everything. But the next day, Concha received him with confusion, biting her lips, until at last she broke out into hearty laughter at the recollection of the follies she had proposed.

"How you must laugh at me! Some days I am perfectly crazy."

Renovales did not conceal his assent. Yes, she was a trifle crazy. But with all her absurdities that made him alternate between hope and despair, she was more attractive, with her merry nonsense, and her transitory fits of anger, than the woman at home, implacable, silent, shunning him with ceaseless repugnance, but following him everywhere with her weeping, uncanny eyes, that became as cutting as steel, as soon as, out of sympathy or remorse, he gave the least evidence of familiarity.

Oh, what a heavy, intolerable comedy! Before his daughter and his friends they had to talk to each other, and he, looking away, so that their eyes might not meet, scolded her gently, for not following the advice of the doctors. At first they had said it was neurasthenia, now it was diabetes, that was increasing the invalid's weakness. The master lamented the passive resistance she opposed to all their curative methods. She would follow them for a few days and then give them up with calm obstinacy. Her health was better than they thought: doctors could not cure her trouble.

At night, when they entered the bed-chamber, a deathly silence fell on them; a leaden wall seemed to rise between their bodies. Here they no longer had to dissemble; they looked at each other face to face with silent hostility. Their life at night was sheer torment,

but neither of them dared to change their mode of living. Their bodies could not leave the common bed;
they found in it the places they had occupied for years.
The habit of their wills subjected them to this room and
its furnishings, with all its memories of the happy days
of their youth.

Renovales would fall into the deep sleep of a healthy
man, tired out with work. His last thoughts were of
the countess. He saw her in that vague mist that
shrouds the portal of unconsciousness; he went to sleep,
thinking of what he would say to her the next day. And
his dreams were in keeping with his desires, for he saw
her standing on a pedestal, in all the majesty of her
nakedness, surpassing the marble of the most famous
statues with the life of her flesh. When he awakened
suddenly and stretched out his arms, he touched the body
of his companion, small, stiff, burning with the fire of
fever or icy with deathly cold. He divined that she was
not asleep. She spent the nights without closing her
eyes, but she did not move, as if all her strength was
concentrated on something that she watched in the darkness with a hypnotic stare. She was like a corpse. There
was the obstacle, the leaden weight, the phantom that
checked the other woman when sometimes in a moment
of hesitation, she leaned toward him, on the point of
falling. And the terrible longing, the hideous thought
came forth again in all its ugliness, announcing that it
was not dead, that it had only hidden in the den of his
brain, to rise more cruelly, more insolently.

"Why not?" argued the rejected spirit, scattering in
his fancy the golden dust of dreams.

Love, fame, joy, a new artistic life, the rejuvenation
of Doctor Faustus; he might expect everything, if kindly
death would but come to help him, breaking the chain
that bound him to sadness and sickness.

But straightway a protest would arise within him. Though he lived like an infidel, he still had a religious soul that in the trying moments of his life led him to call on all the superhuman and miraculous powers as if they were under an inevitable obligation to come to his aid. "Lord, take this horrible thought from me. Take away this temptation. Don't let her die. Let her live, even if I perish."

And the following day, filled with remorse, he would go to some doctors, friends of his, to consult with them minutely. He would stir up the house, organizing the cure according to a vast plan, distributing the medicines by hours. Then he would calmly return to his work, to his artistic prejudices, to his passionate longing, forgetting his determinations, thinking his wife's life was already saved.

One afternoon after luncheon, she came into the studio and as the master looked at her, a sense of anxiety crept over him. It was a long time since Josephina had entered the room while he was working.

She would not sit down; standing beside the easel she spoke slowly and meekly to her husband, without looking at him. Renovales was frightened at this simplicity.

"Mariano, I have come to talk to you about our daughter."

She wanted her to be married: it must come some day and the sooner, the better. She would die before long and she wanted to leave the world with the assurance that her daughter was well settled.

Renovales felt forced to protest loudly with all the vehemence of a man who is not very sure of what he is saying. Shucks! Die! Why should she die? Her health was better now than it had ever been. The only thing she needed was to heed what the doctors told her.

"I shall die before long," she repeated coldly; "I shall die and you will be left in peace. You know it."

The painter tried to protest with a greater show of righteous indignation but his eyes met his wife's cold look. Then he contented himself with shrugging his shoulders in a resigned way. He did not want to argue; he must keep calm. He had to paint; he must go out that afternoon as usual on important business.

"Very well, go ahead. Milita is going to be married. And to whom?"

Led by his desire to maintain his authority, to take the lead, and because of his long-standing affection for his pupil, he hastened to speak of him. Was Soldevilla the suitor? A good boy with a future ahead of him. He worshiped Milita; his dejection when she treated him ill was pitiful. He would make an excellent husband.

Josephina cut short her husband's chatter in a cold, contemptuous tone.

"I don't want any painters for my daughter; you know it. Her mother has had enough of them."

Milita was going to marry López de Sosa. The matter was already settled as far as she was concerned. The boy had spoken to her and, assured of her approval, would ask the father.

"But does she love him? Do you think, Josephina, that these things can be arranged to suit you?"

"Yes, she loves him; she is suited and wants to be married. Besides she is your daughter; she would accept the other man just as readily. What she wants is freedom, to get away from her mother, not to live in the unhappy atmosphere of my ill health. She doesn't say so, she doesn't even know that she thinks it, but I see through her."

And as if, while she spoke of her daughter, she could not maintain the coldness she had toward her husband, she raised her hand to her eyes, to wipe away the silent tears.

Renovales had recourse to rudeness in order to get out of the difficulty. It was all nonsense; an invention of her diseased mind. She ought to think of getting well and nothing else. What was she crying for! Did she want to marry her daughter to that automobile enthusiast? Well, get him. She did not want to? Well, let the girl stay at home.

She was the one who had charge; no one was hindering her. Have the marriage as soon as possible? He was a mere cipher, and there was no reason for asking his advice. But steady, shucks! He had to work; he had to go out. And when he saw Josephina leaving the studio to weep somewhere else, he gave a snort of satisfaction, glad to have escaped from this difficult scene so successfully.

López de Sosa was all right. An excellent boy! Or anyone else. He did not have time to give to such matters. Other things occupied his attention.

He accepted his future son-in-law, and for several evenings he stayed at home to lend a sort of patriarchal air to the family parties. Milita and her betrothed talked at one end of the drawing-room. Cotoner, in the full bliss of digestion, strove with his jests to bring a faint smile to the face of the master's wife, but she stayed in the corner, shivering with cold. Renovales, in a smoking jacket, read the papers, soothed by the charming atmosphere of his quiet home. If the countess could only see him!

One night the Alberca woman's name was mentioned in the drawing-room. Milita was running over from memory the list of friends of the family,—prominent ladies who would not fail to honor her approaching marriage with some magnificent present.

"Concha won't come," said the girl. "It's a long time since she has been here."

There was a painful silence, as if the countess's name chilled the atmosphere. Cotoner hummed a tune, pretending to be thinking of something else; López de Sosa began to look for a piece of music on the piano, talking about it to change the subject. He too seemed to be aware of the matter.

"She doesn't come because she doesn't have to come," said Josephina from her corner. "Your father manages to see her every day, so that she won't forget us."

Renovales raised his eyes in protest, as if he were awakening from a calm sleep. Josephina's gaze was fixed on him, not angry, but mocking and cruel. It reflected the same scorn with which she had wounded him on that unhappy night. She no longer said anything, but the master read in those eyes:

"It is useless, my good man. You are mad over her, you pursue her, but she belongs to other men. I know her of old. I know all about it. Oh, how people laugh at you! How I laugh! How I scorn you!"

IV.

THE beginning of summer saw the wedding of the
daughter of Renovales to López de Sosa. The papers
published whole columns on the event, in which, according to some of the reporters, "the glory and splendor of
art were united with the prestige of aristocracy and
fortune." No one remembered now the nickname
"Pickled Herring."

The master Renovales did things well. He had only
one daughter and he was eager to marry her with royal
pomp; eager that Madrid and all Spain should know of
the affair, that a ray of the glory her father had won
might fall on Milita.

The list of gifts was long. All the friends of the
master, society ladies, political leaders, famous artists,
and even royal personages, appeared in it with their
corresponding presents. There was enough to fill a
store. Both of the studios for visitors were converted
into show rooms with countless tables loaded with articles, a regular fair of clothes and jewelry, that was
visited by all of Milita's girl friends, even the most distant and forgotten, who came to congratulate her, pale
with envy.

The Countess of Alberca, too, sent a huge, showy gift,
as if she did not want to remain unnoticed among the
friends of the house. Doctor Monteverde was represented by a modest remembrance, though he had no other
connection with the family than his friendship with the
master.

The wedding was celebrated at the house, where one

of the studios was converted into a chapel. Cotoner had
a hand in everything that concerned the ceremony, delighted to be able to show his influence with the people
of the Church.

Renovales took charge of the arrangements of the altar, eager to display the touch of an artist even in the
least details. On a background of ancient tapestries he
placed an old triptych, a medieval cross; all the articles
of worship which filled his studio as decorations,
cleaned now from dust and cobwebs, recovered for a
few moments their religious importance.

A variegated flood of flowers filled the master's house.
Renovales insisted on having them everywhere; he had
sent to Valencia and Murcia for them in reckless quan-
tities; they hung on the door-frames, and along the
cornices; they lay in huge clusters on the tables and in
the corners. They even swung in pagan garlands from
one column of the façade to another, arousing the curiosity of the passers-by, who crowded outside of the
iron fence,—women in shawls, boys with great baskets
on their heads who stood in open-mouthed wonder before the strange sight, waiting to see what was going on
in that unusual house, following the coming and going
of the servants who carried in music stands and two
base viols, hidden in varnished cases.

Early in the morning Renovales was hurrying about
with two ribbons across his shirt front and a constella-
tion of golden, flashing stars covering one whole side of
his coat. Cotoner, too, had put on the insignia of his
various Papal Orders. The master looked at himself in
all the mirrors with considerable satisfaction, admiring
equally his friend. They must look handsome; a cel-
ebration like this they would never see again. He plied
his companion with incessant questions, to make sure
that nothing had been overlooked in the preparations.

The master Pedraza, a great friend of Renovales, was to conduct the orchestra. They had gathered all the best players in Madrid, for the most part from the Opera. The choir was a good one, but the only notable artists they had been able to secure were people who made the capital their residence. The season was not the best; the theaters were closed.

Cotoner continued to explain the measures he had taken. Promptly at ten the Nuncio, Monsignore Orlandi, —a great friend of his—would arrive; a handsome chap, still young, whom he had met in Rome when he was attached to the Vatican. A word on Cotoner's part was all that was necessary to persuade him to do them the honor of marrying the children. Friends are useful at times! And the painter of the popes, proud of his sudden rise to importance, went from room to room, arranging everything, followed by the master who approved of his orders.

In the studio, the orchestra and the table for the luncheon were set. The other rooms were for the guests. Was anything forgotten? The two artists looked at the altar with its dark tapestries, and its candelabra, crosses and reliquaries, of dull, old gold that seemed to absorb the light rather than reflect it. Nothing was lacking. Ancient fabrics and garlands of flowers covered the walls, hiding the master's studies in color, unfinished pictures, profane works that could not be tolerated in the discreet, harmonious atmosphere of that chapel-like room. The floor was partly covered with costly rugs, Persian and Moorish. In front of the altar were two praying desks and behind them, for the more important guests, all the luxurious chairs of the studio: white armchairs of the 18th Century, embroidered with pastoral scenes, Greek settles, benches of carved oak and Venetian chairs with high backs, the bizarre confusion of an antique shop.

Suddenly Cotoner started back as if he were shocked. How careless! A fine thing it would have been if he had not noticed it! At the end of the studio, opposite the altar that screened a large part of the window, and directly in its light, stood a huge, white, naked woman. It was the "Venus de Medici," a superb piece of marble that Renovales had brought from Italy. Its pagan beauty in its dazzling whiteness seemed to challenge the deathly yellow of the religious objects that filled the other end of the studio. Accustomed to see it, the two artists had passed in front of it several times without noticing its nakedness that seemed more insolent and triumphant now that the studio was converted into an oratory.

Cotoner began to laugh.

"What a scandal if we hadn't seen it! What would the ladies have said! My friend Orlandi would have thought that you did it on purpose, for he considers you rather lax morally. Come, my boy, let's get something to cover up this lady."

After much searching in the disorder of the studio, they found a piece of Indian cotton, scrawled with elephants and lotus flowers; they stretched it over the goddess's head, so that it covered her down to her feet and there it stood, like a mystery, a riddle for the guests.

They were beginning to arrive. Outside of the house, at the fence sounded the stamping of the horses, the slam of doors as they closed. In the distance rumbled other carriages, drawing nearer every minute. The swish of silk on the floor sounded in the hall, and the servants ran back and forth, receiving wraps and putting numbers on them, as at the theater, to stow them away in the parlor that had been converted into a coat-room. Cotoner directed the servants, smooth shaven or wearing side-whiskers, and clad in faded dress-suits. Renovales meanwhile was wreathed in smiles, bowing graciously, greeting the ladies who came in their black or white mantillas, grasping the hands of the men, some of whom wore brilliant uniforms.

The master felt elated at this procession which ceremoniously passed through his drawing-rooms and studios. In his ears, the swish of skirts, the movement of fans, the greetings, the praise of his good taste sounded like caressing music. Everyone came with the same satisfaction in seeing and being seen, which people reveal on a first night at the theater or at some brilliant reception. Good music, presence of the Nuncio, preparations for the luncheon which they seemed to sniff already, and besides, the certainty of seeing their names in print the next day, perhaps of having their picture in some illustrated magazine. Emilia Renovales' wedding was an event.

Among the crowd of people that continued to pour in were seen several young men, hastily holding up their cameras. They were going to have snap-shots! Those who retained some bitterness against the artist, remembering how dearly they had paid him for a portrait, now pardoned him generously and excused his robbery. There was an artist that lived like a gentleman! And Renovales went from one side to another, shaking hands, bowing, talking incoherently, not knowing in which direction to turn. For a moment, while he stood in the hall, he saw a bit of sunlit garden, covered with flowers and beyond a fence a black mass: the admiring, smiling throng. He breathed the odor of roses and subtle perfumes, and felt the rapture of optimism flood his breast. Life was a great thing. The poor rabble, crowded together outside, made him recall with pride the blacksmith's son. Heavens, how he had risen! He felt grateful to those wealthy, idle people who supported his well-being; he made every effort so that they might lack nothing, and overwhelmed Cotoner with his suggestions. The latter turned on the master with the arrogance of one who is in authority. His place was inside, with the guests. He need not mind him, for he knew his duties. And turning his back on Mariano, he issued orders to the servants and showed the way to the new arrivals, recognizing their station at a glance. "This way, gentlemen."

It was a group of musicians and he led them through a servants' hallway so that they might get to their stands without having to mingle with the guests. Then he turned to scold a crowd of bakerboys, who were late in bringing the last shipments of the luncheon and advanced through the assemblage, raising the great, wicker baskets over the heads of the ladies.

Cotoner left his place when he saw rising from the stairway a plush hat with gold tassels over a pale face, then a silk cassock with purple sash and buttons, flanked by two others, black and modest.

"*Oh, monsignore! Monsignore Orlandi! Va bene? Va bene?*"

He kissed his hand with a profound reverence, and after inquiring anxiously for his health, as if he had not seen him the day before, started off, opening a passage way in the crowded drawing-rooms.

"The Nuncio! The Nuncio of His Holiness!"

The men, with the decorum of decent persons, who know how to show respect for dignitaries, stopped laughing and talking to the ladies, and bent forward, as he passed, to take that delicate, pale hand, which looked like the hand of a lady of the olden days, and kiss the huge stone of its ring. The ladies, with moist eyes, looked for a moment at Monsignor Orlandi,—a distinguished prelate, a diplomat of the Church, a noble of the Old Roman nobility,—tall, thin, pale as chalk, with black hair and imperious eyes in which there was an intense flash of flame.

He moved with the haughty grace of a bull-fighter. The lips of the women rested eagerly on his hand, while he gazed with enigmatical eyes at the line of graceful necks bowed before him. Cotoner continued ahead, opening a passage, proud of his part, elated at the respect which his illustrious friend inspired. What a wonderful thing religion was!

He accompanied him to the sacristy, which once was the dressing-room for the models. He remained outside, discreetly, but every other minute some one of the Nuncio's attendants came out in search of him,—sprightly young fellows with a feminine carriage and a faint suggestion of 'perfume about them, who looked on the artist with respect, believing he was an important personage. They called to Signor Cotoner, asking him to help them find something Monsignor had sent the day before, and the Bohemian, in order to avoid further requests, finally went into the dressing-room, to assist in the sacred toilette of his illustrious friend.

In the drawing-rooms the company suddenly eddied, the conversation ceased, and a throng of people, after crowding in front of one of the doors, opened to leave a passage.

The bride, leaning on the arm of a distinguished gentleman, who was the best man, entered, clad in white, ivory white her dress, snow white her veil, pearl white her flowers. The only bright color she showed was the healthy pink of her cheeks and the red of her lips. She smiled to her friends, not bashfully nor timidly, but with an air of satisfaction at the festivity and the fact that she was its principal object. After her came the groom, giving his arm to his new mother, the painter's wife, smaller than ever in her party-gown that was too large for her, dazed by this noisy event that broke the painful calm of her existence.

And the father? Renovales was missing in the formal entrance; he was very busy attending to the guests; a gracious smile, half hidden behind a fan, detained him at one end of the drawing-room. He had felt some one touch his shoulder and, turning around, he saw the solemn Count of Alberca with his wife on his arm. The count had congratulated him on the appearance of the studios; all very artistic. The countess had congratulated him too, in a jesting tone, on the importance of this event in his life. The moment of retiring, of saying good-by to youth had come.

"They are shelving you, dear master. Pretty soon they will be calling you grandfather."

She laughed with pleasure at the flush of pain these pitying words caused him. But before Mariano could answer the countess, he felt himself dragged away by Cotoner. What was he doing there? The bride and groom were at the altar; Monsignor was beginning the service; the father's chair was still vacant. And Renovales passed a tiresome half-hour following the ceremonies of the prelate with an absent-minded glance. Far away in the last of the studios, the stringed instruments struck a loud chord and a melody of earthly mysticism poured forth from room to room in the atmosphere laden with the perfume of crumpled roses.

Then a sweet voice, supported by others more harsh, began a prayer that had the voluptuous rhythm of an Italian serenade. A passing wave of sentimentality seemed to stir the guests. Cotoner, who stood near the altar, in case Monsignor should need something, felt moved to tenderness by the music, by the sight of that distin-

guished gathering, by the dramatic gravity with which
the Roman prelate conducted the ceremonies of his profession. Seeing Milita so fair, kneeling, with her eyes
lowered under her snowy veil, the poor Bohemian blinked
to keep back the tears. He felt just as if he were marrying his own daughter. He who had not had one!

Renovales sat up, seeking the countess's eyes above the
white and black mantillas. Sometimes he found them
resting on him with a mocking expression, at other times
he saw them seeking Monteverde in the crowd of gentlemen that filled the doorway.

There was one moment when the painter paid attention to the ceremony. How long it was! The music had
ceased; Monsignor, with his back to the altar, advanced
several steps toward the newly married couple, holding
out his hands, as if he were going to speak to them.
There was a profound hush and the voice of the Italian
began to sound in the silence with a sing-song mellow-
ness, hesitating over some words, supplying them with
others of his own language. He explained to the man
and wife their duties and expatiated, with oratorical fire,
in his praises of their families. He spoke little of him;
he was a representative of the upper classes, from which
rise the leaders of men; he knew his duties. She was the
descendant of a great painter whose fame was universal,
of an artist.

As he mentioned art, the Roman prelate was fired with
enthusiasm, as if he were speaking of his own stock, with
the deep interest of a man whose life had been spent
among the splendid half-pagan decorations of the Vatican. "Next to God, there is nothing like art." And after this statement, with which he attributed to the bride a
nobility superior to that of many of the people who were
watching her, he eulogized the virtues of her parents. In
admirable terms, he commended their pure love and

Christian fidelity, ties with which they approached together, Renovales and his wife, the portal of old age and
which surely would accompany them till death. The
painter bowed his head, afraid that he would meet Concha's mocking glance. He could hear Josephina's stifled
sobs, with her face hidden in the lace of her mantilla.
Cotoner felt called upon to second the prelate's praises
with discreet words of approval.

Then the orchestra noisily began Mendelssohn's "Wedding March"; the chairs ground on the floor as they were
pushed back; the ladies rushed toward the bride and a
buzz of congratulations, shouted over the heads of the
company, and of noisy efforts to be the first to reach her,
drowned out the vibration of the strings and the heavy
blast of the brasses. Monsignor, whose importance disappeared as soon as the ceremony was over, made his
way with his attendants to the dressing-room, passing unnoticed through the throng. The bride smiled with a
resigned air amid the circle of feminine arms that
squeezed her and friendly lips that showered kisses on
her. She expressed surprise at the simplicity of the ceremony. Was that all there was to it? Was she really
married?

Cotoner saw Josephina making her way across the
room, looking impatiently among the shoulders of the
guests, her face tinged with a hectic flush. His instinct
of a master of ceremonies warned him that danger was
at hand.

"Take my arm, Josephina. Let's go outside for a
breath of fresh air. This is unbearable."

She took his arm but instead of following him, she
dragged him among the people who crowded around her
daughter until at last, seeing the Countess of Alberca,
she stopped. Her prudent friend trembled. Just what
he thought—she was looking for the other woman.

"Josephina, Josephina! Remember that this is Milita's wedding!"

But his advice was useless. Concha, seeing her old friend, ran toward her. "Dear! So long since I've seen you! A kiss—another." And she kissed her effusively. The little woman made one attempt to resist; but then she submitted, dejectedly, smiling sadly, overcome by habit and training. She returned her kisses coldly with an indifferent expression. She did not hate Concha. If her husband did not go to her, he would go to some one else; the real, the dangerous enemy was within him.

The bride and groom, arm in arm, smiling and somewhat fatigued by the violent congratulations, passed through the groups of people and disappeared, followed by the last chords of the triumphal march.

The music ceased, and the company crowded around the tables covered with bottles, cold meats and confections, behind which the servants hurried in confusion, not knowing how to serve so many a black glove or white hand that seized the gold-bordered plates and the little pearl knives crossed on the dishes. It was a smiling, well-bred riot, but they pushed and trod on the ladies' trains and used their elbows, as if, now the ceremony was over, they were all gnawed with hunger.

Plate in hand, stifled and breathless after the assault, they scattered through the studios, eating even on the very altar. There were not servants enough for so great a gathering; the young men, seizing bottles of champagne, ran in all directions, filling the ladies' glasses. Amid great merriment the tables were pillaged. The servants covered them hastily and with no less speed the pyramids of sandwiches, fruits, and sweets came down and the bottles disappeared. The corks popped two and three at a time, in ceaseless crossfire.

Renovales ran about like a servant, loaded with plates

and glasses, going back and forth from the crowded tables to the corners where some of his friends were seated.
The Alberca woman assumed the airs of a mistress; she
made him go and come with constant requests.

On one of these trips he ran into his beloved pupil,
Soldevilla. He had not seen him for a long time. He
looked rather gloomy, but he found some consolation in
looking at his waistcoat, a novelty that had made a "hit"
among the younger set; of black velvet with embroidered flowers and gold buttons.

The master felt that he ought to console him,—poor
boy! For the first time he gave him to understand that
he was "in the secret."

"I wanted something else for my daughter, but it was
impossible. Work, Soldevilla! Courage! We must not
have any mistress except painting."

And content to have delivered this kindly consolation,
he returned to the countess.

At noon, the reception ended. López de Sosa and his
wife reappeared in traveling costume; he in a fox-skin
overcoat, in spite of the heat, a leather cap and high leg-
gings; she in a long mackintosh that reached to her feet
and a turban of thick veils that hid her face, like a fu-
gitive from a harem.

At the door, the groom's latest acquisition was waiting
for them—an eighty horse-power car that he had bought
for his wedding trip. They intended to spend the night
some hundred miles away in a corner of old Castile, at
an estate inherited from his father which he had never
visited.

A modern wedding, as Cotoner said, a honeymoon at
full speed, without any witness except the discreet back
of the chauffeur. The next day they expected to start
for a tour of Europe. They would go as far as Berlin;
perhaps farther.

López de Sosa shook hands with his friends vigor-
ously, like a proud explorer, and went out to look over his
car, before leaving. Milita submitted to her friends' caresses, carrying away her mother's tears on her veil.

"Good-by, good-by, my daughter!"

And the wedding was over.

Renovales and his wife were left alone. The absence
of their daughter seemed to increase the solitude, widen-
ing the distance between them. They looked at each
other hostilely, reserved and gloomy, without a sound
to break the silence and serve as a bridge to enable them
to exchange a few words. Their life was going to be
like that of convicts, who hate each other and walk side
by side, bound with the same chain, in tormenting union,
forced to share the same necessities of life.

As a remedy for this isolation that filled them with
misgivings they both thought of having the newly married couple come to live with them. The house was
large, there was room for them all. But Milita objected,
gently but firmly, and her husband seconded her. He
must live near his coach house, his garage. Besides,
where could he, without shocking his father-in-law, put
his collection of treasures, his museum of bull's heads and
bloody suits of famous toreadors, which was the envy of
his friends and an object of great curiosity for many foreigners.

When the painter and his wife were alone again, it
seemed as though they had aged many years in a month;
they found their house more huge, more deserted,—with
the echoing silence of abandoned monuments. Renovales
wanted Cotoner to move to the house, but the Bohemian
declined with a sort of fear. He would eat with them;
he would spend a great part of the day at their house;
they were all the family he had; but he wanted to keep his
freedom; he could not give up his numerous friends.

Well along in the summer, the master induced his wife
to take her usual vacation. They would go to a little
known Andalusian watering-place, a fishing village where
the artist had painted many of his pictures. He was tired
of Madrid. The Countess of Alberca was at Biarritz
with her husband. Doctor Monteverde had gone there
too, dragged along by her.

They made the trip, but it did not last more than a
month. The master hardly finished two canvases. Josephina felt ill. When they reached the watering-place,
her health improved greatly. She appeared more cheer-
ful; for hours at a time she would sit in the sand, getting tanned in the sun, craving the warmth with the eagerness of an invalid, watching the sea with her expressionless eyes, near her husband who painted, surrounded
by a semicircle of wretched people. She sang, smiled
sometimes to the master, as if she forgave him everything and wanted to forget, but suddenly a shadow of
sadness had fallen on her; her body seemed paralyzed
once more by weakness. She conceived an aversion to
the bright beach, and the life of the open air, with that
repugnance for light and noise which sometimes seizes
invalids and makes them hide in the seclusion of their
beds. She sighed for her gloomy house in Madrid.
There she was better, she felt stronger, surrounded with
memories; she thought she was safer from the black
danger that hovered about her. Besides, she longed to
see her daughter. Renovales must telegraph to his son-
in-law. They had toured Europe long enough; it was
time for them to come back; she must see Milita.

They returned to Madrid at the end of September, and
a little later the newly married couple joined them, delighted with their trip and still more delighted to be at
home again. López de Sosa had been greatly vexed by
meeting people wealthier than he, who humiliated him

with their luxury. His wife wanted to live among friends who would admire her prosperity. She was grieved at the lack of curiosity in those countries where no one paid any attention to her.

With the presence of her daughter, Josephina seemed to recover her spirits. The latter frequently came in the afternoon, dressed in her showy gowns, which were the more striking at that season when most of the society folk were away from Madrid, and took her mother to ride in the motor in the suburbs of the capital, sweeping along the dusty roads. Sometimes, too, Josephina summoning her courage, overcame her bodily weakness and went to her daughter's house, a second-story apartment in the Calle de Olózaga, admiring the modern comforts that surrounded her.

The master seemed to be bored. He had no portraits to paint; it was impossible for him to do anything in Madrid while he was still saturated with the radiant sun and the brilliant colors of the Mediterranean shore. Besides, he missed the company of Cotoner, who had gone to a historic little town in Castile, where with a comic pride he received the honors due to genius, living in the palace of the prelate and ruining several pictures in the Cathedral by an infamous restoration.

His loneliness made Renovales remember the Alberca woman with all the greater longing. She, on her part, with a constant succession of letters reminded the painter of her every day. She had written to him while he was at the little village on the coast and now she wrote to him in Madrid, asking him what he was doing, taking an interest in the most insignificant details of his daily life and telling him about her own with an exuberance that filled pages and pages, till every envelope contained a veritable history.

The painter followed her life minute by minute, as

if he were with her. She talked to him about Darwin,
concealing Monteverde under this name; she complained
of his coldness, of his indifference, of the air of commiseration with which he submitted to her love. "Oh,
master, I am very unhappy!" At other times her letter
was triumphant, optimistic; she seemed radiant, and the
painter read her satisfaction between the lines; he divined her intoxication after those daring meetings in
her own house, defying the count's blindness. And she
told him everything, with shameless, maddening familiarity, as if he were a woman, as if he could not be
moved in the least by her confidences.

In her last letter, Concha seemed mad with joy. The
count was at San Sebastian, to take leave of the king and
queen,—an important diplomatic mission. Although he
was not "in line," they had chosen him as a representative of the most distinguished Spanish nobility to take
the Fleece to a petty prince of a little German state. The
poor gentleman, since he could not win the golden distinction, had to be contented with taking it to other men
with great pomp. Renovales saw the countess's hand in
all this. Her letters were radiant with joy. She was
going to be left alone with Darwin, for the noble gentleman would be absent for a long time. Married life with
the doctor, free from risk and disturbance!

Renovales read these letters merely out of curiosity;
they no longer awakened in him an intense or lasting
interest. He had grown accustomed to his situation as
a confidant; his desire was cooled by the frankness of
that woman who put herself in his power, telling him all
her secrets. Her body was the only thing he did not
know; her inner life he possessed as did none of her
lovers and he began to feel tired of this possession.
When he finished reading these letters, he would always

think the same thing. "She is mad. What do I care about her secrets?"

A week passed without any news from Biarritz. The papers spoke of the trip of the eminent Count of Alberca. He was already in Germany with all his retinue, getting ready to put the noble lambskin around the princely shoulders. Renovales smiled knowingly, without emotion, without envy, as he thought of the countess's silence. She had a great deal to take up her time, no doubt, since she was left alone.

Suddenly one afternoon he heard from her in the most unexpected manner. He was going out of his house, just at sunset, to take a walk on the heights of the Hippodrome along the Canalillo to view Madrid from the hill, when at the gate a messenger boy in a red coat handed him a letter. The painter started with surprise on recognizing Concha's handwriting. Four hasty, excited lines. She had just arrived that afternoon on the French express with her maid, Marie. She was alone at home. "Come, hurry. Serious news. I am dying." And the master hurried, though the announcement of her death did not make much impression on him. It was probably some trifle. He was used to the countess's exaggeration.

The spacious house of the Albercas was dark, dusty and echoing like all deserted buildings. The only servant who remained was the concierge. His children were playing beside the steps as if they did not know that the lady of the house had returned. Upstairs the furniture was wrapped in gray covers, the chandeliers were veiled with cheese-cloth, the house and glass of the mirrors were dull and lifeless under the coating of dust. Marie opened the door for him and led the way through the dark, musty rooms, the windows closed, and the curtains down, without any light except what came through the cracks.

In the reception hall he ran into several trunks, still unpacked, dropped and forgotten in the haste of arrival.

At the end of this pilgrimage, almost feeling his way through the deserted house, he saw a spot of light, the door of the countess's bedroom, the only room that was alive, lighted up by the glow of the setting sun. Concha was there beside the window, buried in a chair, her brow contracted, her glance lost in the distance, her face tinged with the orange of the dying light.

Seeing the painter she sprang to her feet, stretched out her arms and ran toward him, as if she were fleeing from pursuit.

"Mariano! Master! He has gone! He has left me forever!"

Her voice was a wail; she threw her arms around him, burying her face in his shoulder, wetting his beard with the tears that began to fall from her eyes drop by drop.

Renovales, under the impulse of his surprise, repelled her gently and he made her go back to her chair.

"Who has gone away? Who is it? Darwin?"

Yes; he. It was all over. The countess could hardly talk; a painful sob interrupted her words. She was enraged to see herself deserted and her pride trampled on; her whole body trembled. He had fled at the height of their happiness, when she thought that she was surest of him, when they enjoyed a liberty they had never known. He was tired of her; he still loved her,—as he said in a letter,—but he wanted to be free to continue his studies. He was grateful to her for her kindness, surfeited with so much love, and he fled to go into seclusion abroad and become a great man, not thinking any more about women. This was the purpose of the brief lines he had sent her on his disappearance. A lie, an absolute lie! She saw something else. The wretch had run away with a cocotte who was the cynosure of all eyes on the beach at Biarritz. An ugly thing, who had some vulgar charm about her, for all the men raved over her. That young "sport" was tired of respectable people. He probably was offended because she had not secured him the professorship, because he had not been made a deputy. Heavens! How was she to blame for her failure? Had she not done everything she could?

"Oh, Mariano. I know I am going to die. This is not love; I no longer care for him. I detest him! It is rage, indignation. I would like to get hold of the little whipper-snapper, to choke him. Think of all the foolish things I have done for him. Heavens! Where were my eyes!"

As soon as she discovered that she had been deserted, her only thought was to find her good friend, her counselor, her "brother," to go to Madrid, to see Renovales and tell him everything, everything! impelled by the necessity of confessing to him even secrets whose memory made her blush.

She had no one in the world who loved her disinterestedly, no one except the master, and with the panicky haste of a traveler who is lost at night, in the midst of a desert, she had run to him, seeking warmth and protection.

This longing for protection came back to her in the master's presence. She went to him again, clinging to him, sobbing in hysteric fear, as if she were surrounded by dangers.

"Master, you are all I have; you are my life! You won't ever leave me, will you? You will always be my brother?"

Renovales, bewildered at the unexpectedness of this scene, at the submission of that woman who had always repelled him and now suddenly clung to him, unable to

stand unless her arms were clasped about his neck, tried
to free himself from her arms.

After the first surprise, the old coldness came over
him. He was irritated at this proud despair that was
another's work.

The woman he had longed for, the woman of his
dreams came to him, seemed to give herself to him with
hysteric sobs, eager to overwhelm him, perhaps without
realizing what she was doing in the thoughtlessness of
her abnormal state; but he pushed her back, with sudden terror, hesitating and timid in the face of the deed,
pained that the realization of his dreams came, not volun-
tarily but under the influence of disappointment and de-
sertion.

Concha pressed close to him, eager to feel the protection of his powerful body.

"Master! My friend! You won't leave me! You are
so good!"

And closing her eyes that no longer wept, she kissed
his strong neck, and looked up with her eyes still moist,
seeking his face in the shadow. They could hardly see
each other; the room was dim with mysterious twilight,—
all its objects indistinct as in a dream, the dangerous
hour that had attracted them for the first time in the
seclusion of the studio.

Suddenly she drew away in terror, fleeing from him,
taking refuge in the gloom, pursued by his eager hands.

"No, not that. We'll be sorry for it! Friends!
Nothing more than friends and always!"

Her voice, as she said this, was sincere, but weak, faint,
the voice of a victim who resists and has not the strength
to defend himself.

When the painter awakened it was night. The light
from the street lamps shone through the window with a
distant, reddish glow.

He shivered with a sensation of cold, as if he were emerging from under an enticing wave where he had lain, he could not remember how long. He felt weak, humiliated, with the anxiety of a child who has done something wrong.

Concha was sobbing. What folly! It had been against her will; she knew they would be sorry for it. But she was the first to recover her calmness. Her outline rose on the bright background of the window. She called the painter who stood in the shadow, ashamed.

"After all, there was no escape," she said firmly. "It was a dangerous game and it could not end in any other way. Now I know that I cared for you; that you are the only man for whom I can care."

Renovales was beside her. Their two forms made a single outline on the bright background of the window, in a supreme embrace as though they desired to take refuge in each other.

Her hands gently parted the heavy locks that hid the master's forehead. She gazed at him rapturously. Then she kissed his lips with an endless caress, whispering:

"Mariano, dear. I love you, I worship you. I will be your slave. Don't ever leave me. I will seek you on my knees. You don't know how I will care for you. You shall not escape me. You wanted it,—you ugly darling, you big giant, my love."

V

ONE afternoon at the end of October, Renovales noticed that his friend Cotoner was rather worried.

The master was jesting with him, making him tell about his labors as restorer of paintings in the old church. He had come back fatter and merrier, with a greasy, priestly luster. According to Renovales he had brought back all the health of the clerics. The bishop's table with its succulent abundance was a sweet memory for Cotoner. He extolled it and described it, praising those good gentlemen who, like himself, lived free from passion with no other voluptuousness in life than a refined appetite. The master laughed at the thought of the simplicity of those priests who in the afternoon, after the choir, formed a group around Cotoner's scaffold, following the movements of his hands with wondering eyes; at the respect of the attendants and other servants of the episcopal palace, hanging on Don José's words, astonished to find such modesty in an artist who was a friend of cardinals and had studied in Rome.

When the master saw him so serious and silent that afternoon after luncheon he wanted to know what was worrying him. Had they complained of his restoration? Was his money gone? Cotoner shook his head. It was not his affairs; he was worrying over Josephina's condition. Had he not noticed her?

Renovales shrugged his shoulders. It was the usual trouble: neurasthenia, diabetes, all those chronic ailments of which she did not want to be cured, refusing to obey the physicians. She was thinner, but her nerves seemed calmer; she cried less; she maintained a sad silence, simply wanting to be alone and stay in a corner, staring into space.

Cotoner shook his head again. Renovales' optimism was not to be wondered at.

"You are leading a strange life, Mariano. Since I came back from my trip, you are a different man; I wouldn't know you. Once, you could not live without painting and now you spend weeks at a time without taking up a brush. You smoke, sing, walk up and down the studio and all at once rush off, out of the house and go—well. I know where, and perhaps your wife suspects it. You seem to be having a good time, master. The deuce take the rest! But, man alive, come down from the clouds. See what is around you; have some charity."

And good Cotoner complained bitterly of the life the master was leading—disturbed by sudden impatience and hasty departures, from which he returned absent-minded, with a faint smile on his lips and a vague look in his eyes, as if he still relished the feast of memories he carried in his mind.

The old painter seemed alarmed at Josephina's increasing delicacy, acute consumption that still found matter to destroy in her organism wasted by years of illness. The poor little woman coughed constantly and this cough, that was not dry but prolonged and violent, alarmed Cotoner.

"The doctors ought to see her again."

"The doctors!" exclaimed Renovales, "What's the use? A whole medical faculty has been here and to no avail. She doesn't mind them; she refuses everything, perhaps to annoy me, to oppose me. There's no danger; you don't know her. Weak and small as she is, she will outlive you and me."

His voice shook with wrath, as if he could not stand the atmosphere of that house where the only distractions he found were the pleasant memories that took him away from it.

Cotoner's insistence finally forced him to call a doctor who was a friend of his.

Josephina was provoked, divining the cause of their anxiety. She felt strong. It was nothing but a cold; the coming of winter. And in her glances at the artist there was reproach and insult for his attention which she regarded as hypocrisy.

When the doctor and the painter returned to the studio after the examination of the patient and stood face to face, the former hesitated as if he was afraid to formulate his ideas. He could not say anything with certainty; it was easy to make a mistake in regard to that weak system that maintained itself only by its extraordinary reserve power. Then he had recourse to the usual evasive measure of his profession. He advised him to take her away from Madrid, a change of air,—a change of life.

Renovales objected. Where could she go, now that winter was beginning, when at the height of summer she had wanted to come home? The doctor shrugged his shoulders and wrote out a prescription, revealing in his expression the desire to write something, not to go away without leaving a piece of paper as a trace. He explained various symptoms to the husband in order that he might observe them in the patient and he went away shrugging his shoulders again with a gesture that revealed indecision and dejection.

Pshaw! Who knows? Perhaps! The system sometimes has unexpected reactions, wonderful reserve power to resist disease.

This enigmatic consolation alarmed Renovales. He spied on his wife, studying her cough, watching her closely when she did not see him. They no longer spent the night together. Since Milita's marriage, the father occupied her room. They had broken the slavery of the common bed that tormented their rest. Renovales made up for this departure by going into Josephina's chamber every morning.

"Did you have a good night? Do you want something?"

His wife's eyes greeted him with hostility.

"Nothing."

And she accompanied this brief statement by turning over in the bed, disdainfully, with her back to the master.

The painter received these evidences of hostility with quiet resignation. It was his duty; perhaps she might die! But this possibility of death did not stir him; it left him cold and he was angry at himself, as if two distinct personalities existed within him. He reproached himself for his cruelty, his icy indifference before the invalid who now produced in him only a passing remorse.

One afternoon at the Alberca woman's house, after one of their daring meetings with which they defied the holy calm of the noble, who had now returned from his trip, the painter spoke timidly of his wife.

"I shall have to come less; don't be surprised. Josephina is very ill."

"Very?" asked Concha.

And in the flash of her glance, Renovales thought he saw something familiar, a blue gleam that had danced before him in the darkness of the night with infernal glow, troubling his conscience.

"No, maybe it isn't anything. I don't believe there is any danger."

He felt forced to lie. It consoled him to discount her illness. He felt that, by this voluntary deceit, he was relieving himself of the anxiety that goaded him. It was the lie of the man who justifies himself by pretending not to know the depth of the harm he has caused.

"It isn't anything," he said to his daughter, who, greatly alarmed at her mother's appearance, came to spend every night with her. "Just a cold. It will disappear as soon as good weather comes."

He had a fire in every fireplace in the house; the rooms were as hot as a furnace. He declared loudly, without any show of excitement, that his wife was merely suffering from a slight cold, and as he spoke with such assurance, a strange voice seemed to cry within him: "You lie, she is dying; she is dying and you know it."

The symptoms of which the doctor had spoken began to appear with ominous regularity in fatal succession. At first he noticed only a constant high fever that seemed to grow worse with severe chills at the end of the afternoon. Then he observed sweats that were terrifying in their frequency—sweats at night that left the print of her body on the sheets. And that poor body, which grew more fragile, more like a skeleton, as if the fire of the fever were devouring the last particle of fat and muscle, was left without any other covering and protection than the skin, and that too seemed to be melting away. She coughed frequently; at all hours of the day and night her painful hacking disturbed the silence of the house. She complained of a continual pain in the lower part of her chest. Her daughter made her eat by dint of coaxing, lifting the spoon to her mouth, as if she were a child. But coughing and nausea made nutrition impossible. Her tongue was dry; she complained of an infernal thirst that was devouring her.

Thus passed a month. Renovales, in his optimistic mood, strove to believe that her illness would not last long.

"She is not dying, Pepe," he would say in a convinced

tone, as if he were disposed to quarrel with anyone who opposed this statement. "She is not dying, doctor. You don't think she is, do you?"

The doctor would answer with his everlasting shrug. "Perhaps,—it's possible." And as the patient refused to submit to an internal examination, he was forced to inquire of the daughter and husband about the symptoms.

In spite of her extreme emaciation, some parts of her body seemed to be undergoing an abnormal swelling. Renovales questioned the doctor frankly. What did he think of these symptoms? And the doctor bowed his head. He did not know. They must wait: Nature has surprises. But afterward, with sudden decision, he pretended that he wanted to write a prescription, in order that he might talk with the husband alone in his working studio.

"To tell you the truth, Renovales, this pitiful comedy is getting tiresome. It may be all right for the others but you are a man. It is acute consumption; perhaps a matter of days, perhaps a matter of a few months; but she is dying and I know no remedy. If you want to, get some one else."

"She is dying!" Renovales was dazed with surprise as if the possibility of this outcome had never occurred to him. "She is dying!" And when the doctor had gone away, with a firmer step than usual, as if he had freed himself of a weight, the painter repeated the words to himself, without their producing any other effect than leaving him abstracted in senseless stupidity. She is dying! But was it really possible that that little woman could die, who had so weighed on his life and whose weakness filled him with fear?

Suddenly he found himself walking up and down the studio, repeating aloud,

"She is dying! She is dying!"

He said it to himself in order that he might make himself feel sorry, and break out into sobs of grief, but he remained mute.

Josephina was going to die—and he was calm. He wanted to weep; it seemed to him a duty. He blinked, swelling out his chest, holding his breath, trying to take in the whole meaning of his sorrow; but his eyes remained dry; his lungs breathed the air with pleasure; his thoughts, hard and refractory, did not shudder with any painful image. It was an exterior grief that found expression only in words, gestures and excited walking, his interior continued its old stolidness, as if the certainty of that death had congealed it in peaceful indifference.

The shame of his villainy tormented him. The same instinct that forces ascetics to submit themselves to mortal punishments for their imaginary sins dragged him with the power of remorse to the sick chamber. He would not leave the room; he would face her scornful silence; he would stay with her till the end, forgetting sleep and hunger. He felt that he must purify himself by some noble, generous sacrifice from this blindness of soul that now was terrifying.

Milita no longer spent the nights caring for her mother and would go home, somewhat to the discomfiture of her husband, who had been rather pleased at this unexpected return to a bachelor's life.

Renovales did not sleep. After midnight when Cotoner went away he walked in silence through the brilliantly lighted rooms; he prowled around the chamber— entered it to see Josephina in bed, sweating, shaken from time to time by a fit of coughing or in a deathlike lethargy, so thin and small that the bedclothes hardly showed the childlike outline of her body. Then the master passed the rest of the night in an armchair, smoking, his eyes staring but his brain drowsy with sleep.

His thoughts were far away. There was no use in feeling ashamed of his cruelty; he seemed bewitched by a mysterious power that was superior to his remorse. He forgot the sick woman; he wondered what Concha was doing at that time; he saw her in fancy; he remembered her words, her caresses; he thought of their nights of abandon. And when, with a violent effort, he threw off these dreams, in expiation he would go to the door of the sick chamber and listen to her labored breathing, putting on a gloomy face, but unable to weep or feel the sadness he longed to feel.

After two months of illness, Josephina could no longer stay in bed. Her daughter would lift her out of it without any effort as if she were a feather, and she would sit in a chair,—small, insignificant, unrecognizable, her face so emaciated that its only features seemed to be the deep hollows of her eyes and her nose, sharp as the edge of a knife.

Cotoner could hardly keep back the tears when he saw her.

"There isn't anything left of her!" he would say as he went away. "No one would know her!"

Her harrowing cough scattered a deathly poison about her. White foam came to her lips where it seemed to harden in the corners. Her eyes grew larger, they took on a strange glow as if they saw through persons and things. Oh, those eyes! What a shudder of terror they awakened in Renovales!

One afternoon they fell on him, with the intense, searching glance that had always terrified him. They were eyes that pierced his forehead, that laid bare his thoughts.

They were alone; Milita had gone home; Cotoner was

sleeping in a chair in the studio. The sick woman seemed more animated, eager to talk, looking on her husband with a sort of pity as he sat beside her, almost at her feet.

She was going to die; she was certain of death. And a last revolt of life that recoils from the end, the horror of the unknown, made the tears rise to her eyes.

Renovales protested violently, trying to conceal his deceit by his shouts. Die? She must not think of that! She would live; she still had before her many years of happy existence.

She smiled as if she pitied him. She could not be deceived; her eyes penetrated farther than his; she divined the impalpable, the invisible that hovered about her. She spoke weakly but with that inexplicable solemnity that is characteristic of a voice that emits its last sounds, of a soul that unbosoms itself for the last time.

"I shall die, Mariano, sooner than you think, later than I desire. I shall die and you will be free."

He! He desire her death! His surprise and remorse made him jump to his feet, wave his arms in angry protest, writhe, as if a pair of invisible hands had just laid him bare with a rude wrench.

"Josephina, don't rave. Calm yourself. For God's sake don't talk such nonsense!"

She smiled with a painful, horrible expression, but immediately her poor face became beautiful with the serenity of one who is departing this life without hallucinations or delirium, in perfect mental poise. She spoke to him with the immense sympathy, the superhuman compassion of one who contemplates the wretched stream of life, departing from its current, already touching with her feet the shores of eternal shadow, of eternal peace.

"I should not want to go away without telling you. I die knowing everything. Do not move; do not protest.

You know the power I have over you. More than once
I have seen you watching me in terror, so easily do I read
your thoughts. For years I have been convinced that
all was over between us. We have lived like good creatures of God—eating together, sleeping together, helping
each other in our needs. But I peered within you; I
looked at your heart. Nothing! Not a memory, not a
spark of love. I have been your woman, the good companion who cares for the house, and relieves a man of
the petty cares of life. You have worked hard to surround me with comforts, in order that I might be contented and not disturb you. But Love? Never. Many
people live as we have—many of them; almost all. I
could not; I thought that life was something different
and I am not sorry to go away. Don't go into a rage;
don't shout. You aren't to blame, poor Mariano— It
was a mistake for us to marry."

She excused him gently with a kindness that seemed
not of this world, generously passing over the cruelty
and selfishness of a life she was about to leave. Men
like him were exceptional; they ought to live alone, by
themselves, like those great trees that absorb all the life
from the ground and do not allow a single plant to grow
in the space which their roots reach. She was not strong
enough to stand isolation; in order to live she must have
the shadow of tenderness, the certainty of being loved.
She ought to have married a man like other men; a
simple being like herself, whose only longings were modest and commonplace. The painter had dragged her into
his extraordinary path out of the easy, well-beaten roads
that the rest follow and she was falling by the wayside,
old in the prime of her youth, broken because she had
gone with him in this journey which was beyond her
strength.

Renovales was walking about with ceaseless protests.

"Why, what nonsense you are talking! You are raving! I have always loved you, Josephina. I love you now."

Her eyes suddenly became hard. A flash of anger crossed their pupils.

"Stop; don't lie. I know of a pile of letters that you have in your studio, hidden behind the books in your library.. I have read them one by one. I have been following them as they came; I discovered your hiding place when you had only three of them. You know that I see through you; that I have a power over you, that you can hide nothing from me. I know your love affairs."

Renovales felt his ears buzzing, the floor slipping from under his feet. What astounding witchcraft! Even the letters so carefully hidden had been discovered by that woman's divining instinct!

"It's a lie!" he cried vehemently to conceal his agitation. "It isn't love! If you have read them, you know what it is as well as I; just friendship; the letters of a friend who is somewhat crazy."

The sick woman smiled sadly. At first it was friendship—even less than that, the perverse amusement of a flighty woman who liked to play with a celebrated man, exciting in him the enthusiasm of youth. She knew her childhood companion; she was sure it would not go any farther; and so she pitied the poor man in the midst of his mad love. But afterward something extraordinary had certainly happened; something that she could not explain and which had upset all of her calculations. Now her husband and Concha were lovers.

"Do not deny it; it is useless. It is this certainty that is killing me. I realized it when I saw you distracted, with a happy smile as if you were relishing your thoughts. I realized it in the merry songs you sang when you awoke in the morning, in the perfume with which you were impregnated and which followed you everywhere. I did not need to find any more letters. The odor around you, that perfume of infidelity, of sin, which always accompanied you, was enough. You, poor man, came home thinking that everything was left outside the door, and that odor follows you, denounces you; I think I can still perceive it."

And her nostrils dilated, as she breathed with a pained expression, closing her eyes as though she wished to escape the images which that perfume called up in her. Her husband persisted in his denials, now that he was convinced that she had no other proof of his infidelity. A lie! An hallucination!

"No, Mariano," murmured the sick woman. "She is within you; she fills your head; from here I can see her. Once a thousand mad fancies occupied her place,—illusions of your taste, naked women, a wantonness that was your religion. Now it is she who fills it. It is your desire incarnated. Go on and be happy. I am going away—there is no place for me in the world."

She was silent for a moment and the tears came to her eyes again at the memory of the first years of their life together.

"No one has cared for you as I have, Mariano," she said with tender regret. "I look on you now as a stranger, without affection and without hate. And still, there was never a woman who loved her husband so passionately."

"I worship you. Josephina, I love you just as I did when we first met each other. Do you remember?"

But in spite of the emotion he pretended to show, his voice had a false ring.

"Don't try to bluff, Mariano; it is useless; everything

is over. You do not care for me nor have I either any of the old feeling."

In her face there was an expression of wonder, of surprise; she seemed terror-stricken at her own calmness that made her forgive thus indifferently the man who had caused her so much suffering. In her fancy, she saw a wide garden, flowers that seemed immortal and they were withering and falling with the advent of winter. Then her thoughts went beyond, over the chill of death. The snow was melting; the sun was shining once more; the new spring was coming with its court of love and the dry branches were growing green once more with another life.

"Who knows!" murmured the sick woman with her eyes closed. "Perhaps, after I am dead, you will remember me. Perhaps you will care for me then, and be grateful to one who loved you so. We want a thing when it is lost."

The invalid was silent, exhausted by such an effort; she relapsed into that lethargy which for her took the place of rest. Renovales, after this conversation, felt his vile inferiority beside his wife. She knew everything and forgave him. She had followed the course of his love, letter by letter, look by look, seeing in his smiles the memory of his faithlessness. And she was silent! She was dying without a protest! And he did not fall at her feet to beg her forgiveness! And he remained unmoved, without a tear, without a sigh!

He was afraid to stay alone with her. Milita came back to stay at the house to care for her mother. The master took refuge in his studio; he wanted to forget in work the body that was dying under the same roof.

But in vain he poured colors on his palette and took up brushes and prepared canvases. He did nothing but daub; he could make no progress, as if he had forgotten his art. He kept turning his head anxiously, thinking that Josephina was going to enter suddenly, to continue that interview in which she had laid bare the greatness of her soul and the baseness of his own. He felt forced to return to her apartments, to go on tiptoe to the door of the chamber, in order to be sure that she was there.

Her emaciation was frightful; it had no limits. When it seemed that it must stop, it still surprised them with new shrinking, as if after the disappearance of her flesh, her poor skeleton was melting away.

Sometimes she was tormented with delirium, and her daughter, holding back her tears, approved of the extravagant trips she planned, of her proposals to go far away to live with Milita in a garden, where they would find no men; where there were no painters—no painters.

She lived about two weeks. Renovales, with cruel selfishness, was anxious to rest, complaining of this abnormal existence. If she must die, why did she not end it as soon as possible, and restore the whole house to tranquillity!

The end came one afternoon when the master, lying on a couch in his studio, was re-reading the tender complaints of a scented little letter. So long since she had seen him! How was the patient getting on? She knew that his duty was there; people would talk if he came to see her. But this separation was hard!

He did not have a chance to finish it. Milita came into the studio, in her eyes that expression of horror and fright, which the presence of death, the touch of his passage, always inspires, even if his arrival has been expected.

Her voice came breathlessly, broken. Mamma was talking with her; she was amusing her with the hope of a trip in the near future,—and all at once a hoarse sound,

—her head bent forward before it fell onto her shoulder —a moment—nothing—just like a little bird.

Renovales ran to the bedroom, bumping into his friend Cotoner who came out of the dining-room, running too. They saw her in an armchair, shrunken, wilted, in the deathly abandon that converts the body into a limp mass. All was over.

Milita had to catch her father, to hold him up. She had to be the one who kept her calmness and energy at the critical moment. Renovales let his daughter lead him; he rested his face on her shoulder, with sublime, dramatic grief, with beautiful, artistic despair, still holding absent-mindedly in his hand the letter of the countess.

"Courage, Mariano," said poor Cotoner, his voice choked with tears. "We must be men. Milita, take your father to the studio. Don't let him see her."

The master let his daughter guide him, sighing deeply, trying in vain to weep. The tears would not come. He could not concentrate his attention; a voice within him was distracting him,—the voice of temptation.

She was dead and he was free. He would go on his way, light-hearted, master of himself, relieved of troublesome hindrances. Before him lay life with all its joys, love without a fear or a scruple; glory with its sweet returns.

Life was going to begin again.

PART III

I

Until the beginning of the following winter Renovales did not return to Madrid. The death of his wife
had left him stunned, as if he doubted its reality, as if he
felt strange at finding himself alone and master of his
actions. Cotoner, seeing that he had no ambition for
work and would lie on the couch in the studio with a
blank expression on his face, as if he were in a waking
dream, interpreted his condition as a deep, silent grief.
Besides, it irritated him that as soon as Josephina was
dead, the countess began to come to the house frequently to see the master and her dear Milita.

"You ought to go away,"—the old artist advised.
"You are free; you will be just as well off anywhere as
here. What you need is a long journey; that will take
your mind off your trouble."

And Renovales started on his journey with the eagerness of a school-boy, free for the first time from the
vigilance of a family. Alone, rich, master of his actions, he believed that he was the happiest being on earth.
His daughter had her husband, a family of her own; he
saw himself in welcome seclusion, without cares or duties, without any other ties than the constant letters of
Concha, which met him on his travels. Oh, happy freedom!

He lived in Holland, studying its museums, which he
had never seen: then, with the caprice of a wandering

bird, he went down to Italy where he enjoyed several months of easy life, without any work, visiting studios, receiving the honors due a famous master, in the same places where once he had struggled, poor and unknown. Then he moved to Paris, finally attracted by the countess, who was spending the summer at Biarritz with her husband.

Concha's epistolary style grew more urgent. She had numerous objections to a prolongation of the period of their separation. He must come back; he had traveled enough. She could not stand it without seeing him; she loved him; she could not live without him. Besides, as a last resource, she spoke to him of her husband, the count, who, in his eternal blindness, joined in his wife's requests asking her to invite the artist to spend a while at their house in Biarritz. The poor painter must be very sad in his bereavement and the kindly nobleman insisted on consoling him in his loneliness. In his house, they would divert him; they would be a new family for him.

The painter lived for a great part of the summer and all the autumn in the welcome atmosphere of that home which seemed created for him. The servants respected him, seeing in him the true master. The countess, delirious after his long absence, was so reckless that the artist had to restrain her, urging her to be prudent. The noble Count of Alberca was unceasing in his sympathy. Poor friend! Deprived of his companion! And by his expression he shared the horror he felt at the possibility of being left a widower, without that wife who made him so happy.

At the beginning of winter Renovales returned to his house. He did not experience the slightest emotion on entering the three great studios, on passing through those rooms, which seemed more icy, larger, more hollow, now that they were stirred by no other steps than his own.

He could not believe that a year had passed. All was the same as if he had been absent for only a few days. Cotoner had taken good care of the house, setting to work the concierge and his wife and the old servant who had charge of cleaning the studios,—the only servants that Renovales had kept. There was no dust, none of the close atmosphere of a house that has long been closed. Everything appeared bright and clean, as if life had not been interrupted in that house. The sun and air had been pouring in the windows, driving out that atmosphere of sickness which Renovales had left when he went away and in which he fancied he could feel the trace of the invisible garb of death.

It was a new house, like the one he had known before in form, but as fresh as a recently constructed building.

Outside of his studio nothing reminded him of his dead wife. He avoided going into her chamber; he did not even ask who had the key. He slept in the room that had formerly been his daughter's in a small, iron bed, delighted to lead a modest, sober life in that princely mansion.

He took breakfast in the dining room at one end of the table, on a napkin, oppressed by the size and luxury of the room which now seemed vast and useless. He looked at the chair beside the fireplace, where the dead woman had often sat. That chair with its open arms seemed to be waiting for her trembling, bird-like little body. But the painter did not feel any emotion. He could not even remember Josephina's face exactly. She had changed so much! The last, that skeleton-like mask, was the one he recalled the best, but he thrust it aside, with the selfishness of a strong, happy man, who does not want to sadden his life with unpleasant memories.

He did not see her picture anywhere in the house. She seemed to have evaporated forever without leaving the

least trace of her body on the walls that had so often
supported her tottering steps, on the stairways that hardly felt the weight of her feet. Nothing; she was quite
forgotten. Within Renovales, the only trace of the long
years of their union that remained was an unpleasant
feeling, an annoying memory that made him relish all
the more his new existence.

His first days in the solitude of the house brought new,
intense joys. After luncheon he would lie down on the
couch in the studio, watching the blue spirals of cigar
smoke. Complete liberty! Alone in the world! Life
wholly to himself, without any care or fear. He could
go and come without a pair of eyes spying on his actions, without being reproached with bitter words. That
little door of the studio, which he used to watch in terror, no longer opened, to let in his enemy. He could
close it, shutting out the world; he could open it and
summon in a noisy, scandalous stream, all that he fancied—hosts of naked beauties, to paint in a wild bacchanalian rout, strange, black-eyed Oriental girls to dance
in morbid abandon on the rugs of the studio, all the disordered illusions of his desire—the monstrous feasts of
fancy which he had dreamed of in his days of servitude.
He was not sure where he could find all this, he was not
very eager to look for it. But the consciousness that he
could realize it without any obstacle was enough.

This consciousness of his absolute freedom, instead
of urging him into action, kept him in a state of calm,
satisfied that he could do everything, without the least desire to try anything. Formerly he used to rage, complaining of his fetters. What things he would do if he
were free! What scandals he would cause with his daring! Oh, if he only were not married to a slave of convention who tried to apply rules to his art with the same

formality which she had for her calls and her household expenses!

And now that the slave of convention was gone, the artist remained in sleepy comfort, looking like a timid lover, at the canvases he had begun a year before, at his neglected palette, saying with false energy, "This is the last day. To-morrow I will begin."

And the next day, noon came, and with it luncheon, before Renovales had taken up a brush. He read foreign papers, magazines on art, looking up, with professional interest, what the famous painters of Europe were exhibiting or working on. He received a call from some of his humble companions, and in their presence he lamented the insolence of the younger generation, their disrespectful attacks, with the surliness of a famous artist who is getting old and thinks that talent has died out with him and that no one can take his place. Then the drowsiness of digestion seized him, as it did Cotoner, and he submitted to the bliss of short naps, the happiness of doing nothing. His daughter—all the family he had —would receive more than she expected at his death. He had worked enough. Painting, like all the arts, was a pretty deceit, for the advancement of which men strove as if they were mad, until they hated it like death. What folly! It was better to keep calm, enjoying your own life, intoxicated with the simple animal joys, living for life's sake. What good were a few more pictures in those huge palaces filled with canvases, disfigured by the centuries, in which hardly a single stroke was left as the author had made it? What good did it do the human race, which changes its dwelling place every dozen centuries and has seen the proud works of man, built of marble or granite, fall in ruins,—if a certain Renovales produced a few beautiful toys of cloth and colors, which a cigar stub could destroy, or a puff of wind, a drop of water leaking through the wall, might ruin in a few years?

But this pessimistic attitude disappeared when some one called him "Illustrious Master," or when he saw his name in a paper, and a pupil or admirer manifested an interest in his work.

At present he was resting. He had not yet recovered from the shock. Poor Josephina! But he was going to work a great deal; he felt a new strength for works greater than any that he had thus far produced. And after these exclamations, he would be seized with a mad desire for work and would enumerate the pictures he had in mind, dwelling upon their originality. They were bold problems in color, new technical methods that had occurred to him. But these plans never passed the limits of speech, they never reached the brush. The springs of his will, once vibrant and vigorous, seemed broken or rusted. He did not suffer, he did not desire. Death had taken away his fever for work, his artistic restlessness, leaving him in the limbo of comfort and tranquillity.

In the afternoon, when he succeeded in throwing off his comfortable torpor, he went to see his daughter, if she was in Madrid, for she very frequently went with her husband on his automobile trips. Then he ended the afternoon at the Albercas', where he often stayed till midnight.

He dined there almost every day. The count, accustomed to his society, seemed as eager to see him as his wife. He spoke enthusiastically of the portrait which Renovales was painting of him to go with Concha's. He would make more progress when he secured some insignia of foreign orders that were still lacking in his catalogue of honors. And the artist felt a twinge of remorse as he listened to the good gentleman's simplicity, while his wife, with mad recklessness, caressed him with

her eyes, leaned toward him as if she were on the point
of falling into his arms.

Then, as soon as the husband went away, she would
throw her arms about him, hungry for him, defying the
curiosity of the servants. Love that was threatened with
dangers seemed sweeter to her. And the artist took
pride in letting her worship him. He, who at first was
the one who implored and pursued, assumed now an air
of passive superiority, accepting Concha's homage.

Lacking enthusiasm for work, in order to keep up his
reputation Renovales took refuge in the official honors
which are granted to respected masters. He put off till
the next day the new work, the great work that was to
call forth new cries of admiration over his name. He
would paint his famous picture of Phryne on a beach,
when summer came, and he could retire to the solitary
shore, taking with him the perfect beauty to serve as his
model. Perhaps he could persuade the countess. Who
knows! She smiled with satisfaction every time she
heard from his lips the praise of her beauty. But meanwhile the master demanded that people should remember
his name for his earlier works, that they should admire him for what he had already produced.

He was irritated at the papers, which extolled the
younger generation, remembered him only to mention
him in passing, like a consecrated glory, like a man who
was dead and had his pictures in the Museo del Prado.
He was gnawed with dumb anger, like an actor who is
tortured with envy, seeing the stage occupied by others.

He wanted to work; he was going to work immediately. But as time passed, he felt an increasing laziness, which incapacitated him for work, a numbness in
his hands, which he concealed even from his most intimate friends, ashamed when he recalled his lightness of
touch in the old days.

"This will not last," he said to himself with the confidence of a man who does not doubt his ability.

In one of his fanciful moods, he compared himself with a dog, restless, fierce and aggressive when he is tormented with hunger, but gentle and peaceable when he is surrounded with comforts. He needed his periods of greed and restlessness, when he desired everything, when he could not find peace for his work, and in the midst of his marital troubles attacked the canvas as if it were an enemy, hurling colors on it furiously, in slaps of light. Even after he was rich and famous, he had had something to long for. "If I only were free! If I were master of my time! If I lived alone, without a family, without cares; as a true artist should live!" And now his wishes were fulfilled, he had nothing to hope for, but he was a victim of laziness that amounted to exhaustion, absolutely without desire, as if only wrath and restlessness were for him the internal goad of inspiration.

The longing for fame tormented him; as the days went by and his name was not mentioned, he believed that he had come to an obscure death. He fancied that the youths turned their backs on him, to look in the opposite direction, storing him away among the respected dead, admiring other masters. His artistic pride made him seek opportunities for notoriety, with the guilelessness of a tyro. He, who scoffed so at the official honors and the "sheepfold" of the academies, suddenly remembered that several years before, after one of his successes, they had elected him a member of the Academy of Fine Arts.

Cotoner was astonished to see the importance he began to attach to this unsolicited distinction, at which he had always laughed.

"That was a boy's joking," said the master gravely.

"Life cannot always be taken as a laughing matter. We must be serious, Pepe; we are getting on in years, and we must not always make fun of things that are essentially respectable."

Besides, he charged himself with rudeness. Those worthy personages, whom he had often compared with all kinds of animals, no doubt thought it strange that the years went by without his caring to occupy his seat. He must go to the academic reception. And Cotoner, at his bidding, attended to all the details, from taking the news to those worthies, in order that they might set the date for the function, to arranging the speech of the new Academician. For Renovales learned with some misgiving that he must read a speech. He, accustomed to handling the brush and poorly trained in his childhood, took up the pen with timidity, and even in his letters to the Alberca woman preferred to represent his passionate phrases with amusing pictures, to embodying them in words.

The old Bohemian got him out of this difficulty. He knew his Madrid well. The secrets of the world which are detailed in the newspapers had no mysteries for him. Renovales should have as magnificent a speech as any one.

And one afternoon he brought to the studio a certain Isidro Maltrana,* a diminutive, ugly young fellow with a huge head, and an air of self-satisfaction and boldness that disgusted Renovales from the very first. He was well dressed but the lapels of his coat were dirty with ashes, and its collar was strewn with dandruff. The painter observed that he smelt of wine. At first he pompously styled him master, but after a few words he called him by name with disconcerting familiarity. He

* The life of this character is the theme of *La Horda,* by the same author.

moved about the studio as if it were his own, as if he had spent his whole life in it, indifferent to its beautiful decorations.

It would not be any trouble for him to undertake the preparation of a speech. That was his specialty. Academic receptions and works for members of Congress were his best field. He understood that the master needed him—a painter!

And Renovales, who was beginning to find this Maltrana fellow attractive in spite of his insolence, drew himself up to his full height in the majesty of his fame. If it was a question of doing a picture for admission, he was the man. But a speech!

"Agreed: you shall have the speech," said Maltrana. "It's an easy matter, I know the recipe. We shall speak of the holy traditions of the past, we shall despise certain daring innovations on the part of the inexperienced youth, which were perfectly proper twenty years ago, when you were beginning, but which now are out of place. Do you care for a thrust at modernism?"

Renovales smiled, enchanted at the frankness with which this young fellow spoke of his task, and he moved one hand to suggest a balance. "Man alive! Like this. A just mean is what we want."

"Of course, Renovales; flatter the old men and not quarrel with the young. You are a real master. You will be pleased with my work."

With the calmness of a shopkeeper, before the artist had a chance to speak of the charge, he broached the matter. It would be two thousand *reales;* he had already told Cotoner. The low tariff; the one he set for people he liked.

"A man must live, Renovales. I have a son."

And his voice grew serious as he said this; his face,

ugly and cynical, became noble for a moment, reflecting the cares of paternal love.

"A son, dear master, for whom I do anything that turns up. If it is necessary I will steal. He is the only thing I have in the world. His mother died in misery in the hospital. I dreamt of being something, but you can't think of nonsense when you have a baby. Between the hope of being famous and the certainty of eating—eating is the first."

But his tenderness was not of long duration. He recovered the cold, mercenary expression of a man who goes through life in an armor of cynicism, disillusioned by misfortune, setting a price on all his acts. They agreed on the sum; he should receive it when he handed over the speech.

"And if you print it, as I hope," he said as he went away, "I will read the proof without any extra charge. Of course that is a special favor to you, because I am one of your admirers."

Renovales spent several weeks in the preparations for his reception, as if it were the most important event in his life. The countess also took a great interest in the matter. She would see to it that it was a distinguished function, something like the receptions of the French Academy, described in the papers or in novels. All of her friends would be present. The great painter would read his speech, the cynosure of a hundred interested eyes, amid the fluttering of fans and the buzz of conversation. An immense success which would enrage many artists who were eager to get a foothold in high society.

A few days before the function, Cotoner handed him a bundle of papers. It was a copy of the speech,—in a fair hand; it was already paid for. And Renovales, with the instinct of an actor anxious to make a good show, spent an afternoon, striding from studio to studio, with the manuscript in one hand and making energetic gestures with the other, while he read the paragraphs aloud. That impudent Maltrana was gifted! It was a work that filled the simple artist with enthusiasm, in his ignorance of everything except printing, a series of glorious trumpet blasts, in which were scattered names, many names; appreciations in tremulous rhetoric, historical summaries, so well rounded, so complete that it seemed as though mankind had been living since the beginning of the world with no other thought than Renovales' speech, and judging its acts in order that he might give them a definite interpretation.

The artist felt a thrill of elevation as he repeated in eloquent succession Greek names, many of which were mere sounds to him, for he was not certain whether they were great sculptors or tragic poets. Again, he experienced a sensation of self-satisfaction when he encountered the names of Dante and Shakespeare. He knew that they had not painted, but they ought to appear in every speech which was worthy of respect. And when he came to the paragraphs on modern art, he seemed to touch terra firma, and smiled with a superior air. Maltrana did not know much about that subject; superficial appreciation of a layman; but he wrote well, very well; he could not have done better himself. And he studied his speech, till he could repeat whole paragraphs by heart, paying particular attention to the pronunciation of the difficult names, taking lessons from his most cultured friends.

"It is for appearance's sake," he said naïvely. "It is because I don't want people to poke fun at me, even if I am only a painter."

The day of the reception he had luncheon long before noon. He scarcely touched the food; this ceremony,

which he had never seen, made him rather worried. To
his anxiety was added the irritation he always felt when
he had to attend to the care of his person.

His long years of married life had accustomed him to
neglect all the trivial, everyday needs of life. If he had
to appear in different clothes than usual, the hands of
his wife and daughter deftly arranged them for him.
Even at the times of greatest ill-feeling, when he and
Josephina hardly spoke to each other, he noticed around
him the scrupulous order of that excellent housekeeper
who removed all obstacles from his way, relieving him
of the ordinary cares of life.

Cotoner was away; the servant had gone to the countess's to take her some invitations which she had asked
for, at the last minute, for some friends. Renovales decided to dress alone. His son-in-law and daughter were
going to come for him at two. López de Sosa had insisted on taking him to the Academy in his car, seeking, no doubt, by this a little ray of the splendor of official glory that was to be showered on his father-in-
law.

Renovales dressed himself, after struggling with the
many difficulties that arose from his lack of habit. He
was as awkward as a child without his mother's help.
When at last he looked at himself in the mirror, with
his dress coat on and his cravat neatly tied, he heaved a
sigh of relief. At last! Now the insignia—the ribbon.
Where could he find those honorary trinkets? Since
Milita's wedding he had not had them on, the poor departed had put them away. Where could he find them?
And hastily, fearing the time would go by and his
children would surprise him before he finished the
decoration of his person, out of breath, swearing with
impatience, wandering around in hopeless confusion,
unable to remember anything definitely, he entered

the room his wife had used as a wardrobe. Perhaps she had put away his insignia there. He opened the doors of the great clothes-closets with a nervous pull. Clothes! Nothing but clothes.

The odor of balsam, which made him think of the silent calm of the woods, was mingled with a subtle, mysterious perfume, a perfume of years gone by, of dead beauties, of forgotten memories, like the fragrance of dried flowers. This odor came from the mass of clothes that hung there, white, black, pink and blue dresses, with their colors dull and indistinct, the lace crumpled and yellow, retaining in their folds something of the living fragrance of the form they once had covered. The whole past of the dead woman was there. With superstitious care, she had stored away the gowns of the different periods of her life, as if she had been afraid to get rid of them, to tear out a part of her life.

As the painter looked at some of these gowns, he felt the same emotion as if they were old friends who had suddenly appeared like an unexpected surprise. A pink skirt recalled the happy days in Rome; a blue suit brought to his memory the Piazza di san Marco, and he thought he heard the fluttering of the doves and the distant rumble of the noisy *Ride of the Valkyries*. The dark, cheap suits that belonged to the cruel days of struggle hung at the back of the closet, like the garb of suffering and sacrifice. A straw hat, bright as a summer wood, covered with red flowers and with cherries, seemed to smile to him from a shelf. Oh, he knew that too! Many a time its sharp edge of straw had stuck into his forehead, when at sunset on the roads of the Roman Compagna he used to bend down, with his arm around his little wife's waist, to kiss her lips that trembled softly, while from the distance in the blue mist came the tinkle of the bells of the flocks and the mournful songs of the drivers.

That youthful perfume, grown old in its confinement, which poured from the closets in waves, with the rush of an old wine that escapes from the dusty bottle in spurts, spoke to him of the past, calling up the joys that were dead. His senses trembled, a subtle intoxication crept over him. He fancied he had fallen into a sea of perfume that buffeted him with its waves, playing with him as if he were an inert body. It was the scent of youth that came back to him; the incense of the happy days, fainter, more subtle with the regret of dead years. It was the perfume of her beauty which one night in Rome had made him sigh admiringly.

"I worship you, Josephina. You are as fair as Goya's little *Maja*. You are the *Maja Desnuda*."

Holding his breath like a swimmer, he delved into the depths of the closets, reaching out his hands greedily, yet eager to get out of there, to return, as soon as he could, to the surface, to the pure air. He came upon card-board boxes, bundles of belts and old lace, without finding what he was seeking. And every time that his trembling arms shook the old clothes, the swinging of the skirts seemed to throw in his face a wave of that dead, indefinable perfume which he breathed more with his fancy than with his senses.

He wanted to get out as soon as possible. The insignia were not in the wardrobe. Perhaps he would find them in the chamber. And for the first time since the death of his wife, he ventured to turn the door key. The perfume of the past seemed to go with him; it had penetrated through all the pores of his body. He fancied he felt the pressure of a pair of distant, enormous arms, that came from the infinite. He was no longer afraid to enter the chamber.

He groped his way, looking for one of the windows. When the shutters creaked and the sunlight rushed in, the painter's eyes, after a moment of blinking, saw, like a sweet, faint smile, the glow of the Venetian furniture.

What a beautiful artistic chamber! After a year of absence, the painter admired the great clothes-press with its three mirrors, deep and blue as only the mirror-makers of Murano could make them and the ebony of the furniture inlaid with tiny bits of pearl and bright jewels, a specimen of the artistic genius of ancient Venice in contact with Oriental peoples. This furniture had been for Renovales one of the great undertakings of his youth; the whim of a lover, eager to bestow princely honors on his companion after years of strict economy.

They had always had their luxurious bedroom wherever they were, even at the time of their poverty. In those hard days when he painted in the attic and Josephina did the cooking, they had no chairs, they ate from the same plate; Milita played with rag-dolls; but in their miserable, whitewashed alcove were piled up with sacred respect all that furniture of the fair-haired wife of some Doge, like a hope for the future, a promise of better times. She, poor woman, with her simple faith, cleaned it, worshiped it, waiting for the hour of magic transformation to move them to a palace.

The painter glanced about the chamber calmly. He found nothing unusual there, nothing that moved.him. Cotoner had prudently hidden the chair in which Josephina died.

The princely bed, with its monumental head and foot of carved ebony and brilliant mosaic, looked vulgar with the mattresses piled in a heap. Renovales laughed at the terror which had so often made him stop in front of the locked door. Death had left no trace. Nothing there reminded him of Josephina. In the atmosphere floated that smell of closeness, that odor of dust and dampness which one finds in all rooms that have long been closed.

The time was passing, the insignia must be found, and Renovales, already accustomed to the room, opened the clothespress, expecting to find them in it.

There, too, the wood seemed to scatter, as he opened the door, a perfume like that of the other room. It was fainter, more vague, more distant.

Renovales thought it was an illusion of his senses. But no; from the depths of the clothes-press came an invisible vapor wrapping him in its caressing breath. There were no clothes there. His eyes recognized immediately in the bottom of a compartment the boxes he was looking for; but he did not reach out his hands for them; he stood motionless, lost in the contemplation of a thousand trivial objects that reminded him of Josephina.

She was there, too; she came forth to meet him, more personal, more real than from among the heap of old clothes. Her gloves seemed to preserve the warmth and the outline of those hands which once had run caressingly through the artist's hair, her collars reminded him of her warm ivory neck where he used to place his kisses.

His hands turned over everything with painful curiosity. An old fan, carefully put away, seemed to move him in spite of its sorry appearance. Among its broken folds he could see a trace of old colors—a head he had painted when his wife was only a friend—a gift for Señorita de Torrealta who wanted to have something done by the young artist. At the bottom of a case shone two huge pearls, surrounded by diamonds; a present from Milan, the first jewel of real worth which he had bought for his wife, as they were walking through the Piazza del Duomo; a whole remittance from his manager in Rome invested in this costly trinket which made the little woman flush with pleasure while her eyes rested on him with intense gratitude.

His eager fingers, as they turned over boxes, belts, handkerchiefs and gloves, came upon souvenirs with which her person was forever connected. That poor woman had lived for him, only for him, as if her own existence were nothing, as if it had no meaning unless it were joined with his. He found carefully put away among belts and band-boxes—photographs of the places where she had spent her youth; the buildings of Rome; the mountains of the old Papal States, the canals of Venice—relics of the past which no doubt were of great value to her because they called up the image of her husband. And among these papers he saw dry, crushed flowers, proud roses, or modest wild flowers, withered leaves, nameless souvenirs whose importance Renovales realized, suspecting that they recalled some happy moment completely forgotten by him.

The artist's portraits, at different ages, rose from all the corners, entangled among belts or buried under the piles of handkerchiefs. Then several bundles of letters appeared, the ink reddened with time, written in a hand that made the artist uneasy. He recognized it; it was dimly associated in his memory with some person whose name had escaped him. Fool! It was his own handwriting, the laborious heavy hand of his youth which was dexterous only with the brush. There in those yellow folds was the whole story of his life, his intellectual efforts to say "pretty things" like men who write. Not one was missing; the letters of their early engagement when, after they had seen and talked to each other, they still felt that they must put on paper what their lips did not venture to say; others with Italian stamps, exuberant with extravagant expressions of love, short notes he sent her when he was going to spend a few days with some other artists at Naples, or to visit some dead city in the Marcha; then the letters from Paris to the old Venetian palace, inquiring anxiously for the little girl, asking about the nursing, trembling with fear at the possibility of the inevitable diseases of childhood.

Not one was lacking; all were there, put away like fetishes, perfumed with love, tied up with ribbons like the balsam and swathings of a mummified life. Her letters had had a different fate, her written love had been scattered, lost in the void. They had been left forgotten in old suits, burned in the fireplaces, or had fallen into strange hands, where they provoked laughter at their tender simplicity. The only letters he kept were a few of the other woman's and, as he thought of this, he was seized with remorse, with infinite shame at his evil doings.

He read the first lines of some of them, with a strange feeling, as if they were written by another man, wondering at their passionate tone. And it was he who had written that! How he loved Josephina then! It did not seem possible that this affection could have ended so coldly. He was surprised at the indifference of the last years; he no longer remembered the troubles of their life together; he saw his wife now as she was in her youth, with her calm face, her quiet smile and admiration in her eyes.

He continued to read, passing eagerly from letter to letter. He wondered at his own youth, virtuous in spite of his passionate nature, at the chastity of his devotion to his wife, the only, the unquestionable one. He experienced the joy, tinged with melancholy, which a decrepit old man feels at the contemplation of his youthful portrait. And he had been like that! From the bottom of his soul, a stern voice seemed to rise in a reproachful tone, "Yes, like that, when you were good, when you were honorable."

He became so absorbed in his reading that he did not notice the lapse of time. Suddenly he heard steps in the distant hall-way, the rustle of skirts, his daughter's voice. Outside the house a horn was tooting; his haughty son-in-law telling him to hurry; trembling with fear at the prospect of being discovered, he took the insignia and the ribbons out of their cases and hastily closed the door of the clothes-press.

The reception of the Academy was almost a failure for Renovales. The countess found him very interesting, with his face pale with excitement, his breast starred with jewels and his shirt front cut with several bright lines of colors. But as soon as he stood up amid general curiosity, with his manuscript in his hand, and began to read the first paragraphs, a murmur arose which kept increasing and finally drowned out his voice. He read thickly, with the haste of a schoolboy who wants to have it over, without noticing what he was saying, in a monotonous sing-song. The sonorous rehearsals in the studio, the careful preparation of dramatic gestures was forgotten. His mind seemed to be somewhere else, far away from that ceremony; his eyes saw nothing but the letters. The fashionable assemblage went out, glad they had gathered and seen each other again. Many lips laughed at the speech behind their gauze·fans, delighted to be able to scratch indirectly his friend the Alberca woman.

"Awful, my dear! Insufferably boring!"

II

As soon as he awoke the next day, Renovales felt that he must have open air, light, space, and he went out of the house, not stopping in his walk, up the Castellana, until he reached the clearing near the Exhibition Hall.

The night before he had dined at the Albercas'—almost a formal banquet in honor of his entrance into the Academy, at which many of the distinguished gentlemen who formed the countess's coterie were present. She seemed radiant with joy, as if she were celebrating a triumph of her own. The count treated the famous master with greater respect than ever; he had just advanced another step in glory. His respect for all honorary distinctions made him admire that Academic medal, the only distinction he could not add to his load of insignia.

Renovales spent a bad night. The countess's champagne did not agree with him. He had gone home with a sort of fear, as if something unusual was awaiting him which his uneasiness could not explain. He took off the dress clothes which had been torturing him for several hours and went to bed, surprised at the vague fear that followed him even to the threshhold of his room. He saw nothing unusual around him, his room presented the same appearance it always did. He feel asleep, overcome by weariness, by the digestive torpor of that extraordinary banquet, and he did not awake at all during the night; but his sleep was cruel, tossed with dreams that perhaps made him groan.

On awakening, late in the morning, at the steps of his servant in the dressing room, he realized by the tumbled condition of the bed-clothes, by the cold sweat on his forehead and the weariness of his body what a restless night he had passed amid nervous starts.

His brain, still heavy with sleep, could not unravel the memories of the night. He knew only that he had had unpleasant dreams; perhaps he had wept. The one thing he could recall was a pale face, rising from among the black veils of unconsciousness, around which all his dreams were centered. It was not Josephina; the face had the expression of a person of another world.

But as his mental numbness gradually disappeared, while he was washing and dressing, and while the servant was helping him on with his overcoat, he thought, summoning his memories with an effort, that it might be she. Yes, it was she. Now he remembered that in his dream he had been conscious of that perfume which had followed him since the day before, which accompanied him to the Academy, disturbing his reading, and which had gone with him to the banquet, running between his eyes and Concha's like a mist, through which he looked at her, without seeing her.

The coolness of the morning cleared his mind. The wide prospect from the heights of the Exhibition Hall seemed to blot out instantly the memories of the night.

A wind from the mountains was blowing on the plateau near the Hippodrome. As he walked against the wind, he felt a buzz in his ears, like the distant roar of the sea. In the background, beyond the slopes with their little red houses and wintry poplars, bare as broomsticks, the mountains of Guadarrama stood out, luminously clear against the blue sky, with their snowy crests and their huge peaks which seemed made of salt. In the opposite direction, sunk in a deep cut, appeared the covering of

Madrid; the black roofs, the pointed towers—all indistinct in a haze that gave the buildings in the background the vague blue of the mountains.

The plateau, covered with wretched, thin grass, its furrows stiffly frozen, flashed here and there in the sunlight. The bits of tile on the ground, broken pieces of china and tin cans reflected the light as if they were precious metals.

Renovales looked for a long while at the back of the Exhibition Palace; the yellow walls trimmed with red brick which hardly rose above the edge of the clearing; the flat zinc roofs, shining like dead seas; the central cupola, huge, swollen, cutting the sky with its black curves, like a balloon on the point of rising. From one wing of the Palace came the sound of bugles, prolonging their warlike notes to the accompaniment of the hoof-beats amid clouds of dust. Beside one door swords were flashing and the sun was reflected on patent-leather hats.

The painter smiled. That palace had been erected for them, and now the rural police occupied it. Once every two years Art entered it, claiming the place from the horses of the guardians of peace. Statues were set up in rooms that smelt of oats and stout shoes. But this anomaly did not last long; the intruder was driven out, as soon as the place was beginning to have a semblance of European culture, and there remained in the Exhibition Palace the true, the national, the privileged police, the sorry jades of holy authority which galloped down to the streets of Madrid when its slothful peace was at rare intervals disturbed.

As the master looked at the black cupola, he remembered the days of exhibitions; he saw the long-haired, anxious youths, now gentle and flattering, now angry and iconoclastic, coming from all the cities of Spain with their pictures under their arms and mighty ambitions in

their minds. He smiled at the thought of the unpleasant-
ness and disgust he had suffered under that roof, when
the turbulent throng of artists crowded around him, annoyed him, admiring him more because of his position
as an influential judge than because of his works. It
was he who awarded the prizes in the opinion of those
young fellows who followed him with looks of fear and
hope. On the afternoon when the prizes were awarded,
groups rushed out to meet him in the portico at the news
of his arrival; they greeted him with extravagant demonstrations of respect. Some walked in front of him, talking loudly. "Who? Renovales? The greatest painter in
the world. Next to Velásquez." And at the end of the
afternoon, when the two sheets of paper were placed on
the columns of the rotunda, with the lists of winners, the
master prudently slipped out to avoid the final explosion.
The childish soul that every artist has within him burst
out frankly at the announcement. False pretences were
over; every man showed his true nature. Some hid between the statues, dejected and ashamed, with their fists
in their eyes, weeping at the thought of the return to
their distant home, of the long misery they had suffered
with no other hope than that which had just vanished.
Others stood straight as roosters, their ears red, their
lips pale, looking toward the entrance of the palace with
flaming eyes, as if they wanted to see from there a certain pretentious house with a Greek façade and a gold inscription. "The fossil! It is a shame that the fortunes
of the younger men, who really amount to something, are
entrusted to an old fogey who has run out, a 'four-flusher'
who will never leave anything worth while behind him!"
Oh, from those moments had arisen all the annoyances of his artistic activity. Every time that he
heard of an unjust censure, a brutal denial of his ability, a merciless attack in some obscure paper, he remem-

bered the rotunda of the Exhibition, that stormy crowd
of painters around the bits of paper which contained
their sentences. He thought with wonder and sympathy
of the blindness of those youths who cursed life because
of a failure, and were capable of giving their health,
their vigor, in exchange for the sorry glory of a picture,
less lasting even than the frail canvas. Every medal
was a rung on the ladder; they measured the importance
of these awards, giving them a meaning like that of a
soldier's stripes. And he too had been young! He too
had embittered the best years of his life in these combats,
like amœbæ who struggle together in a drop of water,
fancying they may conquer a huge world! What interest had eternal beauty in these regimental ambitions,
in this ladder-climbing fever of those who strove to be
her interpreters?

The master went home. The walk had made him forget his anxiety of the night before. His body, weakened
by his easy life, seemed to acknowledge this exercise with
a violent reaction. His legs itched slightly, the blood
throbbed in his temples, it seemed to spread through his
body in a wave of warmth. He exulted in his power and
tasted the joy of every organism that is performing its
functions in harmonious regularity.

As he crossed the garden, he was humming a song.
He smiled to the concierge's wife who had opened the
gate for him and to the ugly watchdog who came up
with a caressing whine to lick his trousers. He opened
the glass door, passing from the noise outside into deep,
convent-like silence. His feet sank in the soft rugs; the
only sounds were the mysterious trembling of the pictures which covered the walls up to the ceiling, the
creaking of invisible wood-borers in the picture frames,
the swing of the hangings in a breath of air. Everything that the master had painted; studies or whims,

finished or unfinished, was placed on the ground floor, together with pictures and drawings by some famous companions or favorite pupils. Milita had amused herself for a long time before she was married, in this decoration which reached even to poorly lighted hallways.

As he left his hat and stick on the hat-rack, the eyes of the master fell on a nearby water-color, as if this picture attracted his attention among the others which surrounded it. He was surprised that he should now notice it of a sudden, after passing by it so many times without seeing it. It was not bad; but it was timid; it showed lack of experience. Whose could it be? Perhaps Soldevilla's. But as he drew near to see it better, he smiled. It was his own! How differently he painted then! He tried to remember when and where he had painted it. To help his memory, he looked closely at that charming woman's head, with its dreamy eyes, wondering who the model could have been.

Suddenly a cloud came over his face. The artist seemed confused, ashamed. How stupid! It was his wife, the Josephina of the early days, when he used to gaze at her admiringly, delighting in reproducing her face.

He threw the blame for his slowness on Milita and determined to have the study taken away from there. His wife's portrait ought not be in the hall, beside the hat-rack.

After luncheon he gave orders to the servant to take down the picture and move it into one of the drawing-rooms. The servant looked surprised.

"There are so many portraits of the mistress. You have painted her so many times, sir. The house is full."

Renovales mimicked the servant's expression. "So many! So many!" He knew how many times he had painted her! With a sudden curiosity before going to the studio, he entered the parlor where Josephina received her callers. There, in the place of honor, he saw a large portrait of his wife, painted in Rome, a dainty woman with a lace mantilla, a black ruffled skirt and, in her hand, a tortoise-shell fan—a veritable Goya. He gazed for a moment at that attractive face, shaded by the black lace, its oriental eyes in sharp contrast to its aristocratic pallor. How beautiful Josephina was in those days!

He opened the windows the better to see the portrait and the light fell on the dark red walls making the frames of other smaller pictures flash.

Then the painter saw that the Goyesque picture was not the only one. Other Josephinas accompanied him in the solitude. He gazed with astonishment at the face of his wife, which seemed to rise from all sides of the parlor. Little studies of women of the people or ladies of the 18th century; water-colors of Moorish women; Greek women with the stiff severity of Alma-Tadema's archaic figures; everything in the parlor, everything he had painted, was Josephina, had her face, or showed traces of her with the vagueness of a memory.

He passed to the adjoining parlor and there, too, his wife's face, painted by him, came to meet him among other pictures by his friends.

When had he done all that? He could not remember; he was surprised at the enormous quantity of work he had performed unconsciously. He seemed to have spent his whole life painting Josephina.

Afterwards, in all the hallways, in all the rooms where pictures were hung, his wife met his gaze, under the most varied aspects, frowning or smiling, beautiful or sad with sickness. They were sketched, simple, unfinished charcoal drawings of her head in the corner of a canvas, but always that glance followed him, sometimes with an expression of melancholy tenderness, sometimes with intense reproach. Where had his eyes been? He had lived amid all this without seeing it. Every day he had passed by Josephina without noticing her. His wife was resurrected; henceforth, she would sit down at table, she would enter his chamber, he would pass through the house always under the gaze of two eyes which in the past had pierced into his soul.

The dead woman was not dead; she hovered about him, revived by his hand. He could not take a step without seeing her face on every side. She greeted him from above the doors, from the ends of the rooms she seemed to call him.

In his three studios, his surprise was still greater. All his most intimate painting, which he had done as study, from impulse, without any desire for sale, was stored away there, and all was a memory of the dead woman. The pictures which dazzled the callers were hung low, down on the level of the eyes, on easels, or fastened to the wall, amid the sumptuous furniture; up above, reaching to the ceiling were arranged the studies, memories, unframed canvases, like old, forgotten works, and in this collection at the first glance Renovales saw the enigmatic face rising towards him.

He had lived without lifting his eyes, accustomed as he was to everything about him, and looking around, without seeing, without noticing those women, different in appearance but alike in expression, who watched him from above. And the countess had been there several afternoons, to see him alone in the studio! And the Persian silk draperies, hung on lances before the deep divan, had not hidden them from that sad, fixed gaze which seemed to multiply in the upper stretch of the walls.

To forget his remorse, he amused himself by counting the canvases which reproduced his wife's dainty little face. They were many—the whole life of an artist. He tried to remember when and where he had painted them. In the first days of his love, he felt that he must paint her, with an irresistible impulse to transfer to the canvas everything he delighted to see, everything he loved. Afterwards, it had been a desire to flatter her, to coax her with a false show of affection, to convince her that she was the only object of his artistic worship, copying her in a vague likeness, giving to her features, marred by illness, a soft veil of idealism. He could not live without working and, like many painters, he used as models the people around him. His daughter had carried to her new home a load of paintings, all the pictures, rough sketches, water-colors and panels which represented her from the time she used to play with the cat, dressing him in baby clothes, until she was a proud young lady, courted by Soldevilla and the man who was now her husband.

The mother had remained there, rising after death about the artist in oppressive profusion. All the little incidents in life had given Renovales an occasion to paint new pictures. He recalled his enthusiasm every time he saw her in a new dress. The colors changed her; she was a new woman, so he would declare with a vehemence which his wife took for admiration and which was merely the desire for a model.

Josephina's whole life had been fixed by her husband's hand. In one canvas she appeared dressed in white, walking through a meadow with the poetic dreaminess of an Ophelia; in another, wearing a large, plumed hat covered with jewels, she showed the self-satisfaction of a manufacturer's wife, secure in her well-being; a black curtain served as a background for her bare neck and shoulders. In another picture she had her sleeves rolled up; a white apron covered her from her breast to her feet, on her forehead was a little wrinkle 'of care and weariness, and in her whole mien the carelessness of one who has no time to attend to the adornment of her person. This last was the portrait of the bitter days, the image of the courageous housekeeper, without servants, working with her delicate hands in a wretched attic, striving that the artist might lack nothing, that the petty annoyances of life might not come to distract him from his supreme efforts for success.

This portrait filled the artist with the melancholy which the memory of bitter days inspires in the midst of comfort. His gratitude toward his brave companion brought with it once more remorse.

"Oh, Josephina! Josephina!"

When Cotoner arrived, he found the master lying face down on the couch with his head in his hands, as if he were asleep. He tried to interest him by talking about the function of the day before. A great success; the papers spoke of him and his speech, declaring that he was a great writer and could win as marked a success in literature as in art. Had he not read them?

Renovales answered with a bored expression. He had found them, when he went out in the morning, on a table in the reception-room. He had cast a glance at his picture surrounded by the solid columns of his speech but he had put off reading the praises until later. They did not interest him; he was thinking of something else—he was sad.

And in answer to Cotoner's anxious questions, who thought he must be ill, he said quietly:

"I am well enough. It's melancholy. I'm tired of doing nothing. I want to work and haven't the strength."

Suddenly he interrupted his old friend, pointing to

all the portraits of Josephina, as if they were new works which he had just produced.

Cotoner expressed surprise. He knew them all; they had been there for years. What was strange about them?

The master told him of his recent surprise. He had lived beside them without seeing them, he had just discovered them two hours before. And Cotoner laughed.

"You are rather unsettled, Mariano. You live without noticing what is around you. That is why you don't know of Soldevilla's marriage to a rich girl. The poor boy was disappointed because his master was not present at the wedding."

Renovales shrugged his shoulders. What did he care for such follies? There was a long pause and the master, pensive and sad, suddenly raised his head with a determined expression.

"What do you think of those portraits, Pepe?" he asked anxiously. "Is it she? I couldn't have made a mistake in painting them, I couldn't have seen her different from what she really was, could I?"

Cotoner broke out laughing. Really, the master was out of his mind. What questions! Those portraits were marvels, like all of his work. But Renovales insisted with the impatience of doubt. His opinion! Were those Josephinas like his wife!

"Exactly," said the Bohemian. "Why, man alive, their fidelity to life is the most astonishing thing about your portraits!"

He declared this confidently, but a shadow of doubt worried him. Yes, it was Josephina, but there was something unusual, idealized about her. Her features looked the same, but they had an inner light that made them more beautiful. It was a defect he had always found in these pictures, but he said nothing.

"And she," insisted the master, "was she really beau-

tiful? What did you think of her as a woman? Tell
me, Pepe,—without hesitating. It's strange, I can't remember very well what she was like."

Cotoner was disconcerted by these questions, and answered with some embarrassment. What an odd thing!
Josephina was very good—an angel; he always remembered her with gratitude. He had wept for her as for
a mother, though she might almost have been his daughter. She had always been very considerate and thought-
ful of the poor Bohemian.

"Not that," interrupted the master. "I want to know
if you thought she was beautiful, if she really was
beautiful."

"Why, man, yes," said Cotoner resolutely. "She was
beautiful or, rather, attractive. At the end she seemed
a bit changed. Her illness! But all in all, an angel."

And the master, calmed by these words, stood looking
at his own works.

"Yes, she was very beautiful," he said slowly, without
turning his eyes from the canvases. "Now I recognize it;
now I see her better. It's strange, Pepe. It seems as
if I have found Josephina to-day after a long journey.
I had forgotten her; I was no longer certain what her
face was like."

There was another long pause, and once more the
master began to ply his friend with anxious questions.

"Did she love me? Do you think she really loved me?
Was it love that made her sometimes act so—strangely?"

This time Cotoner did not hesitate as he had at the
former questions.

"Love you? Wildly, Mariano. As no man has been
loved in this world. All that there was between you was
jealousy—too much affection. I know it better than
anyone else; old friends, like me, who go in and out of
the house just like old dogs, are treated with intimacy

and hear things the husband does not know. Believe
me, Mariano, no one will ever love you as she did. Her
sulky words were only passing clouds. I am sure you no
longer remember them. What did not pass, was the
other, the love she bore you. I am positive; you know
that she told me everything, that I was the only person
she could tolerate toward the end."

Renovales seemed to thank his friend for these words
with a glance of joy.

They went out to walk at the end of the afternoon,
going toward the center of Madrid. Renovales talked
of their youth, of their days in Rome. He laughed as
he reminded Cotoner of his famous stock of Popes, he
recalled the funny shows in the studios, the noisy entertainments, and then, after he was married, the evenings of friendly intercourse in that pretty little dining-
room on the Via Margutta; the arrival of the Bohemian
and the other artists of his circle to drink a cup of tea
with the young couple; the loud discussions over painting, which made the neighbors protest, while she, his
Josephina, still surprised at finding herself the mistress
of a household, without her mother, and surrounded by
men, smiled timidly to them all, thinking that those fearful comrades, with hair like highwaymen but as innocent
and peevish as children, were very funny and interesting.

"Those were the days, Pepe! Youth, which we never
appreciate till it has gone!"

Walking straight ahead, without knowing where they
were going, absorbed in their conversation and their
memories, they suddenly found themselves at the Puerta
del Sol. Night had fallen; the electric lights were coming out; the shop windows threw patches of light on the
sidewalks.

Cotoner looked at the clock on the Government Building.

"Aren't you going to the Alberca woman's house to-night?"

Renovales seemed to awaken. Yes, he must go; they expected him. But he was not going. His friend looked at him with a shocked expression, as if he considered it a serious error to scorn a dinner.

The painter seemed to lack the courage to spend the evening between Concha and her husband. He thought of her with a sort of aversion; he felt as if he might brutally repel her constant caresses and tell everything to the husband in an outburst of frankness. It was a disgrace, treachery—that life *à trois* which the society woman accepted as the happiest of states.

"It's intolerable," he said to dissipate his friend's surprise. "I can't stand her. She's a regular barnacle, and won't let me go for a minute."

He had never spoken to Cotoner of his affair with the Alberca woman, but he did not have to tell him anything, he assumed that he knew.

"But she's pretty, Mariano," said he. "A wonderful woman! You know I admire her. You might use her for your Greek picture."

The master cast at him a glance of pity for his ignorance. He felt a desire to scoff at her, to injure her, thus justifying his indifference.

"Nothing but a façade. A face and a figure."

And bending over toward his friend he whispered to him seriously as if he were revealing the secret of a terrible crime.

"She's knock-kneed. A regular swindle."

A satyr-like smile spread over Cotoner's lips and his ears wriggled. It was the joy of a chaste man; the satisfaction of knowing the secret defects of a beauty who was out of his reach.

The master did not want to leave his friend. He

needed him, he looked at him with tender sympathy, seeing in him something of his dead wife. When she was sad, he had been her confidant. When her nerves were on edge, this simple man's words ended the crisis in a flood of tears. With whom could he talk about her better?

"We will dine together, Pepe; we will go to the *Italianos*—a Roman banquet, *ravioli, piccata,* anything you want and a bottle of Chianti or two, as many as you can drink, and at the end sparkling Asti, better than champagne. Does that suit you, old man?"

Arm in arm they walked along, their heads high, a smile on their lips, like two young painters, eager to celebrate a recent sale with a gluttonous relief from their misery.

Renovales went back into his memories and poured them out in a torrent. He reminded Cotoner of a *trattoria* in an alley in Rome, beyond the statue of Pasquino, before you reach the Via Governo Vecchio, a chop house of ecclesiastical quiet, run by the former cook of a cardinal. The shelves of the establishment were always covered with the headgear of the profession, priestly tiles. The merriment of the artists shocked the sedate frugality of the habitués, priests of the Papal palace or visitors who were in Rome scheming advancement; loud-mouthed lawyers in dirty frock-coats from the nearby Palace of Justice, loaded with papers.

"What *maccheroni!* Remember, Pepe? How poor Josephina liked it!"

They used to reach the *trattoria* at night in a merry company—she on his arm and around them the friends whose admiration for the promising young painter attracted them to him. Josephina worshiped the mysteries of the kitchen, the traditional secrets of the solemn table of the princes of the Church, which had come down

to the street, taking refuge in that little room. On the
white table cloth trembled the amber reflection of the
wine of Orvieto in decanters, a thick, yellow, golden
liquid, of clerical sweetness, a drink of old-time pontiffs,
which descended to the stomach like fire and more than
once had mounted to heads covered with the tiara.

On moonlit nights, they used to go from there and
walk to the Colosseum to look at the gigantic, monstrous
ruin under the flood of blue light. Josephina, shaking
with nervous excitement, went down into the dark tun-
nels, groping along among the fallen stones, till she was
on the open slope, facing the silent circle, which seemed
to enclose the corpse of a whole people. Looking around
with anxiety, she thought of the terrible beasts which had
trod upon that sand. Suddenly came a frightful roar
and a black beast leaped forth from the deep vomitory.
Josephina clung to her husband, with a shriek of terror,
and all laughed. It was Simpson, an American painter,
who bent over, walking on all fours, to attack his companions with fierce cries.

"Do you remember, Pepe?" Renovales kept saying,
"What days! What joy! What a fine companion the
little girl was before her illness saddened her!"

They dined, talking of their youth, mingling with their
memories the image of the dead. Afterwards, they
walked the streets till midnight, and Renovales was always going back to those days, recalling his Josephina,
as if he had spent his life worshiping her. Cotoner
was tired of the conversation and said "Good-by" to
the master. What new hobby was this? Poor Josephina
was very interesting, but they had spent the whole evening without talking of anything else, as though memory of her was the only thing in the world.

Renovales started home impatiently; he took a cab to
get there sooner. He felt as anxious as if some one

were waiting for him; that showy house, cold and solitary before, seemed animated with a spirit he could not define, a beloved soul which filled it, pervading all like perfume.

As he entered, preceded by the sleepy servant, his first glance was for the watercolor. He smiled; he wanted to bid good-night to that head whose eyes rested on him.

For all the Josephinas who met his gaze, rising from the shadow of the walls, as he turned on the electric lights in the parlors and hallways, he had the same smile and greeting. He no longer was uneasy in the presence of those faces which he had looked at in the morning with surprise and fear. She saw him; she read his thoughts; she forgave him, surely. She had always been so good!

He hesitated a moment on his way, wishing to go to the studios and turn on the lights. There he could see her full length, in all her grace; he would talk to her, he would ask her forgiveness in the deep silence of those great rooms. But the master stopped. What was he thinking of? Was he going to lose his senses? He drew his hand across his forehead, as if he wanted to wipe these ideas out of his mind. No doubt it was the Asti that led him to such absurdities. To sleep!

When he was in the dark, lying in his daughter's little bed, he felt uneasy. He could not sleep, he was uncomfortable. He was tempted to go out of the room and take refuge in the deserted bed-chamber as if only there could he find rest and sleep. Oh, the Venetian bed, that princely piece of furniture which kept his whole history, where he had whispered words of love; where they had talked so many times in low tones of his longing for glory and wealth; where his daughter was born!

With the energy which showed in all his whims, the master put on his clothes, and quietly, as if he feared

to be overheard by his servant who slept nearby, made
his way to the chamber.

He turned the key with the caution of a thief, and
advanced on tiptoe, under the soft, pink light which an
old lantern shed from the center of the ceiling.   He
carefully stretched out the mattresses on the abandoned
bed.   There were no sheets nor pillows.   The room so
long deserted was cold.   What a pleasant night he was
going to spend!   How well he would sleep there!   The
gold-embroidered cushions from a sofa would serve as
a pillow.   He wrapped himself in an overcoat and got
into bed, dressed, putting out the light so as not to see
reality, to dream, peopling the darkness with the sweet
deceits of his fancy.

On those mattresses, Josephina had slept.   He did not
see her as in the last days,—sick, emaciated, worn with
physical suffering.   His mind repelled that painful image,
bent on beautiful illusions.   The Josephina whom he saw,
the Josephina within him, was the other, of the first
days of their love, and not as she had been in reality but
as he had seen her, as he had painted her.

His memory passed over a great stretch of time, dark
and stormy; it leaped from the regret of the present to
the happy days of youth.   He no longer recalled the
years of trying confinement, when they quarreled together, unable to follow the same path.   They were unimportant disturbances in life.   He thought only of her smiling kindness, her generosity, and submissiveness.   How
tenderly they had lived together for a part of their life, in
that bed which now knew only the loneliness of his body..

The artist shivered under his inadequate covering.   In
this abnormal situation, exterior impressions called up
memories—fragments of the past that slowly came to
his mind.   The cold made him think of the rainy nights
in Venice, when it poured for hour after hour on the

narrow alleys and deserted canals in the deep, solemn
silence of a city without horses, without wheels, without
any sound of life, except the lapping of the solitary
water on the marble stairways. They were in the same
calm, under the warm eider-down, amid the same furniture which he now half saw in the shadow.

Through the slits of the lowered blind shone the glow
of the lamp which lighted the nearby canal. On the ceiling a spot of light flickered with the reflection of the dead
water, constantly crossed by lines of shadow. They,
closely embraced, watched this play of light and water
above them. They knew that outside it was cold and
damp; they exulted in their physical warmth, in the selfishness of being together, with that delicious sense of
comfort, buried in silence as if the world were a thing of
the past, as if their chamber were a warm oasis, in the
midst of cold and darkness.

Sometimes they heard a mournful cry in the silence.
Aooo! It was the gondolier giving warning before he
turned the corner. Across the spot of light which shim-
mered on the ceiling slipped a black, Lilliputian gondola,
a shadow toy, on the stern of which bent a manikin the
size of a fly, wielding the oar. And, thinking of those
who passed in the rain, lashed by the icy gusts, they experienced a new pleasure and clung closer to each other
under the soft eider-down and their lips met, disturbing
the calm of their rest with the noisy insolence of youth
and love.

Renovales no longer felt cold. He turned restlessly
on the mattresses; the metallic embroidery of the cushions stuck in his face; he stretched out his arms in the
darkness, and the silence was broken by a despairing
cry, the lament of a child who demands the impossible,
who asks for the moon.

"Josephina! Josephina!"

III

One morning the painter sent an urgent summons to Cotoner and the latter arrived in great alarm at the terms of the message.

"It's nothing serious," said Renovales. "I want you to tell me where Josephina was buried. I want to see her."

It was a desire which had been slowly taking form in his mind during several nights; a whim of the long hours of sleeplessness through which he dragged in the darkness.

More than a week before, he had moved into the large chamber, choosing among the bed linen, with a painstaking care that surprised the servants, the most worn sheets, which called up old memories with their embroidery. He did not find in this linen that perfume of the closets which had disturbed him so deeply; but there was something in them, the illusion, the certainty that she had many a time touched them.

After soberly and severely telling Cotoner of his wish, Renovales felt that he must offer some excuse. It was disgraceful that he did not know where Josephina was; that he had not yet gone to visit her. His grief at her death had left him helpless and afterward, the long journey.

"You always know things, Pepe! You had charge of the funeral arrangements. Tell me where she is; take me to see her."

Up to that time he had not thought of her remains. He remembered the day of the funeral, his dramatic grief which kept him in a corner with his face buried in his hands. His intimate friends, the elect, who penetrated to his retreat, clad in black, and wearing gloomy faces, caught his hand and pressed it effusively. "Courage, Mariano. Be strong, master." And outside the house, a constant trampling of horses' feet; the iron fence black with the curious crowd, a double file of carriages as far as the eye could see; reporters going from group to group, taking down names.

All Madrid was there. And they had carried her away to the slow step of a pair of horses with waving plumes, amid the undertaker's men in white wigs and gold batons —and he had forgotten her, had felt no interest in seeing the corner of the cemetery where she was buried forever, under the glare of the sun, under the night rains that dripped upon her grave. He cursed himself now for this outrageous neglect.

"Tell me where she is, Pepe. Take me. I want to see her."

He implored with the eagerness of remorse; he wanted to see her once, as soon as possible, like a sinner who fears death and cries for absolution.

Cotoner acceded to this immediate trip. She was in the Almudena cemetery, which had been closed for some time. Only those who had long standing titles to a lot went there now. Cotoner had desired to bury Josephina beside her mother in the same inclosure where the stone that covered the "lamented genius of diplomacy" was growing tarnished. He wanted her to rest among her own.

On the way, Renovales felt a sort of anguish. Like a sleep-walker he saw the streets of the city passing by the carriage window, then they went down a steep hill, ill-kempt gardens, where loafers were sleeping, leaning against the trees, or women were combing their hair in the sun; a bridge; wretched suburbs with tumble-down houses; then the open country, hilly roads and at last a grove of cypress trees beyond an adobe wall and the tops of marble buildings, angels stretching out their wings with a trumpet at their lips, great crosses, torch-holders mounted on tripods, and a pure, blue sky which seemed to smile with superhuman indifference at the excitement of that ant, named Renovales.

He was going to see her; to step on the ground which covered her body; to breathe an atmosphere in which there was still perhaps some of that warmth which was the breath of the dead woman's soul. What would he say to her?

As he entered the graveyard he looked at the keeper, an ugly, dismal old fellow, as pale and yellow and greasy as a wax candle. That man lived constantly near Josephina! He was seized with generous gratitude; he had to restrain himself, thinking of his companion, or he would have given him all the money he had with him.

Their steps resounded in the silence. They felt the murmuring calm of an abandoned garden about them, where there were more pavilions and statues than trees. They went down ruined colonnades, which echoed their steps strangely; over slabs which sounded hollow under their feet,—the void, trembling at the light touch of life.

The dead who slept there were dead indeed, without the least resurrection of memory, completely deserted, sharing in the universal decay,—unnamed, separated from life forever. From the beehive close by, no one came to give new life with tears and offerings to the ephemeral personality they once had, to the name which marked them for a moment.

Wreaths hung from the crosses, black and unraveled, with a swarm of insects in their fragments. The exuberant vegetation, where no one ever passed, stretched in every direction, loosening the tombstones with its roots, springing the steps of the resounding stairways. The rain, slowly filtering through the ground, had produced hollows. Some of the slabs were cracked open, revealing deep holes.

They had to walk carefully, fearing that the hollow ground would suddenly open; they had to avoid the depressions where a stone with letters of pale gold and noble coats-of-arms lay half on its side.

The painter walked trembling with the sadness of an immense disappointment, questioning the value of his greatest interests. And this was life! Human beauty ended like this! This was all that the human mind came to and here it must stop in all its pride!

"Here it is!" said Cotoner.

They had entered between two rows of tombs so close together that as they passed they brushed against the old ornaments which crumbled and fell at the touch.

It was a simple tomb, a sort of coffin of white marble which rose a few inches above the ground, with an elevation at one end, like the bolster of a bed and surmounted by a cross.

Renovales was cold. There was Josephina! He read the inscription several times, as if he could not convince himself. It was she; the letters reproduced her name, with a brief lament of her inconsolable husband, which seemed to him senseless, artificial, disgraceful.

He had come trembling with anxiety at the thought of the terrible moment when he should behold Josephina's last resting place. To feel that he was near her, to tread upon the ground in which she rested! He would not be able to resist this critical moment, he would weep like a child, he would fall on his knees, sobbing in deadly anguish.

Well, he was there; the tomb was before his eyes and still, they were dry; they looked about coldly in surprise.

She was there! He knew it from his friend's statement, from the declamatory inscription on the tomb, but nothing warned him of her presence. He remained indifferent, looking curiously at the adjoining graves, filled with a monstrous desire to laugh, seeing in death only his sardonic buffoon's mask.

At one side, a gentleman who rested under the endless list of his titles and honors, a sort of Count of Alberca, who had fallen asleep in the solemnity of his greatness, waiting for the angel's trumpet-blast to appear before the Lord with all his parchments and crosses. On the other, a general who rotted under a marble slab, engraved with cannon, guns and banners, as though he hoped to terrify death. In what ludicrous promiscuity Josephina had come to sleep her last sleep, mingled with forms she had not known in life! They were her eternal, her final lovers; they carried her off from his very presence and forever, indifferent to the pressing concerns of the living. Oh, Death! What a cruel mocker! The earth! How cold and cynical!

He was sad and disgusted at human insignificance—but he did not weep. He saw only the external and material—the form, always the concern of his thoughts. Standing before the tomb he felt merely his vulgar meanness, with a sort of shame. She was his wife; the wife of a great artist.

He thought of the most famous sculptors, all friends of his; he would talk to them, they should erect an imposing sepulcher with weeping statues, symbolical of fidelity, gentleness and love, a sepulcher worthy of the companion of Renovales. And nothing more; his thought went no farther; his imagination could not pass beyond the hard marble nor penetrate the hidden mystery. The grave was speechless and empty, in the air there was nothing which spoke to the soul of the painter.

He remained indifferent, unmoved by any emotion, without ceasing for a single moment to see reality. The cemetery was a hideous, gloomy, repulsive place, with an odor of decay. Renovales thought he could perceive a stench of putrefaction scattered in the wind which bent the pointed tops of the cypresses, and swayed the old wreaths and the branches of the rose bushes.

He looked at Cotoner with a sort of displeasure. He was to blame for his coldness. His presence was a check on him which prevented him from showing his feelings. Though a friend, he was a stranger, an obstacle between him and the dead. He interfered with that silent dialogue of love and forgiveness of which the master had dreamed as he came. He would come back alone. Perhaps the cemetery would be different in solitude.

And he came back; he came back the next day. The keeper greeted him with a smile, realizing that he was a profitable visitor.

The cemetery seemed larger, more imposing in the silence of the bright, quiet morning. He had no one to talk with; he heard no human sound but that of his own steps. He went up stairways, crossed galleries, leaving behind him his indifference, thinking anxiously that every step took him farther from the living, that the gate with its greedy keeper was already far away and that he was the only living being, the only one who thought and could feel fear in the mournful city of thousands and thousands of beings, wrapped in a mystery which made them imposing amid the strange, dull sounds of the land beyond that terrifies with the blackness of its bottomless abyss.

When he reached Josephina's grave, he took off his hat.

No one. The trees and the rose bushes trembled in the wind among the cross paths. Some birds were twittering above him in an acacia, and the sound of life, disturbing the rustling of the solitary vegetation, shed a certain calm over the painter's spirit, blotted out the childish fear he had felt before he reached there, as he crossed the echoing pavements of the colonnades.

For a long time he remained motionless, absorbed in the contemplation of that marble case obliquely cut by a ray of sunlight, one part golden, the other blue in the shadow. Suddenly he shivered, as if he had awakened at the sound of a voice,—his own. He was talking, aloud, driven to cry out his thoughts, to stir this deathly silence with something that meant life.

"Josephina. It is I. Do you forgive me?"

It was a childish longing to hear the voice from beyond that might pour on his soul a balm of forgiveness and forgetting; a desire of humbling himself, of weeping, of having her listen to him, smile to him from the depth of the void, at the great revolution which had been carried out in his spirit. He wanted to tell her—and he did tell her silently with the speech of his feelings—that he loved her, that he had resuscitated her in his thoughts, now that he had lost her forever, with a love which he had never had for her in her earthly life. He felt ashamed before her grave; ashamed of the difference of their fates.

He begged her forgiveness for living, for still feeling vigorous and young, for now loving her without reality, in a wild hope, when he had been cold and indifferent at her departure, with his thoughts on another woman, hoping for her death with criminal craving. Wretch! And he was still alive! And she, so kind, so sweet, buried forever, lost in the depths of eternal, ruthless death!

He wept; at last he wept those hot, sincere tears which compel forgiveness. It was the weeping which he had so long desired. Now he felt that they approached each other, that they were almost together, separated only by a strip of marble and a little earth. His fancy saw her poor remains and in their decay he loved them, he worshiped them with a calm passion that rose above earthly miseries. Nothing which had once been Josephina's could cause him repugnance or horror. If he could but open that white case! If he could kiss her, take her ashes with him, that they might go with him on his pilgrimage, like the household gods of the ancients! He no longer saw the cemetery, he did not hear the birds nor the rustling of the branches; he seemed to live in a cloud, looking only at that white grave, the marble slab,—the last resting place of his beloved.

She forgave him; her body rose before him, such as it had been in her youth, as he had painted it. Her deep eyes were fixed on his, eyes that shone with love. He seemed to hear her childish voice laughing, admiring little trifles, as in the happy days. It was a resurrection,— the image of the dead woman was before him, formed no doubt by the invisible atoms of her being which floated over her grave, by something of the essence of her life which still fluttered around the material remains, reluctant to say farewell before they started on the way that leads to the depths of the infinite.

His tears continued to fall in the silence, in sweet relief; his voice, broken by sobs, stilled the birds with fear. "Josephina! Josephina!" And the echo answered with dull, mocking cries, from the smooth walls of the mausoleums, from the invisible end of the colonnades.

The artist could not resist the temptation to step over

the rusted chains which surrounded the grave. To feel her nearer! To overcome the short distance which separated them! To mock death with a loving kiss of intense gratitude for forgiveness!

The huge frame of the master covered the slab of marble, his arms encircled it as if he would pick it up from the ground and carry it away with him. His lips eagerly sought the highest part of the stone.

He wished to find the spot which covered her face and he began to kiss it, moving his head as if he were going to dash it against the marble.

A sensation of stone, warmed by the sun, on his lips; a taste of dust, insipid and repulsive in his mouth. Renovales sat up, rose to his feet as if he had awakened, as if the cemetery, until then invisible, was suddenly restored to reality. The faint odor of decay once more struck him.

Now he saw the grave, as he had seen it the day before. He no longer wept. The immense disappointment dried his tears, though within him he felt the longing for weeping increased. Horrible awakening! Josephina was not there; only the void was about him. It was useless to seek the past in the field of death. Memories could not be aroused in that cold ground, stirred by worms and decay. Oh, where had he come to seek his dreams! From what a foul dunghill he had tried to raise the roses of his memories!

In fancy he saw her beneath that repugnant marble in all the repulsiveness of death, and this vision left him cold, indifferent. What had he to do with such wretchedness? No; Josephina was not there. She was truly dead, and if he ever was to see her it would not be beside her grave.

Once more he wept—not with external tears but within; he mourned the bitterness of solitude, the inability to exchange a single thought with her. He had so many things to tell her which were burning his soul! How he would talk with her, if some mysterious power would bring her back for an instant. He would implore her forgiveness; he would throw himself at her feet, lamenting the error of his life, the painful deceit of having remained beside her, indifferent, fostering hopes which had no fulfillment, only to groan now in the torment of irreparable loss, with a mad, thirsting love which worshiped the woman in death after scoring her in life.

He would swear a thousand times the truth of this posthumous worship, this desire aroused by death. And then he would lay her once more in her eternal bed, and would depart in peace after his wild confession.

But it was impossible. The silence between them would last forever. He must remain for all eternity with this confession of his thoughts, unable to tell it to her, crushed beneath its weight. She had gone away with rancor and scorn in her soul, forgetting their first love, and she would never know that it had blossomed once more after her death.

She could not cast one glance back; she did not exist; she would never again exist. All that he was doing and thinking, the sleepless nights when he called to her in loving appeal, the long hours when he stood gazing at her pictures,—all would be unknown to her. And when he died in his turn, the silence and loneliness would be still greater. The things which he had been unable to tell her would die with him and they would both crumble away in the earth, strangers to each other, prolonging their grievous error in eternity, unable to approach each other, or see each other, without a saving word, condemned to the fearful, unbounded void, over whose limitless firmament passed unnoticed the desires and griefs of men.

The unhappy artist walked up and down enraged at

his impotence. What cruelty surrounded them? What dark, hard-hearted, implacable mockery was that which drove them toward one another and then separated them forever, forever! forbidding them to exchange a look of forgiveness, a word to rectify their errors and to permit them to return to their eternal sleep with new peace?

Lies—deceit that hovers about man, like a protecting atmosphere that shields him in his path through the void of life. That grave with its inscription was a lie; she was not there; it contained merely a few remnants, like those of all the others, which no one could recognize, not even he, who had loved her so dearly.

His despair made him lift his eyes to the pure, shining sky. Ah, the heavens! A lie, too! That heavenly blue with its golden rays and fanciful clouds was an imperceptible film, an illusion of the eyes. Beyond the deceitful web which wraps the earth was the true heaven, endless space, and it was black, ominously obscure, with the sputtering spark of burning tears, of infinite worlds, little lamps of eternity in whose flame lived other swarms of invisible atoms, and the icy, blind, and cruel soul of shadowy space laughed at their passions and longings, at the lies they fabricated incessantly to protect their ephemeral existence, striving to prolong it with the illusion of an immortal soul.

All were lies which death came to unmask, interrupting men's course on the pleasant path of their illusions, throwing them out of it with as much indifference as their feet had crushed and driven to flight the lines of ants which advanced amid the grass that was sowed with bony remains.

Renovales was forced to flee. What was he doing there? What did that deserted, empty spot of earth mean to him? Before he went away, with the firm determination not to return again, he looked around the grave for a flower, a few blades of grass, something to take with him as a remembrance. No, Josephina was not there; he was sure, but like a lover, he felt that longing, that passionate respect for anything which the woman he loves had touched.

He scorned a cluster of wild-flowers which grew in abundance at the foot of the grave. He wanted them from near the head and he picked a few white buds close to the cross, thinking that perhaps their roots had touched her face, that they preserved in their petals something of her eyes, of her lips.

He went home downcast and sad, with a void in his mind and death in his soul.

But in the warm air of the house, his love came forth to meet him; he saw her beside him, smiling from the walls, rising out of the great canvases. Renovales felt a warm breath on his face, as if those pictures were breathing at once, filling the house with the essence of memories which seemed to float in the atmosphere. Everything spoke to him of her, everything was filled with that vague perfume of the past. Over there on the graveyard hill was the wretched perishable covering. He would not return. What was the use? He felt her around him, all that was left of her in the world was enclosed in the house, as the strong odor remains in a broken, forgotten perfume bottle. No, not in the house. She was in him, he felt her presence within him, like those wandering souls of the legends who took refuge in another's body, struggling to share the dwelling with the soul which was mistress of the body. They had not lived in vain so many years together—at first united by love and afterward by habit. For half a lifetime, their bodies had slept in close contact, exchanging through their open pores that warmth which is like the breath of the soul. She had taken away a part of the artist's life. In her remains, crumbling in the lonely cemetery, there was a part of the master and he, in turn, felt something strange and mysterious which chained him to her memory, which made him always long for that body—the complement of his own—which had already vanished in the void.

Renovales shut himself up in the house, with a taciturn air and a gloomy expression which terrified his valet. If Señor Cotoner came, he was to tell him that the master had gone out. If letters came from the countess, he could leave them in an old terra-cotta jar in the anteroom, where the neglected calling cards were piling up. If it was she who came, he was to close the door. He did not want anything to distract him. Dinner should be served in the studio.

And he worked alone, without a model, with a tenacity which kept him standing before the canvas until it was dark. Sometimes, when the servant entered at nightfall, he found the luncheon untouched on the table. In the evening the master ate in silence in the dining-room, from sheer animal necessity, not seeing what he was eating, his eyes gazing into space.

Cotoner, somewhat piqued at this unusual régime which prevented him from entering the studio, would call in the evening and try in vain to interest him with news of the world outside. He observed in the master's eyes a strange light, a gleam of insanity.

"How goes the work?"

Renovales answered vaguely. He could see it soon—in a few days.

His expression of indifference was repeated when he heard the Countess of Alberca mentioned. Cotoner described her alarm and astonishment at the master's behavior. She had sent for him to find out about Mariano, to complain, with tears in her eyes, of his absence. She had twice been to the door of his house and had not been

able to get in; she complained of the servant and that
mysterious work.   At least he ought to write to her, answer her letters, full of tender laments, which she did not
suspect were lying unopened and neglected in a pile of yellow cards.   The artist listened to this with a shrug of the
shoulders as if he was hearing about the sorrows of a
distant planet.

"Let's go and see Milita," he said.   "There isn't any
opera to-night."

In his retirement the only thing which connected him
with the outside world was his desire to see his daughter, to talk to her, as if he loved her with new affection.
She was his Josephina's flesh, she had lived in her.   She
was healthy and strong, like him, nothing in her appearance reminded him of the other, but her sex bound her
closely with the beloved image of her mother.

He listened to Milita with smiles of pleasure, grateful
for the interest she manifested in his health.

"Are you ill, papa?   You look poorly.   I don't like
your appearance.   You are working too much."

But he calmed her, swinging his strong arms, swelling
out his lusty chest.   He had never felt better.   And with
the minuteness of a good-natured grandfather he inquired about all the little displeasures of her life.   Her
husband spent the day with his friends.   She grew tired
of staying at home and her only amusement was making
calls or going shopping.   And after that came a complaint, always the same, which the father divined at her
first words.   López de Sosa was selfish, niggardly toward
her.   His spendthrift habits never went beyond his own
pleasures and his own person; he economized in his wife's
expenses.   He loved her in spite of that.   Milita did not
venture to deny it; no mistresses or unfaithfulness.   She
would be likely to stand that!   But he had no money except for his horses and automobiles; she even suspected

that he was gambling, and his poor wife lived without a thing to her back, and had to weep her requests every time she received a bill, little trifles of a thousand pesetas or two.

The father was as generous to her as a lover. He felt like pouring at her feet all that he had piled up in long years of labor. She must live in happiness, since she loved her husband! Her worries made him smile scornfully. Money! Josephina's daughter sad because she needed things, when in his house there were so many dirty, insignificant papers which he had worked so hard to win and which he now looked at with indifference! He always went away from these visits amid hugs and a shower of kisses from that big girl who expressed her joy by shaking him disrespectfully, as if he were a child.

"Papa, dear, how good you are! How I love you!"

One night as he left his daughter's house with Cotoner, he said mysteriously:

"Come in the morning, I will show it to you. It isn't finished but I want you to see it. Just you. No one can judge better."

Then he added with the satisfaction of an artist:

"Once I could paint only what I saw. Now I am different. It has cost me a good deal, but you shall judge."

And in his voice there was the joy of difficulties overcome, the certainty that he had produced a great work.

Cotoner came the next day, with the haste of curiosity, and entered the studio closed to others.

"Look!" said the master with a proud gesture.

His friend looked. Opposite the window was a canvas on an easel; a canvas for the most part gray, and on this, confused, interlaced lines revealing some hesitancy over the various contours of a body. At one end was a spot of color, to which the master pointed—a woman's head which stood out sharply on the rough background of the cloth.

Cotoner stood in silent contemplation. Had the great artist really painted that? He did not see the master's hand. Although he was an unimportant painter, he had a good eye, and he saw in the canvas hesitancy, fear, awkwardness, the struggle with something unreal which was beyond his reach, which refused to enter the mold of form. He was struck by the lack of likeness, by the forced exaggeration of the strokes; the eyes unnaturally large, the tiny mouth, almost a point, the bright skin with its supernatural pallor. Only in the pupils of the eyes was there something remarkable—a glance that came from afar, an extraordinary light which seemed to pass through the canvas.

"It has cost me a great deal. No work ever made me suffer so. This is only the head; the easiest part. The body will come later; a divine nude, such as has never been seen. And only you shall see it, only you!"

The Bohemian no longer looked at the picture. He was gazing at the master, astonished at the work, disconcerted by its mystery.

"You see, without a model. Without the real before me," continued the master. "*They* were all the guide I had; but it is my best, my supreme work."

They were all the portraits of the dead woman, taken down from the walls and placed on easels or chairs in a close circle around the canvas.

His friend could not contain his astonishment, he could not pretend any longer, overcome by surprise.

"Oh, but it is—— But you have been trying to paint Josephina!"

Renovales started back violently.

"Josephina, yes. Who else should it be? Where are your eyes?"

And his angry glance flashed at Cotoner.

The latter looked at the head again. Yes, it was she, with a beauty that was not of this world,—uncanny, spiritualized, as if it belonged to a new humanity, free from coarse necessities, in which the last traces of animal descent have died out. He gazed at the numerous portraits of other times and recognized parts of them in the new work, but animated by a light which came from within and changed the value of the colors, giving to the face a strange unfamiliarity.

"You recognize her at last!" said the master, anxiously following the impressions of his work in the eyes of his friend. "Is it she? Tell me, don't you think it is like her?"

Cotoner lied compassionately. Yes, it was she, at last he saw her well enough. She, but more beautiful than in life. Josephina had never looked like that.

Now it was Renovales who looked with surprise and pity. Poor Cotoner! Unhappy failure—pariah of art, who could not rise above the nameless crowd and whose only feeling was in his stomach! What did he know about such things? What was the use of asking his opinion?

He had not recognized Josephina, and nevertheless this canvas was his best portrait, the most exact.

Renovales bore her within him, he saw her merely by retiring into his thoughts. No one could know her better than he. The rest had forgotten her. That was the way he saw her and that was what she had been.

IV

THE Countess of Alberca succeeded in making her way, one afternoon, to the master's studio.

The servant saw her arrive as usual in a cab, cross the garden, come up the steps, and enter the reception room with the hasty step of a resolute woman who goes straight ahead without hesitating. He tried to block her way respectfully, going from side to side, meeting her every time she started to one side to pass this obstacle. The master was working! The master was not receiving callers! It was a strict order; he could not make an exception! But she continued ahead with a frown, a flash of cold wrath in her eyes, an evident determination to strike down the servant, if it was necessary, and to pass over his body.

"Come, my good man, get out of the way."

And her haughty, irritated accent made the poor servant tremble and at a loss to stop this invasion of rustling skirts and strong perfumes. In one of her evolutions the fair lady ran into an Italian mosaic table, on the center of which was the old jar. Her glance fell instinctively to the bottom of the jar.

It was only an instant, but enough for her woman's curiosity to recognize the blue envelopes with white borders, whose sealed ends stuck out, untouched, from the pile of cards. The last straw! Her paleness grew intense, almost greenish, and she started forward with such a rush that the servant could not stop her and was left behind her, dejected, confused, fearful of his master's wrath.

Renovales, alarmed by the sharp click of heels on
the hard floor, and the rustling of skirts, turned toward
the door just as the countess made her entrance with a
dramatic expression.

"It's me."

"You? You, dear?"

Excitement, surprise, fear made the master stammer.

"Sit down," he said coldly.

She sat down on a couch and the artist remained standing in front of her.

They looked at each other as if they did not recognize
each other after this absence of weeks which weighed
on their memories as if it were of years.

Renovales looked at her coldly, without the least tremble of desire, as if it were an ordinary visitor whom he
must get rid of as soon as possible. He was surprised
at her greenish pallor, at her mouth, drawn with irritation, at her hard eyes which flashed yellow flames, at her
nose which curved down to her upper lip. She was
angry, but when her eyes fell on him, they lost their
hardness.

Her woman's instinct was calmed when she gazed at
him. He, too, looked different in the carelessness of the
seclusion; his hair tangled, revealing the preoccupation,
the fixed, absorbing idea, which made him neglect the
neatness of his person.

Her jealousy vanished instantly, her cruel suspicion
that she would surprise him in love with another woman,
with the fickleness of an artist. She knew the external
evidence of love, the necessity a man feels of making
himself attractive, refining the care of his dress.

She surveyed his neglect with satisfaction, noticing
his dirty clothes, his long fingernails, stained with paint,
all the details which revealed lack of tidiness, forgetful-
ness of his person. No doubt it was a passing artist's

whim, a craze for work, but they did not reveal what she had suspected.

In spite of this calming certainty, as Concha was ready to shed the tears which were all prepared, waiting impatiently on the edge of her eyelids, she raised her hands to her eyes, curling up on one end of the couch, with a tragic expression. She was very unhappy; she was suffering terribly. She had passed several horrible weeks. What was the matter? Why had he disappeared without a word of explanation, when she loved him more than ever, when she was ready to give up everything, to cause a perfect scandal, by coming to live with him, as his companion, his slave? And her letters, her poor letters, neglected, unopened, as if they were annoying requests for alms. She had spent the nights awake, putting her whole soul into their pages! And in her accent there was a tremble of literary pique, of bitterness, that all the pretty things, which she wrote down with a smile of satisfaction after long reflection, remained unknown. Men! Their selfishness and cruelty! How stupid women were to worship them!

She continued to weep and Renovales looked at her as if she were another woman. She seemed ridiculous to him in that grief, which distorted her face, which made her ugly, destroying her smiling, doll-like impassibility.

He tried to offer excuses, that he might not seem cruel by keeping silent, but they lacked warmth and the desire to carry conviction. He was working hard; it was time for him to return to his former life of creative activity. She forgot that he was an artist, a master of some reputation, who had his duty to the public. He was not like those young fops who could devote the whole day to her and pass their life at her feet, like enamored pages.

"We must be serious, Concha," he added with pedantic coldness. "Life is not play. I must work and I am working. I haven't been out of here for I don't know how many days."

She stood up angrily, took her hands from her eyes, looked at him, rebuking him. He lied; he had been out and it had never occurred to him to come to her house for a moment.

"Just to say 'Good morning,' nothing more. So that I may see you for an instant, Mariano, long enough to be sure that you are the same, that you still love me. But you have gone out often; you have been seen. I have my detectives who tell me everything. You are too well known to pass unnoticed. You have been in the Museo del Prado mornings. You have been seen gazing at a picture of Goya's, a nude, for hours at a time, like an idiot. Your hobby is coming back again, Mariano! And it hasn't occurred to you to come and see me; you haven't answered my letters. You feel proud, it seems, content with being loved, and submit to being worshiped like an idol, certain that the more uncivil you are, the more you will be loved. Oh, these men! These artists!"

She sobbed, but her voice no longer preserved the irritated tone of the first few moments. The certainty that she did not have to struggle with the influence of another woman softened her pride, leaving in her only the gentle complaint of a victim who is eager to sacrifice herself anew.

"But sit down," she exclaimed amid her sobs, pointing to a place on the couch beside her. "Don't stand up. You look as if you wanted me to go away."

The painter sat down timidly, taking care not to touch her, avoiding those hands which reached out to him, longing for a pretext to seize him. He saw her desire to weep on his shoulder, to forget everything, and to banish her last tears with a smile. That was what always happened, but Renovales, knowing the game, drew back

roughly. That must not begin again; it could not be repeated, even if he wanted to. He must tell her the truth
at any cost, end it forever, throw off the burden from
his shoulders.

He spoke hoarsely, stammering, with his eyes on the
floor, not daring to lift them for fear of meeting Concha's which he felt were fixed upon him.

For several days he had been meaning to write to her.
He had been afraid that he might not express his ideas
clearly and so he had put off the letter until the next
day. Now he was glad she had come; he rejoiced at the
weakness of his valet, in letting her enter.

They must talk like good comrades who examine the
future together. It was time to put an end to their folly.
They would be what Concha once desired, friends—good
friends. She was beautiful; she still had the freshness
of youth, but time leaves its mark, and he felt that he was
getting old; he looked at life from a height, as we look
at the water of a stream, without dipping into it.

Concha listened to him in astonishment, refusing to
understand his words. What did these scruples mean?
After some digressions, the painter spoke remorsefully
of his friend, the Count of Alberca, a man whom he respected for his very guilelessness. His conscience rose
in protest at the simple admiration of the good man.
This daring deceit in his own house, under his own roof,
was infamous. He could not go on; they must purify
themselves from the past by being good friends, must say
good-by as lovers, without spite or antipathy, grateful
to each other for the happy past, taking with them, like
dead lovers, their pleasant memories.

Concha's laugh, nervous, sarcastic, insolent, interrupted
the artist. Her cruel spirit of fun was aroused at the
thought that her husband was the pretext of this break.
Her husband! And once more she began to laugh up-

roariously, revealing the count's insignificance, the absolute lack of respect which he inspired in his wife, or her
habit of adjusting her life as her fancy dictated, with
never a thought of what that man might say or think.
Her husband did not exist for her; she never feared him;
she had never thought that he might serve as an obstacle,
and yet her lover spoke of him, presented *him* as a jus-
tification for leaving her!

"My husband!" she repeated amid the peals of her
cruel laughter. "Poor thing! Leave him in peace; he
has nothing to do with us. Don't lie; don't be a coward.
Speak. You've something else on your mind. I don't
know what it is; but I have a presentiment, I see it from
here. If you loved another woman! If you loved another woman!"

But she broke off this threatening exclamation. She
needed only to look at him to be convinced that it was
impossible. His body was not perfumed with love;
everything about him revealed calm peace, without interests or desires. Perhaps it was a whim of his fancy,
some unbalanced caprice which led him to repel her.
And encouraged by this belief, she relaxed, forgetting her
anger, speaking to him affectionately, caressing him with
a fervor in which there was something at once of the
mother and of the mistress.

Renovales suddenly saw her beside him with her arms
around his neck, burying her hands in his tangled hair.

She was not proud; men worshiped her, but her heart,
her body, all of her belonged to the master, the ungrateful
brute, who returned so ill her affection that she was getting old with her trouble.

Suddenly filled with tenderness, she kissed his forehead generously and purely. Poor boy! He was working so hard! The only thing the matter was that he was
tired out, distracted with too much painting. He must

leave his brushes alone, live, love her, be happy, rest his wrinkled forehead behind which, like a curtain, an invisible world passed and repassed in perpetual revolution.

"Let me kiss your pretty forehead again, so that the hobgoblins within may be silent and sleep."

And she kissed once more his *pretty* forehead, delighting in caressing with her lips the furrows and prominences of its irregular surface, rough as volcanic ground.

For a long time her wheedling voice, with an exaggerated childish lisp, sounded in the silence of the studio. She was jealous of painting, the cruel mistress, exacting and repugnant, who seemed to drive her poor baby mad. One of these days, master, the studio would catch on fire together with all its pictures. She tried to draw him to her, to make him sit on her lap, so that she might rock him like a child.

"Look here, Mariano, dear. Laugh for your Concha. Laugh, you big stupid! Laugh, or I'll whip you."

He laughed, but it was forced. He tried to resist her fondling, tired of those childish tricks which once were his delight. He remained indifferent to those hands, those lips, to the warmth of that body which rubbed against him without awakening the least desire. And he had loved that woman! For her he had committed the terrible, irreparable crime which would make him drag the chain of remorse forever! What surprises life has in store!

The painter's coldness finally had its effect on the Alberca woman. She seemed to awaken from the dream, in which she was lulling herself. She drew back from her lover, and looked at him fixedly with imperious eyes, in which a spark of pride was once more beginning to flash.

"Say that you love me! Say it at once! I need it!"

But in vain did she show her authority; in vain she brought her eyes close to him, as if she wished to look within him. The artist smiled faintly, murmured evasive words, refused to comply with her demands.

"Say it out loud, so that I can hear it. Say that you love me. Call me Phryne, as you used to when you worshiped me on your knees, kissing my body!"

He said nothing. He hung his head in shame at the memory, so as not to see her.

The countess stood up nervously. In her anger, she drew back to the middle of the studio, her hands clenched, her lips quivering, her eyes flashing. She wanted to destroy something, to fall on the floor in a convulsion. She hesitated whether to break an Arabic amphora close by, or to fall on that bowed head and scratch it with her nails. Wretch! She had loved him so dearly; she still cared for him so, feeling bound to him by both vanity and habit!

"Say whether you love me," she cried. "Say it once and for all! Yes or no?"

Still she obtained no answer. The silence was trying. Once more she believed there was another love, a woman who had come to occupy her place. But who was it? Where could he have found her? Her woman's instinct made her turn her head and glance into the next studio and beyond into the last, the real workshop of the master. Warned by a mysterious intuition, she started to run toward it. There! Perhaps there! The painter's steps sounded behind her. He had started from his dejection when he saw her fleeing; he followed her in a frenzy of fear. Concha foresaw that she was going to know the truth; a cruel truth with all the crudeness of a discovery in broad daylight. She stopped, scowling with a mental effort before that portrait which seemed to dominate the studio, occupying the best easel, in the most advantageous position, in spite of the solitary gray of its canvas.

The master saw in Concha's face the same expression of doubt and surprise which he had seen in Cotoner's. Who was that? But the hesitation was shorter; her woman's pride sharpened her senses. She saw beyond that unrecognizable head the circle of older portraits which seemed to guard it.

Ah! The immense surprise in her eyes; the cold astonishment in the glance she fixed on the painter as she surveyed him from head to foot!

"Is it Josephina?"

He bowed his head in mute assent. But his silence seemed to him cowardly; he felt that he must cry out in the presence of those canvases, what he had not dared to say outside. It was a longing to flatter the dead woman, to implore her forgiveness, by confessing his hopeless love.

"Yes, it is Josephina."

And he said it with spirit, going forward a step, looking at Concha as if she were an enemy, with a sort of hostility in his eyes which did not escape her notice.

They did not say anything more. The countess could not speak. Her surprise passed the limits of the probable, the known.

In love with his wife,—and after she was dead! Shut up like a hermit in order to paint her with a beauty which she had never had. Life brings surprises, but this surely had never been seen before.

She felt as if she were falling, falling, driven by astonishment and, at the end of the fall, she found that she was changed, without a complaint or pang of grief. Everything about her seemed strange—the room, the man, the pictures. This whole affair went beyond her power of conception. Had she found a woman there, it would have made her weep and shriek with grief, roll on the floor, love the master still more with the stimulus of jealousy. But to find that her rival was a dead woman! And more than that—his wife! It seemed supremely ridiculous, she felt a mad desire to laugh. But she did not laugh. She recalled the unusual expression she had noticed on the master's face, when she entered the studio; she thought that now she saw in his eyes a spark of that same gleam.

Suddenly she felt afraid; afraid of the man who looked at her in silence as if he did not know her and toward whom she felt the same strangeness.

Still she had for him a glance of sympathy, of that tenderness which every woman feels in the presence of unhappiness, even if it afflicts a stranger. Poor Mariano! All was over between them; she took care not to speak intimately to him; she held out her gloved hand with the gesture of an unapproachable lady. For a long time they stood in this position, speaking only with their eyes.

"Good-by, master; take care of yourself! Don't bother to come with me. I know the way. Go on with your work. Paint——"

Her heels clicked nervously on the waxed floor as she left the room, which she was never to enter again. The swish of her skirts scattered their wake of perfumes in the studio for the last time.

Renovales breathed more freely when he was left alone. He had ended forever the error of his life. The only thing in this visit that left a sting was the countess's hesitation before the portrait. She had recognized it sooner than Cotoner, but she too had hesitated. No one remembered Josephina; he alone kept her image.

That same afternoon, before his old friend came, the master received another call. His daughter appeared in the studio. Renovales had divined that it was she before she entered, by the whirl of joy and overflowing life which seemed to precede her.

She had come to see him; she had promised him a visit months ago. And her father smiled indulgently, recalling some of her complaints when he last visited her. Just to see him?

Milita pretended to be absorbed in examining the studio which she had not entered for a long time.

"Look!" she exclaimed. "Why, it's mamma!"

She looked at the picture with astonishment, but the master seemed pleased at the readiness with which she had recognized her. At last, his daughter! The instinct of blood! The poor master did not see the hasty glance at the other portraits which had guided the girl in her induction.

"Do you like it? Is it she?" he asked as anxiously as a novice.

Milita answered rather vaguely. Yes, it was good; perhaps a little more beautiful than she was. She never knew her like that.

"That is true," said the master. "You never saw her in her good days. But she was like that before you were born. Your poor mother was very beautiful."

But his daughter did not manifest any great enthusiasm over the picture. It seemed strange to her. Why was the head at one end of the canvas? What was he going to add? What did those lines mean? The master tried to explain, almost blushing, afraid to tell his intention to his daughter, suddenly overcome by paternal modesty. He was not sure as yet what he would do; he had to decide on a dress to suit her. And in a sudden access of tenderness, his eyes grew moist and he kissed his daughter.

"Do you remember her well, Milita? She was very good, wasn't she?"

His daughter felt infected by her father's sadness, but only for a moment. Her strength, health and joy of life soon threw off these sad impressions. Yes, very good. She often thought about her. Perhaps she spoke the truth; but these memories were not deep nor painful. Death seemed to her a thing without meaning, a remote incident without much terror which did not disturb the serene calm of her physical perfection.

"Poor mamma," she added in a forced tone. "It was a relief for her to go. Always sick, always sad! With such a life it is better to die!"

In her words there was a trace of bitterness, the memory of her youth, spent with that touchy invalid, in an atmosphere made the more unpleasant by the hostile chill with which her parents treated each other. Besides, her expression was icy. We all must die. The weak must go first and leave their place to the strong. It was the unconscious, cruel selfishness of health. Renovales suddenly saw his daughter's soul through this rent of frankness. The dead woman had known them both. The daughter was his, wholly his. He, too, possessed that selfishness in his strength which had made him crush weakness and delicacy placed under his protection. Poor Josephina had only him left, repentant and adoring. For the other people, she had not passed through the world; not even his daughter felt any lasting sorrow at her death.

Milita turned her back to the portrait. She forgot her mother and her father's work. An artist's hobby! She had come for something else.

She sat down beside him, almost in the same way that another woman had sat down, a few hours before. She coaxed him with her rich voice, which took on a sort of

cat-like purring. Papa,—papa, dear,—she was very unhappy. She came to see him, to tell him her troubles.

"Yes, money," said the master, somewhat annoyed at
the indifference with which she had spoken of her
mother.

"Money, papa, you've said it; I told you the other day.
But that isn't all. Rafael—my husband—I can't stand
this sort of life."

And she related all the petty trials of her existence.
In order not to feel that she was prematurely a widow,
she had to go with her husband in his automobile and
show an interest in his trips which once had amused her
but now were growing unbearable.

"It's the life of a section-hand, papa, always swallowing dust and counting kilometers. When I love Madrid
so much! When I can't live out of it!"

She had sat down on her father's knees, she talked to
him, looking into his eyes, smoothing his hair, pulling
his mustache, like a mischievous child,—almost as the
other had.

"Besides, he's stingy; if he had his way, I'd look like a
frump. He thinks everything is too much. Papa, help
me out of this difficulty, it's only two thousand pesetas.
With that I can get on my feet and then I won't bother
you with any more loans. Come, that's a dear papa. I
need them right away, because I waited till the last minute, so as not to inconvenience you."

Renovales moved about uneasily under the weight of
his daughter, a strapping girl who fell on him like a child.
Her filial confidences annoyed him. Her perfume made
him think of that other perfume, which disturbed his
nights, spreading through the solitude of the rooms. She
seemed to have inherited her mother's flesh.

He pushed her away roughly, and she took this movement for a refusal. Her face grew sad, tears came to

her eyes, and her father repented his brusqueness. He
was surprised at her constant requests for money. What
did she want it for? He recalled the wedding-presents,
that princely abundance of clothes and jewels which had
been on exhibition in this very room. What did she need?
But Milita looked at her father in astonishment. More
than a year had gone by since then. It was clear enough
that her father was ignorant in such matters. Was she
going to wear the same gowns, the same hats, the same
ornaments for an endless length of time, more than
twelve months? Horrible! That was too commonplace.
And overcome at the thought of such a monstrosity, she
began to shed her tender tears to the great disturbance
of the master.

"There, there, Milita, there's no use in crying. What
do you want? Money? I'll send you all you need to-
morrow. I haven't much at the house. I shall have to get
it at the bank—operations you don't understand."

But Milita, encouraged by her victory, insisted on·her
request with desperate obstinacy. He was deceiving her;
he would not remember it the next day; she knew her
father. Besides, she needed the money at once,—her
honor was at stake (she declared it seriously) if her
friends discovered that she was in debt.

"This very minute, papa. Don't be horrid. Don't
amuse yourself by making me worry. You must have
money, lots of it, perhaps you have it on you. Let's see,
you naughty papa, let me search your pockets, let me look
at your wallet. Don't say no; you have it with you. You
have it with you!"

She plunged her hands in her father's breast, unbutton-
ing his working jacket, tickling him to get at the inside
pocket. Renovales resisted feebly. "You foolish girl.
You're wasting your time. Where do you think the wallet is? I never carry it in this suit."

"It's here, you fibber," his daughter cried merrily, persisting in her search. "I feel it! I have it! Look at it!"

She was right. The painter had forgotten that he had picked it up that morning to pay a bill and then had put it absent-mindedly in the pocket of his serge coat.

Milita opened it with a greediness that hurt her father. Oh, those woman's hands, trembling in the search for money! He grew calmer when he thought of the fortune he had amassed, of the different colored papers which he kept in his desk. All would be his daughter's and perhaps this would save her from the danger toward which her longing to live amid the vanities and tinsel of feminine slavery was leading her.

In an instant she had her hands on a number of bills of different denominations, forming a roll which she squeezed tight between her fingers.

Renovales protested.

"Let me have it, Milita, don't be childish. You're leaving me without a cent. I'll send it to you to-morrow; give it up now. It's robbery."

She avoided him; she had stood up; she kept at a distance, raising her hand above her hat to save her booty. She laughed boisterously at her trick. She did not mean to give him back a single one! She did not know how many there were, she would count them at home, she would be out of difficulty for the nonce, and the next day she would ask him for what was lacking.

The master finally began to laugh, finding her merriment contagious. He chased Milita without trying to catch her; he threatened her with mock severity, called her a robber, shouting "help," and so they ran from one studio to another. Before she disappeared, Milita stopped on the last doorsill, raising her gloved finger authoritatively:

"To-morrow, the rest. You mustn't forget. Really, papa, this is very important. Good-by; I shall expect you to-morrow."

And she disappeared, leaving in her father some of the merriment with which they had chased each other.

The twilight was gloomy. Renovales sat in front of his wife's portrait, gazing at that extravagantly beautiful head which seemed to him the most faithful of his portraits. His thoughts were lost in the shadow which rose from the corners and enveloped the canvases. Only on the windows trembled a pale, hazy light, cut across by the black lines of the branches outside.

Alone—alone forever. He had the affection of that big girl who had just gone away, merry, indifferent to everything which did not flatter her youthful vanity, her healthy beauty. He had the devotion of his friend Cotoner, who, like an old dog, could not live without seeing him, but was incapable of wholly devoting his life to him, and shared it between him and other friends, jealous of his Bohemian freedom.

And that was all. Very little.

On the verge of old age, he gazed at a cruel, reddish light which seemed to irritate his eyes; the solitary, monotonous road which awaited him—and at the end, death! No one was ignorant of that; it was the only certainty, and still he had spent the greater part of his life without thinking of it, without seeing it.

It was like one of those epidemics in distant lands which destroy millions of lives. People talk of it as of a definite fact, but without a start of horror, or a tremble of fear. "It is too far away; it will take it a long time to reach us."

He had often named Death, but with his lips; his thoughts had not grasped the meaning of the word, feeling that he was alive, bound to life by his dreams and desires.

Death stood at the end of the road; no one could avoid meeting it, but all are long in seeing it. Ambition, desire, love, the cruel animal needs distracted man in his course toward it; they were like the woods, valleys, blue sky and winding crystal streams which diverted the traveler, hiding the boundary of the landscape, the fatal goal, the black bottomless gorge to which all roads lead.

He was on the last days' march. The path of his life was growing desolate and gloomy; the vegetation was dwindling; the great groves diminished into sparse, miserable lichens. From the murky abyss came an icy breath; he saw it in the distance, he walked without escape toward its gorge. The fields of dreams with their sunlit heights which once bounded the horizon, were left behind and it was impossible to return. In this path no one retraced his steps.

He had wasted half his life, struggling for wealth and fame, hoping sometimes to receive their revenues in the pleasures of love. Die! Who thought of that? Then it was a remote, unmeaning threat. He believed that he was provided with a mission by Providence. Death would take no liberties with him, would not come till his work was finished. He still had many things to do. Well, all was done now; human desires did not exist for him. He had everything. No longer did fanciful towers rise before his steps, for him to assault. On the horizon, free from obstacles, appeared the great forgotten,—Death.

He did not want to see it. There was still a long journey on that road which might grow longer and longer, according to the strength of the traveler, and his legs were still strong.

But, ah, to walk, walk, year after year, with his gaze fixed on that murky abyss, contemplating it always at the edge of the horizon, unable to escape for an instant the certainty that it was there, was a superhuman torture which would force him to hurry his steps, to run in order to reach the end as soon as possible. Oh, for deceitful clouds which might veil the horizon, concealing the reality which embitters our bread, which casts its shadows over our souls and makes us curse the futility of our birth! Oh, for lying, pleasant illusions to make a paradise rise from the desert shadows of the last journey! Oh, for dreams!

And in his mind the poor master enlarged the last fancy of his desire; he connected with the beloved likeness of his dead wife all the flights of his imagination, longing to infuse into it new life with a part of his own. He piled up by handfuls the clay of the past, the mass of memory, to make it greater that it might occupy the whole way, shut off the horizon like a huge hill, hide till the last moment the murky abyss which ended the journey.

V

RENOVALES' behavior was a source of surprise and even scandal for all his friends.

The Countess of Alberca took especial care to let every one know that her only relation with the painter was a friendship which grew constantly colder and more formal.

"He's crazy," she said. "He's finished. There's nothing left of him but a memory of what he once was."

Cotoner in his unswerving friendship was indignant at hearing such comment on the famous master.

"He isn't drinking. All that people say about him is a lie; the usual legend about a celebrated man."

He had his own ideas about Mariano; he knew his longing for a stirring life, his desire to imitate the habits of youth in the prime of life, with a thirst for all the mysteries which he fancied were hidden in this evil life, of which he had heard without ever daring till then to join in them.

Cotoner accepted the master's new habits indulgently. Poor fellow!

"You are putting into action the pictures of 'The Rake's Progress,'" he said to his friend. "You're going the way of all virtuous men when they cease to be so, on the verge of old age. You are making a fool of yourself, Mariano."

But his loyalty led him to acquiesce in the new life of the master. At last he had given in to his requests and had come to live with him. With his few pieces of luggage he occupied a room in the house and cared for

Renovales with almost paternal solicitude. The Bohemian showed great sympathy for him. It was the same
old story: "He who does not do it at the beginning
does it at the end," and Renovales, after a life of hard
work, was rushing into a life of dissipation with the
blindness of a youth, admiring vulgar pleasures, clothing them with the most fanciful seductions.

Cotoner frequently harassed him with complaints.
What had he brought him to live at his house for? He
deserted him for days at a time; he wanted to go out
alone; he left him at home like a trusty steward. The old
Bohemian posted himself minutely on his life. Often the
students in the Art School, gathered at nightfall beside
the entrance to the Academy, saw him going down the
Calle de Alcalá, muffled in his cloak with an affected air
of mystery that attracted attention.

"There goes Renovales. That one, the one in the
cloak."

And they followed him out of curiosity—in his com-
ings and goings through the broad street where he circled
about like a silent dove as if he were waiting for something. Sometimes, no doubt tired of these evolutions, he
went into a café and the curious admirers followed him,
pressing their faces against the window-panes. They
saw him drop into a chair, looking vaguely at the glass
before him; always the same thing: brandy. Suddenly
he would drink it at one gulp, pay the waiter and go out,
with the haste of one who has swallowed a drug. And
once more he would begin his explorations, peering with
greedy eyes at all the women who passed alone, turning
around to follow the course of run-down heels, the flutter
of dark and mud-splashed skirts. At last he would start
with sudden determination, he would disappear almost
on the heel of some woman always of the same appearance. The boys knew the great artist's preference: little,

weak, sickly women, graceful as faded flowers, with large eyes, dull and sorrowful.

A story of strange mental aberration was forming about him. His enemies repeated it in the studios; the throng which cannot imagine that celebrated men lead the same life as other people, and like to think that they are capricious, tormented by extraordinary habits, began to talk with delight about the hobby of the painter Renovales.

In all the houses of prostitution, from the middle class apartments, scattered in the most respectable streets, to the damp, ill-smelling dens which cast out their wares at night on the Calle de Peligros, circulated the story of a certain gentleman, provoking shouts of laughter. He always came muffled up mysteriously, following hastily the rustle of some poor starched skirts which preceded him. He entered the dark doorway with a sort of terror, climbed the winding staircase which seemed to smell of the residues of life, hastened the disrobing with eager hands, as if he had no time to waste, as if he was afraid of dying before he realized his desire, and all at once the poor women who looked askance at his feverish silence and the savage hunger which shone in his eyes, were tempted to laugh, seeing him drop dejectedly into a chair in silence, unmindful of the brutal words which they in their astonishment hurled at him; without paying any attention to their gestures and invitations, not coming out of his stupor till the woman, cold and somewhat offended, started to put on her clothes. "One moment more."* This scene almost always ended with an expression of disgust, of bitter disappointment. Sometimes the poor puppets of flesh thought they saw in his eyes a sorrowful expression, as if he were going to weep. Then he fled precipitously, hidden under his cloak in sudden shame, with the firm determination not to return, to resist that demon of hungry curiosity which dwelt within him and could not see a woman's form in the street, without feeling a violent desire to disrobe it.

These stories came to Cotoner's ears. Mariano! Mariano! He did not dare to rebuke him openly for these shameful nocturnal adventures; he was afraid of a violent explosion of anger on the part of the master. He must direct him prudently. But what most aroused his old friend's censure was the people with whom the artist associated.

This false rejuvenation made him seek the company of the younger men and Cotoner cursed roundly when at the close of the theater he found him in a café, surrounded by his new comrades, all of whom might be his sons. Most of them were painters, novices, some with considerable talent, others whose only merit was their evil tongue, all of them proud of their friendship with the famous man, delighting like pigmies in treating him as an equal, jesting over his weaknesses. Great Heavens! Some of the bolder even went so far as to call him by his first name, treating him like a glorious failure, presuming to make comparisons between his paintings and what they would do when they could. "Mariano, art moves in different paths, now."

"Aren't you ashamed of yourself!" Cotoner would exclaim. "You look like a schoolmaster surrounded by children. You ought to be spanked. A man like you tolerating the insolence of those shabby fellows!"

Renovales' good nature was unshaken. They were very interesting; they amused him; he found in them the joy of youth. They went together to the theaters and music halls, they knew women; they knew where the good models were; with them he could enter many places where he would not venture to go alone. His years and ugliness passed unnoticed amid that youthful merry crowd.

"They are of service to me," the poor man said with a sly wink. "I am amused and they tell me lots of things. Besides,' this isn't Rome; there are hardly any models; it is very difficult to find them and these boys are my guides."

And he went on to speak of his great artistic plans, of that picture of Phryne, with her divine nakedness, which had once more risen in his mind, of the beloved portrait which was still in the same condition as his brush had left it when he finished the head.

He was not working. His old energy, which had made painting a necessary element in his life, now found vent in words, in the desire to see everything, to know "new phases of life."

Soldevilla, his favorite pupil, found himself a target for the master's questions when he appeared at rare intervals in the studio.

"You must know good women, Soldevilla: You have been around a great deal in spite of that angel face of yours. You must take me with you. You must introduce me."

"Master!" the youth would exclaim in surprise, "it isn't yet six months since I was married! I never go out at night! How you joke!"

Renovales answered with a scornful glance. A fine life! No youth, no joy! He spent all his money on variegated waistcoats and high collars. What a perfect ant! He had married a rich woman, since he couldn't catch the master's daughter. Besides, he was an ungrateful scamp. Now he was joining the master's enemies, convinced that he could get nothing more out of him. He scorned him. It was too bad that his protection had caused him so much inconvenience! He was no artist.

And the master went back with new affection to his companions, those merry youths, slandering and disrespectful as they were. He recognized talent in them all.

The gossip about his extraordinary life reached even his daughter, with the rapid spread which anything prejudicial to a famous man acquires.

Milita scowled, trying to restrain the laughter which the strangeness of this change aroused. Her father becoming a rake!

"Papa! Papa!" she exclaimed in a comic tone of reproach.

And papa made excuses like a naughty, hypocritical little boy, increasing by his perturbation his daughter's desire to laugh.

López de Sosa seemed inclined to be indulgent toward his father-in-law. Poor old gentleman! All his life working, with a sick wife, who was very good and kind, to be sure, but who had embittered his life! She did well to die, and the artist did quite as well in making up for the time he had lost.

With the instinctive freemasonry of all those who lead an easy, merry life, the sport defended his father-in-law, supported him, found him more attractive, more congenial, as a result of his new habits. A man must not always stay shut up in his studio with the irritated air of a prophet, talking about things which nobody would understand.

They met each other in the evening during the last acts at the theaters and music halls, when the songs and dances were accompanied by the audience with a storm of cries and stamping. They greeted each other, the father inquired for Milita, they smiled with the sympathy of two good fellows and each went back to his group; the son-in-law to his club-mates in a box, still wearing the dress suits of the respectable gatherings from which they came

—the painter to the orchestra seats with the long-haired young fellows who were his escort.

Renovales was gratified to see López de Sosa greeting the most fashionable, highest-priced *cocottes* and smiling to comic-opera stars with the familiarity of an old friend.

That boy had excellent connections, and he regarded this as an indirect honor to his position as a father.

Cotoner frequently found himself dragged out of his orbit of serious, substantial dinners and evening-parties, which he continued to frequent in order not to lose his friendships which were his only source of income.

"You are coming with me to-night," the master would say mysteriously. "We will dine wherever you like, and afterwards I will show you something."

And he took him to the theater where he sat restless and impatient until the chorus came on the stage. Then he would nudge Cotoner, who was sunk in his seat, with his eyes wide open, but asleep inside, in the sweet pleasure of good digestion.

"Listen, look! the third from the right, the little girl— the one in the yellow shawl!"

"I see her. What about her?" said his friend in a sour voice.

"Look at her closely. Who does she look like? Who does she remind you of?"

Cotoner answered with a grunt of indifference. She probably looked like her mother. What did he care about such resemblances. But his astonishment aroused him from his quiet when he heard Renovales say he thought her a rare likeness of his wife, and was indignant at him because he did not recognize it.

"Why, Mariano, where are your eyes?" he exclaimed with no less sourness. "What resemblance is there between that scraggly girl with her starved face and your poor, dead wife. If you see a sorry-looking bean pole you

will give it a name, Josephina,—and there's nothing more
to say."

Although Renovales was at first irritated at his friend's
blindness, he was finally convinced. He had probably deceived himself, as long as Cotoner did not find the likeness. He must remember the dead woman better than he
himself; love did not disturb *his* memory.

But a few days later he would once more besiege
Cotoner with a mysterious air. "I have something to
show you." And leaving the company of the merry lads
who annoyed his old friend, he would take him to a music
hall and point out another scandalous woman who was
kicking a fling or doing a *danse du ventre,* and revealed
her anemic emaciation under a mask of rouge.

"How about this one?" the master would implore, almost in terror as if he doubted his own eyes. "Don't
you think she looks something like her? Doesn't she
remind you of her?"

His friend broke out angrily:

"You're crazy. What likeness is there between that
poor little woman, so good, so sweet and so refined, and
this low creature?"

Renovales, after several failures which made him doubt
the accuracy of his memory, did not dare to consult his
friend. As soon as he tried to take him to a new show,
Cotoner would draw back.

"Another discovery? Come, Mariano, get these ideas
out of your head. If people found out about it, they
would think that you were crazy."

But defying his wrath, the master insisted one evening
with great obstinacy that he must go with him to see the
"Bella Fregolina," a Spanish girl, who was singing at a
little theater in the low quarter, and whose name was dis-
played in letters a meter high in the shop windows of

Madrid. He had spent more than two weeks watching her every evening.

"I must have you see her, Pepe. Just for a minute. I beg you. I am sure that this time you won't say that I am mistaken."

Cotoner gave in, persuaded by the imploring tone of his friend. They waited for the appearance of the "Bella Fregolina" for a long time, watching dances and listening to songs accompanied by the howls of the audience. The wonder was reserved till the last. At last, with a sort of solemnity, amid a murmur of expectation, the orchestra began to play a piece well known to all the admirers of the "star," a ray of rosy light crossed the little stage and the "Bella" entered.

She was a slight little girl, so thin that she was almost emaciated. Her face, of a sweet melancholy beauty, was the most striking thing about her. Beneath her black dress, covered with silver threads, which spread out like a broad bell, you could see her slender legs, so thin that the flesh seemed hardly to cover the bones. Above the lace of her gown her skin, painted white, marked the slight curve of her breasts and the prominent collar bones. The first thing you saw about her were her eyes, large, clear, and girlish, but the eyes of a depraved girl, in which a licentious expression flickered, without, however, hurting their pure surface. She moved like an overgrown schoolgirl, arms akimbo, bashful and blushing and in this position she sang in a thin, high voice, obscene verses which contrasted strangely with her apparent timidity. This was her charm and the audience received her atrocious words with roars of delight, contenting themselves with this, without demanding that she dance, respecting her hieratic stiffness.

When the painter saw her appear he nudged his friend. He did not dare to speak, waiting for his opinion anxiously. He followed his inspection out of the corner of his eye.

His friend was merciful.

Yes, she is something like her. Her eyes,—figure,— expression; she reminds me of her. She is very much like her. But the monkey face she is making now! The words! No, that destroys all likeness."

And as if he were angry that that little girl without any voice and without any sense of shame, should be compared to the sweet Josephina, he commented with sarcastic admiration on all the cynical expressions with which she ended her couplets.

"Very pretty! Very refined!"

But Renovales, deaf to these ironical remarks, absorbed in the contemplation of "Fregolina," kept on poking him and whispering:

"It's she, isn't it? Just exactly; the same body. And besides, the girl has some talent; she's funny."

Cotoner nodded ironically: "Yes, very." And when he found that Mariano wanted to stay for the next act and did not move from his seat, he though of leaving him. Finally he stayed, stretching out in his seat with the determination to have a nap, lulled by the music and the cries of the audience.

An impatient hand aroused him from his comfortable doze. "Pepe, Pepe." He shook his head and opened his eyes ill-naturedly. "What's the matter?" In Renovales' face he saw a honeyed, treacherous smile, some folly that he wanted to propose in the most pleasing manner.

"I thought we might go behind the scenes for a minute: we could see her at close range."

His friend answered him indignantly. Mariano thought he was a young buck; he forgot how he looked. That woman would laugh at them, she would assume the air of the Chaste Susanna, besieged by the two old men.

Renovales was silent, but in a little while he once more aroused his friend from his nap.

"You might go in alone, Pepe. You know more about these things than I do. You are more daring. You might tell her that I want to paint her portrait. Think, a portrait with my signature!"

Cotoner started to laugh, in sheer admiration of the princely simplicity with which the master gave him the commission.

"Thank you, sir; I am highly honored by such a favor, but I am not going. You confounded fool. Do you suppose that girl knows who Renovales is or has ever even heard of his name?"

The master expressed his astonishment with childlike simplicity.

"Man alive. I believe that the name Renovales—that what the papers have said—that my portraits—— Be frank, say that you don't want to."

And he was silent, offended at his companion's refusal and his doubt that his fame had reached this corner. Friends sometimes abuse us with unexpected scorn and great injustice.

At the end of the show the master felt that he must do something, not go away without sending the "Bella Fregolina" some evidence of his presence. He bought an elaborate basket of flowers from a flower vendor who was starting home, discouraged at the poor business. She should deliver it immediately to Señorita—"Fregolina."

"Yes, to Pepita," said the woman with a knowing air, as if she were one of her friends.

"And tell her it is from Señor Renovales—from Renovales, the painter."

The woman nodded, repeating the name. "Very well, Renovales," just as she would have said any other name. And without the least emotion she took the five dollars which the painter gave her.

"Five dollars! You idiot," muttered his friend, losing all respect for him.

Good Cotoner refused to go with him after that. In vain Renovales talked to him enthusiastically every night about that girl, deeply impressed by her different impersonations. Now she appeared in a pale pink dress, almost like some clothes put away in the closets of his house; now she entered in a hat trimmed with flowers and cherries, much larger, but still something like a certain straw hat which he could find amid the confusion of Josephina's old finery. Oh, how it reminded him of her! Every night he was struck with some renewed memory.

Lacking Cotoner's assistance, he went to see the "Bella" with some of the young fellows of his disrespectful court. These boys spoke of the "star" with respectful scorn, as the fox in the fable gazed at the distant grapes, consoling himself at the thought of their sourness. They praised her beauty, seen from a distance; according to them she was "lily-like"; she had the holy beauty of sin. She was out of their reach; she wore costly jewels and according to all reports had influential friends, all those young gentlemen in' dress clothes who occupied the boxes during the last act, and waited for her at the stage door to take her to dinner.

Renovales was gnawed with impatience, unable to find a way to meet her. Every night he sent his little baskets of flowers, or huge bouquets. The "star" must be informed whence these gifts came, for she looked around the audience for the ugly elderly gentleman, deigning to grant him a smile.

One night the master saw López de Sosa speak to the

singer. Perhaps his son-in-law was acquainted with her. And boldly as a lover, he waited for him when he came out to implore his help.

He wanted to paint her; she was a magnificent model for a certain work he had in mind. He said it blushingly, stammering, but López laughed at his timidity and seemed disposed to protect him.

"Oh, Pepita? A wonderful woman, in spite of the fact that she is on the decline. With all her school-girl face, if you could only see her at a party! She drinks like a fish. She's a terror!"

But afterwards, with a serious expression, he explained the difficulties. She "belonged" to one of his friends, a lad from the provinces who, eager to win notoriety, was losing one-half his fortune gambling at the Casino and was calmly letting that girl devour the other half,—she gave him some reputation. He would speak to her; they were old friends; nothing wrong—eh, father? It would not be hard to persuade her. This Pepita had a predilection for anything that was unusual; she was rather— romantic. He would explain to her who the great artist was, enhancing the honor of acting as his model.

"Don't stint on the money," said the master anxiously. "All that she wants. Don't be afraid to be generous."

One morning Renovales called Cotoner to talk to him with wild expressions of joy.

"She's going to come! She's going to come this very afternoon!"

The old painter looked surprised.

"Who?"

"The 'Bella Fregolina.' Pepita. My son-in-law tells me he has persuaded her. She will come this afternoon at three. He is coming with her himself."

Then he cast a worried glance at his workshop. For some time it had been deserted; it must be set in order.

And the servant on one side and the two artists on the other, began to tidy up the room hastily.

The portraits of Josephina and the canvas with nothing but her head were piled up in a corner by the master's feverish hands. What was the use of those phantoms when the real thing was going to appear. In their place he put a large white canvas, gazing at its untouched surface with hopeful eyes. What things he was going to do that afternoon! What a power for work he felt!

When the two artists were left alone, Renovales seemed restless, dissatisfied, constantly suspecting that something had been overlooked for this visit, toward which he looked with chills of anxiety. Flowers; they must get some flowers, fill all the old vases in the studio, create an atmosphere of delicate perfume.

And Cotoner ran through the garden with the servant, plundered the greenhouse and came in with an armful of flowers, obedient and submissive as a faithful friend, but with a sarcastic reproach in his eyes. All that for the "Bella Fregolina"! The master was cracked; he was in his second childhood! If only this visit would cure him of his mania, which was almost madness!

Afterwards the master had further orders. He must provide on one of the tables in the studio sweets, champagne, anything good he could find. Cotoner spoke of sending for the valet, complaining of the tasks which were imposed on him as a result of the visit of this girl of the guileless smile and the vile songs, who stood with arms akimbo.

"No, Pepe," the master implored. "Listen—I don't want the valet to know. He talks afterward; my daughter probes him with questions."

Cotoner went away with a resigned expression and

when he returned an hour later, he found Renovales in the model's room arranging some clothes.

The old painter lined up his packages on the table. He put the confectionery in antique plates and took the bottles out of their wrappers.

"You are served, sir," he said with ironical respect. "Do you wish anything else, sir? The whole family is in a state of revolution over this noble lady; your son-in-law is bringing her; I am acting as your valet; all you need now is to send for your daughter to help her undress."

"Thanks, Pepe, thanks ever so much," said the master with naïve gratitude, apparently undisturbed by his jests.

At luncheon time Cotoner saw him come into the dining-room with his hair carefully combed, his mustache curled, wearing his best suit with a rose in the buttonhole. The Bohemian laughed boisterously. The last straw! He was crazy; they would make sport of him!

The master scarcely touched the meal. Afterwards he walked up and down alone in the studio. How slowly the time went! At each turn through the three studios he looked at the hands of an old clock of Saxon china, which stood on a table of colored marble, with its back reflected in a tall, Venetian mirror.

It was already three. The master wondered if she was not going to come. Quarter past three,—half-past three. No, she was not coming; it was past the time. Those women who live amid obligations and demands, without a minute to themselves!

Suddenly he heard steps and Cotoner entered.

"She is here; here she comes. Good luck, master. Have a good time! I guess you have imposed on me long enough and will not expect me to stay."

He went out waving him an ironical farewell and a

little later Renovales heard López de Sosa's voice, approaching slowly, explaining to his companion the pictures and furniture which attracted her attention.

They entered. The "Bella Fregolina" looked astonished; she seemed intimidated by the majestic silence of the studio. What a big, princely house, so different from all those she had seen! That ancient, solid, historic luxury with its rare furniture filled her with fear! She looked at Renovales with great respect. He seemed to her more distinguished than that other man whom she had seen indistinctly in the orchestra of her little theater. He was awe-inspiring, as if he were a great personage, different from all the men with whom she had had to do. To her fear was added a sort of admiration. How much money that old boy must have, living in such style!

Renovales, too, was deeply moved when he saw her so close at hand.

At first he hesitated. Was she really like the other? The paint on her face disconcerted him—the layer of rouge with black lines about the eyes—visible through the veil. The *other* did not paint. But when he looked at her eyes, the striking resemblance rose again, and starting from them he gradually restored the beloved face under the layers of pomade.

The "star" examined the canvases which covered the walls. How pretty! And did this gentleman do all that? She wanted to see herself like that, proud and beautiful in a canvas. Did he truly want to paint her? And she drew herself up vainly, delighted that people thought she was beautiful, that she would enjoy the emotion until then unknown of seeing her image reproduced by a great artist.

López de Sosa excused himself to his father-in-law. She was to blame for their being late. You could never get a woman like that to hurry. She went to bed at day-break; he had found her in bed.

Then he said good-by, understanding the embarrassment his presence might cause. Pepita was a good girl, she was dazzled by his works and the appearance of the house. The master could do what he wanted with her.

"Well, little girl, you stay here. The gentleman is my father; I told you already. Be sure and be a good girl."

And he went out, followed by the forced laugh of them both, who greeted this recommendation with uneasy merriment.

A long and painful silence followed. The master did not know what to say. Timidity and emotion weighed on his will. She seemed no less disturbed. That great room, so silent and imposing with its massive, superb decorations, different from anything she had seen, frightened her. She felt the vague terror which precedes an unknown operation. Besides, she was disturbed by the man's glowing eyes fixed on her, with a quiver on his cheeks and a twitching of his lips, as if they were tormented by thirst.

She soon recovered from her timidity. She was used to these moments of shamefaced silence which came with the lone meeting of two strangers. She knew these interviews which begin hesitatingly and end in rough familiarity.

She looked around with a professional smile, eager to end the unpleasant situation as soon as possible.

"When you will. Where shall I undress?"

Renovales started at the sound of her voice, as if he had forgotten that that image could speak. The simplicity with which she dispensed with explanations surprised him likewise.

His son-in-law did things well; he had brought her well coached, callous to all surprises.

The master showed her the way to the model's room and remained outside, prudently, turning his head without knowing why, so as not to see-through the half-opened door. There was a long silence, broken by the rustle of falling clothes, the metallic click of buttons and hooks. Suddenly her voice came to the master, smothered, distant with a sort of timidity.

"My stockings too? Must I take them off?"

Renovales knew this objection of all models when they undressed for the first time. López de Sosa, carrying his desire of pleasing his father to the extreme, had spoken to her of giving her body wholly and she undressed without asking any further explanations, with the calm of accepted duty, thinking that her presence there was absurd for any other purpose.

The painter came out of his silence; he called to her uneasily. She must not stay undressed. In the room there were clothes for her to put on. And without turning his head, reaching his arm through the half open door he pointed out blindly what he had left. There was a pink dress, a hat, shoes, stockings, a shirt.

Pepita protested when she saw these cast-off garments, showing an aversion to putting on those underclothes which seemed worn and old.

"The shirt, too? The stockings? No, the dress is enough."

But the master begged her impatiently. She must put them all on; his painting demanded it. The long silence of the girl proved that she was complying, putting on these old garments, overcoming her repugnance.

When she came out of the room she smiled with a sort of pity, as if she were laughing at herself. Renovales drew back, stirred by his own work, bewildered, feeling his temples throbbing, fancying that the pictures and furniture were whirling about him.

Poor "Fregolina"! What a delightful clown! She felt like laughing at the thought of the storm of cries which would burst out in her theater if she should appear on the stage dressed in this fashion, of the jests of her friends if she should come into one of their dinners in these clothes of twenty years ago. She did not know these styles, and to her they seemed to belong to a remote antiquity. The master leaned over the back of a chair.

"Josephina! Josephina!"

It was she, such as he kept her in his memory—as she was that happy summer in the Roman mountains, in her pink dress and that rustic hat which gave her the dainty air of a village girl in the opera. Those fashions at which the younger generation laughed were for him the most beautiful, the most artistic that feminine taste had ever produced; they recalled the spring of his life.

"Josephina! Josephina!"

He remained silent, for these exclamations were born and died in his thoughts. He did not dare to move or speak, for fear this apparition of his dreams would vanish. She, smiling, was delighted at the effect her appearance had on the painter and seeing her reflection in a distant mirror, recognized that in this strange costume she did not look at all badly.

"Where shall I go? Sitting or standing?"

The master could hardly speak; his voice was hoarse, labored.

She could pose as she wished. And she sat down in a chair adopting a posture which she considered very graceful—her cheek on one hand, her legs crossed, just as she was wont to sit in the green room of the theater, showing a bit of open-work pink silk stocking under her skirt. That too reminded the painter of the other.

It was she! She sat before his eyes in bodily form, with the perfume of the form he loved.

From instinct, from habit, he took up his palette and a brush stained with black, trying to trace the outlines of that figure. Ah, his hand was old, heavy, trembling! Where had his old time skill fled, his drawing, his striking qualities? Had he really ever painted? Was he truly the painter Renovales? He had suddenly forgotten everything. His head seemed empty, his hand paralyzed, the white canvas filled him with a terror of the unknown. He did not know how to paint; he could not paint. His efforts were useless; his mind was deadened. Perhaps,— some other day. Now his ears hummed, his face was pale, his ears were red, purple, as if they were on the point of dripping blood. In his mouth he felt the torment of a deathly thirst.

The "Bella Fregolina" saw him throw down his palette and come toward her with a wild expression.

But she felt no fear; she knew those distorted faces. This sudden rush was no doubt part of the program; she was warned when she went there after her friendly conversation with the son-in-law. That gentleman, so serious and so imposing, was like all the men she knew, as brutal as the rest.

She saw him come to her with open arms, take her in a close embrace, fall at her feet with a hoarse cry, as if he were stifling; and she, gently and sympathetically encouraged him, bending her head, offering her lips with an automatic loving expression which was the implement of her profession.

The kiss was enough to overcome the master completely.

"Josephina! Josephina!"

The perfume of the happy days rose from her clothes, surrounding her adorable person. It was her form, her flesh! He was going to die at her feet, suffocated by the immense desire that swelled within him. It was she; her very eyes—her eyes! And as he raised his glance to lose himself in their soft pupils, to gaze at himself in their trembling mirror, he saw two cold eyes, which examined him, half closed with professional curiosity, taking a scornful delight from their calm height in this intoxication of the flesh, this madness which groveled, moaning with desire.

Renovales was thunderstruck with surprise; he felt something icy run down his back, paralyzing him; his eyes were veiled with a cloud of disappointment and sorrow.

Was it really Josephina whom he had in his arms? It was her body, her perfume, her clothes, her beauty, pale as a dying flower. But no, it was not she! Those eyes! In vain did they look at him differently, alarmed at this sudden reaction; in vain they softened with a tender light, trained by habit. The deceit was useless; he saw beyond, he penetrated through those bright windows into the depths; he found only emptiness. The other's soul was not there. That maddening perfume no longer moved him; it was a false essence. He had before him merely a reproduction of the beloved vase, but the incense, the soul, lost forever.

Renovales, standing up, drew away from her, looking at that woman with terror in his eyes, and finally threw himself on a couch, with his face in his hands.

The girl, hearing him sob, was afraid and ran toward the models' room to take off those clothes, to flee. The man must be mad.

The master was weeping. Farewell, youth! Farewell desire! Farewell dreams; enchanting sirens of life, that have fled forever. 'Useless the search, useless the struggle in the solitude of life. Death had him in his grasp, he was his and only through him could he renew his youth. These images were useless. He could not find another to call up the memory of the dead like this hired woman whom he had held in his arms—and still, it was not she!

At the supreme moment, on the verge of reality, that indefinable something had vanished, that something which had been enclosed in the body of his Josephina, of his *maja,* whom he had worshiped in the nights of his youth.

Immense, irreparable disappointment flooded his body with the icy calm of old age.

Fall, ye towers of illusion! Sink, ye castles of fancy, built with the longing to make the way fair, to hide the horizon! The path still remained unbroken, barren and deserted. In vain would he sit by the roadside, putting off the hour of his departure, in vain would he bow his head that he might not see. The longer his rest, the longer his fearful torment. At every hour he was destined to gaze at the dreaded end of the last journey—unclouded, undisturbed—the dwelling from which there is no return—the black, greedy abyss—death!

ImTheStory.com

CPSIA information can be obtained
at www.ICGtesting.com
Printed in the USA
BVOW06s0855070217
475515BV00012B/127/P